P9-DDI-071

LINCOLN CHRISTIAN COLLEGE AND SEMINARY

Leadership and Performance Beyond Expectations

ALSO BY BERNARD M. BASS

1960   *Leadership, Psychology, and Organizational Behavior*

1965   *Organizational Psychology*

1966   *Training in Industry: The Management of Learning* (with J. A. Vaughan)

1979   *Assessment of Managers: An International Comparison* (with P. C. Burger)

1981   *People, Work, and Organizations* (with G. V. Barrett)

1981   *Stogdill's Handbook of Leadership*

1982   *Interpersonal Communications in Industry* (with R. Klauss)

1983   *Organizational Decision-Making*

EDITED WORKS

1959   *Objective Approaches to Personality Assessment* (with I. A. Berg)

1959   *Leadership and Interpersonal Behavior* (with L. Petrullo)

1961   *Conformity and Deviation* (with I. A. Berg)

1970   *Managing for Accomplishment* (with R. C. Cooper and J. A. Haas)

1972   *Studies in Organizational Psychology* (with S. D. Deep)

Leadership
and Performance
Beyond Expectations

Bernard M. Bass

THE FREE PRESS
A Division of Macmillan, Inc.
NEW YORK

Collier Macmillan Publishers
LONDON

Copyright © 1985 by The Free Press
            A Division of Macmillan, Inc.

All rights reserved. No part of this book may be reproduced
or transmitted in any form or by any means, electronic or
mechanical, including photocopying, recording, or by any
information storage and retrieval system, without permission
in writing from the Publisher.

The Free Press
A Division of Macmillan, Inc.
866 Third Avenue, New York, N. Y. 10022

Collier Macmillan Canada, Inc.

Printed in the United States of America

printing number

    4 5 6 7 8 9 10

Library of Congress Cataloging in Publication Data

Bass, Bernard M.
   Leadership and performance beyond expectations.

   Bibliography: p.
   Includes indexes.
   1. Leadership.   I. Title.
HM141.B33   1985   303.3′4   84–24724
ISBN 0–02–901810–2

The material quoted from G. A. Yukl, *Leadership in Organizations,* © 1981, pp. 61, 121, 125, 193,
194, and 195, is reprinted by permission of Prentice-Hall, Inc., Englewood Cliffs, New Jersey.

To James MacGregor Burns

2 6 64

92958

Contents

List of Illustrations

List of Tables

Preface

The hope is that this book will represent a major breakthrough in understanding what it takes for leaders to have great effects on their followers. But breakthroughs come slowly in leadership practice, theory, and research. The past half-century has seen the refinement of the use of more carrot and less stick. Contingent reinforcement has been the fundamental concept of consequence. Followers are rewarded for fulfilling roles based on agreements reached with their leaders. Reaching such agreements through democratic processes have been encouraged. But even in the best of circumstances there seem to be limits on what contingent reinforcement of followers can achieve with this transactional arrangement between followers and leaders. A shift in paradigm is in order. Another concept is required to go beyond these limits. To achieve follower performance beyond the ordinary limits, leadership must be transformational. Followers' attitudes, beliefs, motives, and confidence need to be transformed from a lower to a higher plane of arousal and maturity.

Management is not only leadership nor is leadership only management; however, those appointed to a position of responsibility as managers need to appreciate what leadership is expected of them. If they are to be transactional leaders, they will need to provide their subordinates with a clear understanding of what is expected of them and what they can hope to receive in exchange for fulfilling these expectations. Such clarification generates confidence in subordinates that they can fulfill the expectations and achieve the mutually valued outcomes. But employees' confidence and how much value they attach to the potential outcomes can be increased further through transformational leadership. Such an increase in employees' confidence and valuing of outcomes will produce a noticeable step-up in their efforts to fulfill expectations. Leadership can become an inspiration to extraordinary effort on the part of followers.

As subordinates become competent, a development that transformational leaders encourage and support, leaders delegate as much as they can to their subordinates. Managers who aspire to become transformational leaders must pay attention to each of their subordinates, sharing their concerns and development needs, and treating them as individuals.

Charismatic leadership is central to the transformational leadership process. Charismatic leaders have great power and influence. Followers want to identify with them, to develop intense feelings about them, and above all to have trust and confidence in them. But if leaders can command such love, trust, and confidence, they can also use their power for evil ends, for selfish aggrandizement at the expense of others, as well as for good, for satisfying the positive needs of their followers. As another important aspect of effective transformation, leaders intellectually stimulate their subordinates. Finally, transformational leaders may excite, arouse, and inspire their subordinates, imparting to them a vision of what they might be able to accomplish with extra effort.

Their own personality goes a long way in explaining whether leaders will or will not be transformational. But in addition, transformational leadership is more likely to emerge in times of stress and disorganization, and in organizations more open to growth and change.

In studying leadership behavior over the past 35 years, early on, I became aware of the continuing gap in theory and research between social and organizational psychology, on the one hand, and political science and psychohistory, on the other. Social and organizational psychology focus on leaders in small groups and complex organizations; political science and psychohistory focus on world-class leaders.

Without losing focus on leadership in small groups and complex organizations, this book attempts to understand some of what makes the performance of these charismatic world-class leaders so remarkable and what seems so often to be missing when we try to understand leadership performance in small groups and complex organizations. What we shall see are the transformational processes by which the effort expected from followers based on their own confidence and their valuing of what they can achieve is elevated into extra effort beyond expectations.

The book was inspired by leaders such as President John F. Kennedy whose legend two decades after his assassination is still growing. In style at least, Kennedy exemplified what a transformational national leader should be and could become. The errors and contradictions in his performance during the 1,000 days of his leadership cannot dim the memory of his contribution to the transformation of U.S. society from a state of benign neglect of its social problems and international responsibilities to a growing awareness of the need for change; to the transformation of world consciousness from a climate of resignation about nuclear confrontation to one of increased expectation and hope for negotiated settlements of the nuclear issue; and to the transformation of global consciousness from Earth-boundedness to an awareness of the possibilities of space exploration. Finally, Kennedy had a transformational effect on the character of world-class leadership itself, and caused his own qualities of wit, charm, intellect, vision, and reason to be valued even more highly in leaders of this caliber. The result was a pride in President and country which we are still hard-pressed to begin to restore after the assassinations of the 1960s, the Vietnam War, the Watergate cover-up, and the Iranian hostage crisis.

As will be seen, the work of certain scholars is particularly important in my study. To James McGregor Burns, I am indebted for the initial ideas about transformational and transactional leadership. Abraham Zaleznik's and Warren Bennis's observations and interpretations of transformational leadership phenomena greatly increased my confidence in the approach I pursued. I also wish to thank Gary Yukl, Jane Saxton, Robert House, Robert Caro, Lloyd Demause, Sam Hayes, and Robert Quinn for valuable ideas which helped shape this book.

The book is an initial statement of what we can do to study and determine the antecedents and effects of transformational leadership. The models that are presented should be seen as preliminary scaffolding. They suggest a variety of relationships about which much empirical testing still remains to be done. Although they are useful as they are, the measurements used here to test the relationships are likely to undergo much further refinement. But as will be seen, transformational leadership is not a rare phenomenon limited to a few world-class leaders. Rather, it is to be found in varying degrees in all walks of life. The problem remains as to how to identify and encourage its appearance in the military, in business and industry, and in educational and governmental agencies.

It is important to keep in mind that transformational leadership is a two-edged sword. In the hands of a Theodore Roosevelt, it slices up the world for the imperialist powers to bring civilization to their underprivileged brothers; in the hands of a Mahatma Gandhi, it carves out a national identity.

This book is in six parts. After an introduction building on earlier theories of motivation to work, the meaning of transformational leadership is detailed in terms of charisma, inspirational leadership, individualized consideration, and intellectual stimulation. In the same way, transactional leadership is examined in terms of contingent reinforcement. Also considered are the societal, organizational, and personal elements that promote or thwart the occurrence of transformational leadership. Quantitative explanations and exploratory analyses follow which describe measurements designed to quantify the amount of transformational and transactional leadership displayed and their factor composition.

I wish to thank Dr. James Lester for his encouragement and the Organizational Effectiveness Branch of the Office of Naval Research for its support of the review and theory formulation. Colonel Philip Saulnier, of the Army War College, was most helpful in arranging for the gathering of the survey data. Colleagues Bruce Avolio and David Waldman are to be thanked for their support and Susan Harrington for editorial assistance. I also wish to thank Laurie Goodheim, Penny Brander, and Robert Halliday for help in data processing. The book also benefited from the reactions of an international audience to the main themes presented which were in a preliminary reading at the Harvard Business School symposium on leadership, March 4–9, 1984.

I would like to point out that in this book ''he'' stands for ''he'' and ''she,'' with apologies. In no way, have I, by this, wished to disregard women as leaders. As can be seen in the text, I have not ignored women either as leaders or followers nor implied that leadership was for men only. Generally, I used the plural construction to eliminate the sexual identity of leaders and followers. However, pluralizing everything makes for ambiguities and dull reading.

B. M. B.

Part I

Introduction

As ACTING GENERAL MANAGER, Henderson was first in line for the position to head the plant, but the Management Committee had reservations about him. He had applied cost accounting to examining each section of the plant and correcting what was needed to improve operational efficiency. He was good at getting agreements with each unit supervisor on specific production targets and working to see that they were met. People knew what they were to do and whether they had achieved the agreed-upon goals. He made the situation comfortable and smooth-running. He was liked by those around him, but he was colorless and did not inspire anyone to exert themselves to come up with new ideas or to feel or see that they and the plant could become the best in the business under his leadership. Doubts were expressed about how he would handle a crisis.

Henderson was satisfactory as a transactional leader but the committee was looking for something additional in the leader they were seeking for the plant.

Chapter 1

New Models
of Leadership

FOR A HALF-CENTURY, the study of leadership has centered on autocratic versus democratic approaches; on questions about the locus of decision-making—directive versus participative; on questions about the focus—tasks versus relationships; or on questions about the behavior—initiation versus consideration. At the same time, springing from the same source has been the attention to the promotion of change in individuals, groups, and organizations. Promoting change and dealing with resistance to it was seen to call for democratic, participative, relations-oriented, considerate leadership. Nevertheless, in many contingencies such as in emergencies or when leading inexperienced followers, more direction, task-orientation, and initiation were seen to be the more effective way to lead.

Changing Approaches to Leadership

Higher-Order Change in Effort and Performance

Often, the desired change which was the target was primarily an increase in quantity or quality of performance, a substitution of one goal for another, a shift of attention from one action to another, or a reduction in the resistance to particular actions or the implementation of decisions within a contextual framework. A higher order of change is also possible. We may see an accelerated increase in effort and/or a change in the rate in which a group's speed and accuracy are improving. Such higher-order changes also may be revolutionary. They may involve large changes in attitudes, beliefs, values, and needs. Quantum leaps in performance may be seen such as when a group is roused out of its despair by a new leader who articulates revolutionary new ideas about what may be possible. A new paradigm is introduced. More quantity is no longer enough; quality must improve dramatically. Leaders may help bring about a radical shift in attention. For instance, groups oriented toward traditional beliefs will be shifted so that they come to value modern approaches. The contextual framework may be changed by leaders. They may influence a perceptual change in followers reversing what is figure and what is ground. Finally, as Burns (1978) suggested, leadership may result in increasing the maturity level of followers' needs. Followers may be elevated from concerns for security and affiliation to concerns for recognition, achievement, and self-actualization.

The first order of change—changes of degree—can be handled adequately by the current emphasis on leadership as an exchange process, a transactional relationship in which followers' needs can be met if their performance measures up to their contracts with their leader. But the higher order of change calls for something distinguishable from such an exchange relationship—transformational leadership. Thus, we see another important distinction for leadership theory and research—transactional versus transformational leadership. Questions about this distinction are what we want to address here. What are the differences between? For what reasons do each emerge or disappear? Which is more effective and/or satisfying for followers? Under what conditions is one type of leadership more advisable to employ than the other? New answers to new questions will be pursued here using a new paradigm or new pattern of inquiry.

Limitations of Cost–Benefit Exchange Theories

The study of leadership as an experimental social science and in organizational psychology has proceeded from trait to situational theories and thence to their interaction in contingency theories. The leader–group relationship has been replaced in importance by the individual leader/follower dyad. From the practicing organizational leader's view, a parallel historical change in attitude toward leadership has taken place. In the first part of this century, leadership was mainly a matter of how and when to give directions and orders to obedient subordinates. The strong directed the weak. Valuing equalitarianism, the opposing Human Relations Movement emphasized participative and consultative group processes, and shared leadership. The dialectic merged into a synthesis. The behavior of leaders was now to be seen as initiating structure and/or showing consideration for human relationships. Leader decision-making was directive and/or participative. Leader focus was on the task to be done and/or the human relations to be maintained. These are now what experimental social science studies as its dependent variables as it contemplates leader/follower dyads and group leadership in situational contexts and combinations of leaders and followers. Throughout, the approach has built on the economic cost–benefit assumptions about motivation, energization, and direction of perception and behavior. For behaviorists, cues, available repertoires, and reinforcements (or rewards and punishments) have been the building blocks. For perceptual and cognitive theorists, expectations of achieving valued goals have been the grist for their mills. For example, the currently popular path–goal model of leadership effectiveness explains leadership effectiveness as an extension of the expectancy theory of motivation and cost–benefit formulations. Subordinates' satisfaction and work motivation are seen to depend on their expectancy that their effort will result in their better performance which in turn will result in desired outcomes for them. When the superior initiates structure, this enhances and reinforces the subordinates' expectancy that their efforts will succeed. Consideration by the superior is a desired benefit reinforcing the subordinate performance. Unfortunately, empirical tests in different work situations have yielded mixed support for the path–goal model (Schriesheim & Von Glinow, 1977).

Some of What Is Missing

By limiting survey and experimental leadership research to the effects of leadership on first-order changes, what has been excluded from experimental social science, partly for the sake of scientific advancement, and partly because results could be explained in terms of simple cost–benefit exchanges, may be the more important phenomena of leadership —leadership that accomplishes second-order changes. Currently these phenomena largely remain outside what is usually incorporated in testable leadership models. Yet, experimental psychology itself has long abandoned the purely cost–benefit approach to motivation. The path of least effort was not the path a rat necessarily chose to reach the goal box. As early as 1918, R. S. Woodworth had declared that "capacity was its own motivation." Nevertheless, the study of leadership has been dominated by logical positivism and operationalism, and it is the economic cost–benefit exchange models of leadership that have been most likely to be tested in laboratory or field. Exchanges are easier to sense, observe, record, and measure. They are logically compelling as long as we can posit that man is a rational and economic being. But exchange theories and experiments fail to account for what may be some of the more important phenomena of leadership such as the effects on leader–follower relations of symbolism, mysticism, imaging, and fantasy.

Consider the Jim Jones tragedy in Guyana where a combination of coercion and misguided ideals led to mass suicide. Consider the millions who hear repeated policies in person from Pope John Paul that are diametrically opposed to their own self-interest, yet adore his leadership performance. Consider Lee Iacocca's success in rescuing a near-bankrupt Chrysler Corporation by convincing all its respective constituencies—suppliers, employees, government, shareholders, management—of the need to transcend their own immediate self-interests for the chancy promise of corporate survival. Consider how the elevation of Walter Wriston to chief executive officer of Citicorp resulted in its remarkable growth. Consider those who as adults accomplished leadership missions they had continuously proclaimed as children: Charles de Gaulle, to restore the glory of France; Lyndon Johnson, to become President of the United States; Alexander the Great, to conquer the known world.

Exchange theories direct us toward situational emphasis. They fail to account for the DeGaulles, Johnsons, and Alexanders and the many others who emerge as leaders with particular styles no matter where the leaders find themselves. From age 6 to 60, Lyndon Johnson had to dominate and be acknowledged as a leader among his peers and associates. He sought power in whatever situations he placed himself. (Caro, 1982). There are alternatives to exchange theories available. For psychoanalytic theory, for example, the immediate situation confronting a person's leadership efforts are far less of consequence than a balanced id and superego which give opportunity for the ego to pursue its ideals.

Most important of all, consider the relatively modest statistical associations we find in repeated studies of the antecedent conditions: external environment, organizations, team, personality of leader and follower, differential power and information, and so on; and the two dependent leader behaviors usually studied, decision styles or task-versus-relations orientation with their consequences in unit satisfaction and effectiveness. The effects are there to see but so often leave us after exhaustive investigation with more error than explained variance. A correlation of .40 means we still account for only 16 percent of the variance leaving 84 percent unexplained. We can either applaud the 16 percent explained or remain dissatisfied with the 84 percent unexplained. In this book, we begin in a dissatisfied state believing that there is much in the unexplained portion of variance in leadership which can be explained if we are willing to go deeper and higher in entertaining conceptualizations about it. Physics talks about strong and weak forces. Social and organizational psychology have offered leadership theories and research about weak forces. By incorporating into organizational psychology more of what has been in the domain of sociology, political science, and psychohistory, we hope to direct more attention of experimental social science and organizational psychology to the strong forces.

Alternative Approaches to Motivation

Alternative views about motivation are available which may better explain the sharp reversals in direction and changes in rate of second-order changes. Two of these are homeostasis and opponent process theory. Instead of motivation being a matter of seeking rewards and avoiding punishments, the homeostatic model sees subordinates or followers as being in a steady state to which they will strive to return if they are forced to deviate from it. Starting with this view, we would look at leaders in the context of their group's reactions to deviations from the steady state, their leadership performance in such circumstances, and the leader–subordinate processes by which a new higher (or lower) steady state is achieved.

The level of motivational response is seen by Berlyne (1967) as a matter of stimulus intensity. No overt response is evoked until the stimulus increases in intensity beyond a given threshold. Response is activated only if the stimulus event evokes a stronger hedonic disturbance. If the stimulus event becomes too strong, the disturbance is stressful and the individual will attempt to psychologically withdraw from the situation. But the disturbance may linger long after the event as a consequence of a slower opponent process which arises opposing the original stimulus arousal process (Landy, 1978). Sheridan et al. (1982) deduce from this the likelihood that the intensity of leadership acts may be much more influential than the frequency with which the acts occur. Yet it has mainly been the frequency of leader behavior that has been studied quantitatively rather than its intensity.

Furthermore, to the degree that leaders engage in the arousal of emotions in their followers, much of the effects of the leaders may be better understood as disinhibition of current follower tendencies rather than as merely further stimulation of such tendencies. Such leadership triggers release of followers from controls which may have been holding them back from being creative, taking risks, and broadening their horizons.

Need to Qualify Theories of Motivation to Work

Minimally, we need to qualify considerably the simple carrot-and-stick formulations of exchange theories. Expectancy theories of motivation to work such as Vroom's (1964) postulate that effort is a function of the value of goals and the expectancy of attaining them through the required effort. It follows that the easier the goals to attain, the greater the expectancy in doing so. Greater effort is induced by easier goals. Nevertheless, Locke (1968) argues just the opposite with empirical evidence to support his position. Harder goals stimulate more effort. Need achievement theorists such as Atkinson (1964) take a third position. Challenging but not too difficult goals are most stimulating, particularly among those with strong needs to achieve. Shapira (1975) seems to have resolved the issue by showing that it all depends on whether the goal is of intrinsic or extrinsic value to the individual. The higher and more frequent the extrinsic payoff, the more we will be willing to continue the easy task of playing a slot machine although the activity itself lacks intrinsic interest or intellectual challenge for us. We will stop if convinced there will be little or no payoff. On the other hand, we will work inordinate amounts of time to work at a difficult and challenging task such as solving an intriguing, intrinsically interesting puzzle despite the lack of any extrinsic payoff. Deci (1975) argues further that adding extrinsic rewards to intrinsically valued work may reduce the intrinsic value of the work. Amateurs who turn professional may lose their intrinsic interest in the activity which now becomes more a matter of extrinsic reinforcement.

According to Maslow's (1954) theory of work motivation, people have a hierarchy of needs. Only if lower-level needs such as safety and security have been fulfilled will they be ignored in favor of higher-level social and personal needs such as the need for affiliation and recognition. Self-actualization, the need to become what one has the capacity to become, is at the highest level of need.

In addition, there are the many well-recognized Freudian phenomena which further distort any simple exchange possibilities. Instead of effort to achieve leader-promised gains, depending on the maturity and level of the subordinate one may see independent or counterdependent actions, projections, and denials, fantasy-substitutions for effort, displacements, and reaction formations.

We argue, therefore, that subordinate motivation to work cannot be fully accounted for by any notion of a simple swap of desired material and psychic payments from a superior in exchange for satisfactory services rendered by the subordinate. This exchange is common and apparent in leader–subordinate relationships but it fails to account for an important portion. Expanded views of motivation and leadership must be added on to the basic postulate that effort is a function of the value for us of outcomes and our confidence (subjective probability) that we will obtain them.

A Broader View of Leadership Sought

The need for a broader view of leadership has been voiced by many others. Hambrick and Mason (1983) noted that when the question is asked, "Why do organizations act as they do," analysts concentrate on explanations in terms of market share, life cycle of products, competition, and portfolios. The strategic processes are seen as flows of information and decisions by reified organizations. Hambrick and Mason suggested that both the strategies and effectiveness of organizations can be better understood as "reflecting the values and perceptions of powerful actors in the organizations." They uncovered evidence to show that when firms were led by younger rather than older top managers, they were more likely to grow and to exhibit more volatile sales and earnings. They also noted that newcomers brought in from the outside to head the organization will make more changes in structure, procedures, and people than executives promoted from within the organization. The education and financial position of the top executives was also seen to be likely to strongly influence the direction of the organization. Yet, research in social and organizational psychology on leadership has focused on the readily observable, usually short-time, leader–subordinate relations and ignored the much more important aspects of leadership to be seen in the charismatic movers and shakers of our time (McCall, 1977). Equal dissatisfaction has been expressed about the practice of organizational leadership in the military setting:

> we have been lavish in our rewards to those who have demonstrated excellence in sophisticated business and management techniques. These talents are worthwhile to a leader, but, of themselves, they are not leadership. [Meyer, 1980, p. 4]

Good management, General Eugene Meyer, a former U.S. Army Chief of Staff, noted, may sometimes even be at cross-purposes with good leadership.

> Strong personal leadership is as necessary today as at anytime in our history. That which soldiers are willing to sacrifice their lives for—loyalty, team spirit, morale, trust and confidence cannot be infused by managing. The attention we need to invest in our soldiers far exceeds that which is possible through any centralized management system. To the degree that such systems assist efficient operation, they are good. To the degree that they interfere with essential relationships between the unit and its leader, they are disruptive. Management techniques have limitations which leaders need to identify and curb to preclude destructive side effects. [p. 6]

For Meyer, "overmanagement can be the death of an Army," but undermanagement will deprive units of essential resources. Therefore, "leaders need to be able to identify either extreme."

Robert K. Mueller (1980), Chairman of the Board of Arthur D. Little, Inc., has seen the need in industry for leaders who can

> initiate structure in group expectation and show us how to master and motivate institutions and individuals within a complex environment experiencing excessive internal and external stresses and changes. [p. 19]

For Mueller (1980) such "leading-edge" leadership deals with "fuzzy futures." It is able to simplify problems and to jump to the (correct) crux of complex matters while the rest of the crowd is still trying to identify the problem. He sees the need for research on this "rapid reification." Second, he sees the need for leadership research on how "to integrate and relate a charismatic component with the logical and intuitive attributes which is vital to leading-edge leadership." [p. 21]

As seen by Zaleznik (1977), leaders of the sort called for by Mueller arouse intense feelings and generate turbulent one-to-one relationships. They are inspirational and concerned with ideas rather than process. They heighten expectations and engender excitement at work. They "react to the mundane as to an affliction." They are committed to their own destinies and are likely to be dramatic and unpredictable.

Asked what qualities their client companies are seeking in candidates for a top job, executive recruiters comment that "they're hearing our old friend 'charisma' a great deal more than they used to." "The need for vision" also seems in increasing demand (along with) new and much-sought-after skills in motivating people" (Kiechel, 1983, p. 135). "Vision" heads the list, according to Bennis (1982), of the characteristics of chief executive officers who can translate their intentions into reality. They have "the capacity to create and communicate a compelling vision of a desired state of affairs." Furthermore, they can gain understanding and commitment to their vision from their followers to "harness the energies and abilities of their followers making it possible for the dream to come true."

Transactional and Transformational Leadership Defined

For Burns (1978), the transactional political leader motivated followers by exchanging with them rewards for services rendered. This was distinguished from leadership that motivates followers to work for transcendental goals and for aroused higher-level needs for self-actualization rather than for immediate self-interest.

For Burns, transactional leaders "approach followers with an eye to exchanging one thing for another: jobs for votes, or subsidies for campaign contributions. Such transactions comprise the bulk of the relationships among leaders and followers, especially in groups, legislatures, and parties." (p. 3)

Our purpose here is to extend the definition to supervisory–subordinate relations in general. With this aim in mind, the transactional leader can be described in his relations with subordinates as follows:

1. Recognizes what it is we want to get from our work and tries to see that we get what we want if our performance warrants it.
2. Exchanges rewards and promises of reward for our effort.
3. Is responsive to our immediate self-interests if they can be met by our getting the work done.

The Model of Transactional Leadership

Figure 1 shows the relationship between transactional leadership and what Vroom called the "force on a person to exert a given amount of effort in performance of his job" (Vroom, 1964, p. 284). The force is

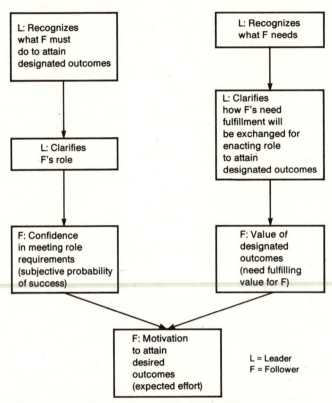

Figure 1 Transactional Leadership and Follower Effort

equal to the expectation that one's effort will result in attaining desired outcomes. One's effort then depends on two elements: (1) one's confidence or subjective probability or expectation that an outcome can and will be attained by means of one's performance, and (2) the value of the outcome—how much it, in itself, is desired and valued or how much it is perceived as instrumental in realizing other desired outcomes. For our purposes here, we will propose that subordinates' or followers' level of effort depends on their confidence that such effort will yield desired outcomes. Furthermore, we assume that the subordinate has the capability to perform as required. Thus, the expected effort is translated into the expected performance. As shown in Figure 1, transactional leaders serve to recognize and clarify the role and task requirements for the subordinates' reaching the desired outcomes. This gives the subordinates sufficient confidence to exert the necessary effort. Transactional leaders also recognize what the subordinates need and want and clarify how these needs and wants will be satisfied if the necessary effort is expended by the subordinate. Such effort to perform or motivation to work implies a sense of direction in the subordinate as well as some degree of energization.

Like all models, Figure 1 is a simplified replica of reality. It is an attempt to describe the most important variables affecting the dependent outcome of expected effort and performance. The leader recognizes the role the follower must play to attain the outcomes desired by the leader. The leader clarifies this role. This clarification provides the follower with the confidence necessary to carry it out to meet the objectives. In parallel, the leader recognizes what the follower needs and clarifies for the follower how these needs will be fulfilled in exchange for the follower's satisfactory effort and performance. This makes the designated outcome of sufficient value to the follower to result in his effort to attain the outcome. This is the transactional process at its simplest.

Zaleznik's (1983) "managers" are transactional leaders. They tend to survey their subordinates' needs and set goals for them on the basis of the effort they can rationally expect from their subordinates. Such "managers" do not question the goals of their organization. They assume their subordinates maintain a constant motivation to support the managers' plans. The managers, as transactional leaders, concentrate on compromise, intrigue, and control. Because they focus on the process, not the substance of issues, if they are newcomers, such managers are seen as inscrutable, detached, and manipulative.

This focus on process by the transactional leader or Zaleznik's manager may have unintended consequences. Twenty-five years later, I vividly recall seeing a group of young managers from a large multinational firm emerging from a sensitivity training session which concentrated on the need for understanding group processes and the importance of shared leadership. Half in earnest, they were collectively muttering "I must not be a leader, I must not be a leader, I must not be a leader!" Twenty years later, one of them became chairman of the board. Fortunately for both his company and himself, he did not fully absorb the unintended lesson.

Chapter 2

Transformational Leadership

THE TRANSACTIONAL LEADER pursues a cost–benefit, economic exchange to meet subordinates' current material and psychic needs in return for "contracted" services rendered by the subordinate. For Burns, the transformational leader also recog.nizes these existing needs in potential followers but tends to go further, seeking to arouse and satisfy higher needs, to engage the full person of the follower. Transformational leaders can attempt and succeed in elevating those influenced from a lower to a higher level of need according to Maslow's (1954) hierarchy of needs.

Maslow's Hierarchy

An individual must satisfy his needs for physiologic survival to some reasonable degree before he becomes primarily concerned about his safety and security. Only with some minimum achievement of safety and security can he be aroused to focus on needs for love and affiliation with family and friends. When these needs are reasonably satisfied, recognition and esteem can be sought. At the top of this hierarchy is the need for self-actualization, for realizing one's own potential, for becoming what one is capable of being. As the highest need in the hierarchy, when need for self-actualization is fulfilled, the lower needs have also been satisfied. Creative contributions are likely to be highest in an organization when the members feel themselves to be self-actualizing.

Maslow did not view the hierarchy of need satisfactions as independent steps, each of which has to be completed before an individual progresses to a higher level of needs. The levels of needs are overlapping and interdependent. Each higher-need level emerges before the lower-level needs have been fully satisfied. Maslow (1943) estimated that the average person (in the United States in 1943, that is) was satisfied 85 percent in his physiologic needs, 70 percent in his safety needs, 50 percent in his affiliative needs, 40 percent in his esteem needs, and 10 percent in his self-actualization needs.

Empirical investigation by Aldefer (1969) of workers' responses about their needs indicated that Maslow's hierarchy was an observable phenomenon but that it could be simplified into a hierarchy of three levels of need instead of Maslow's five levels: existence needs (safety and security), need for relatedness (love and affiliation), and need for growth (esteem and self-actualization).

If Maslow's percentages have any truth to them, it would seem that opportunities for transformational leaders in modern affluent society would lie mainly at the higher levels, with such leaders moving followers toward a greater concern for their own relatedness and growth. But even where basic existence needs were far less fulfilled, as in India, Mahatma Gandhi was repeatedly able to convince his followers to sacrifice their own safety and security interests for the greater good of an independent India. The inaugural exhortation of President John F. Kennedy: "Ask not what your country can do for you; ask what you can do for your country" had (pre-Vietnam) an exhilarating impact on American society. The transformational leader can move those influenced to transcend their own self-interest for the good of the group, organization, or country.

Increased awareness and the arousal of higher-level needs which transcend self-interests can produce extraordinary effort. This level of effort will be beyond expectations derived from earlier lack of consciousness, lower-level needs, and self-interest. The financial markets had already declared the near-bankrupt Chrysler Corporation "a basket case" but Lee Iacocca succeeded in completely turning the enterprise around, partly at least by generating confidence among its creditors and by convincing employees of the need for sacrifice and extra effort.

While both transactional and transformational leadership involve sensing followers' felt needs, it is the transformational leader who raises consciousness about higher considerations through articulation and role modeling. For Burns, a political scientist, aspiration levels are raised, legitimatized, and turned into political demands by the transformational leader. Such leadership can have similar effects in the world of the highly structured worlds of industry, government, and the military.

The Hierarchy Is Sufficient but Not Necessary

Maslow's hierarchy of needs was seen by Burns (1978) as fundamental to the transformational process. However we suggest that although such an upward shift in level of need is sufficient evidence of a transformation occurring, it is not a necessary condition. Needs may be expanded at the same hierarchical level or even shifted downward. For example, political leaders can transform the economic and technological processes, moving people from a traditional "higher-level" socially oriented culture to a modern culture dominated by crass materialism. As a further example, a law-abiding group of adolescents may be moved by a strong informal leader who induces more concern for lower-level existence and affiliative needs from abiding by a higher code of morality to engaging in criminal activities. However, in the world of work, transformational processes usually involve the upgrading of needs. As a consequence of this upgrading of needs, subordinates and followers become self-directing and self-reinforcing. They take on greater responsibilities. They themselves are "converted into leaders" (Burns, 1978, p. 3).

Bandura (1982) has provided evidence of the importance of self-regulation. People can create their own inducements to action. They can generate cognitive support for doing one thing rather than another. They can supply their own reinforcers and feelings of satisfaction for what they decide to do. They can regulate their own behavior by rewarding themselves for meeting self-prescribed standards of performance. In some sense, transformational leaders work themselves out of a job to the extent that they elevate their subordinates into becoming self-actualizers, self-regulators, and self-controllers. The transforming leaders provide the high standards of performance and accomplishment and the inspiration to reach such standards. To the degree their followers become self-actualizing, the achievements become self-reinforcing.

Some Characteristics of the Transformational Process

Consider the following prime example of transformational leadership:

> What are the sources of fundamental change in our society? From what spring will justice roll down like water? . . . Martin Luther King, Jr. in his

"I Have a Dream" speech . . . and in a hundred other sermons—located that spring inside people: in their hearts, or souls, or whatever the organ is called that can override selfish calculation. . . . His strategy called for conversion—if not of the policeman brandishing the club, then at least of the bystanders watching on TV. At its root, the strategy, a new one to this nation, involved an attempt to fundamentally alter the moral anatomy of Americans. Far more than he wanted the Voting Rights Act, far more then he wanted the freedom to eat at dimestore lunch counters, far more then he wanted black elected officials, King wanted the change of heart in individual Americans which would make those political developments possible. [Anonymous, 1983A, p. 37]

What we see here is much more than the desire for superficial change in attitudes or for minor increments in the level of motivation which can be accomplished by transactional leadership.

Unlike the transactional leader who indicates how current needs of followers can be fulfilled, the transformational leader sharply arouses or alters the strength of needs which may have lain dormant. This is illustrated by Dwight D. Eisenhower's and Harry Truman's definitions of leadership. According to Eisenhower, "Leadership is the ability to decide what is to be done, and then to get others to want to do it" (Larson, 1968, p. 21). According to Truman (1958, p. 139), "A leader is a man who has the ability to get other people to do what they don't want to do, and like it." It is leadership that is transformational that can bring about the big differences and big changes in groups, organizations, and societies. Franklin Delano Roosevelt sensed what the country needed in 1932, raised people's awareness about what was possible, and put into words for us (with the aid of speech writers) what we could do. The role of the Federal government would never be the same again. It was transformed into involvement with our social and economic welfare, involvement which remains mostly in place 50 years after Roosevelt's inspiring inaugural message that the only thing we have to fear (from the economic depression) is fear itself.

As we will detail in a later section, transformational leaders attempt and succeed in raising colleagues, subordinates, followers, clients, or constituencies to a greater awareness about the issues of consequence. This heightening of awareness requires a leader with vision, self-confidence, and inner strength to argue successfully for what he sees is right or good, not for what is popular or is acceptable according to the established wisdom of the time. Henry Ford had this sense about the affordable, mass-produced automobile. Although an ardent economic determinist (as a good Communist should be), Leon Trotsky (1963) reminisced that without Lenin's incredible determination and persuasive talents, there probably would have been no October Revolution in Russia. Often this vision of the transformational leader involves symbolic solutions of conflicts which reconcile psychological contradictions inherent in the experience of those influenced. A coherent, meaningful symbolic context is provided, for example, by the song "We Shall Overcome" which states the contradictions inherent in America, land of equality, versus America, land of oppression of the blacks, yet still provides motivation for action to change the situation and resolve the contradictions. Unfortunately, symbolism may most readily be used by the demagogue to support oversimplified solutions. For example, the transformational industrial leader Henry Ford helped publicize the fraudulent *Protocols of the Elders of Zion* which became the symbol of a supposed Jewish plot to control the world, and thereby provided a simple but untrue means of explaining political and economic difficulties in the 1920s as a consequence of a Jewish conspiracy. On a more positive note, the "New Deal" in 1933 became symbolic of a whole, seemingly coherent, new approach to Federal intervention in the U.S. economy which incorporated many aspects of the Populist movement of the preceding 50 years to stimulate the economy and to regulate business. What people believe and understand is restructured into a new equilibrium incorporating old and new beliefs (Eoyang, 1983). Individual initiative and entrepreneurship was still prized in the United States, but the New Deal brought a new configuration of economic stimulation, social security, government regulation of banking, securities exchange, and agriculture.

Transformation Through Coercion

Transformational political leaders may also use their authority and power to radically reshape through coercive means the social and physical environment, thus destroying the old way of life and making way for a new one. Physical and social patterns and symbols of the old regime are prohibited; new physical and social forms are required. Peter the Great forced his nobility to build a new capital and move into it; Kemal Ataturk forced the Turks to adopt Roman script; Sun Yat-sen proscribed the pigtail (a symbol of Manchu supremacy over China); Habib Bourguiba made parks of Tunisia's former city cemeteries; Alexander the Great organized the mass marriage of his Greek soldiers with Persian women to create an ecumenical society.

Similar coercive means were used by industrialists such as Henry

Ford to transform their workforces. There was forced acculturation and Americanization of Ford's immigrant and formerly agrarian employees. Investigators from a "sociological department" visited workers' homes to check for hygiene and sobriety. Hundreds of orthodox Christian workers were fired for taking time off to celebrate their Christmas in January.

Using force and terror, the tyrants of history from Ivan the Terrible to Idi Amin achieve command and control, but rather than transforming followers, they reduce them to focused concern over their own personal survival. There is a point in coercion when leadership, transformational or transactional, disappears as such, and becomes a matter of physical force, of control with whips and shackles. Prisoners do not follow their jailer as a leader, but rather succumb to overpowering force or threat of it from their jailer. Jailers don't lead their victims any more than doormen lead visitors by opening one door rather than another for them. The time came when members of the Politburo met with Stalin not knowing if what they said or was said about them at the meeting would result in their being led off to face a firing squad. Stalin ceased to be transformational but was transfigured into a most dangerous, deranged, uncontrollable, omnipotent fiend.

Relation to Political Change

Paige (1977, p. 103) conceives of three patterns of political leadership and their effects:

Minimal change ("conservative") leadership; tending toward maintenance of existing political institutions and policies

Moderate change ("reformist") leadership; tending toward moderate change in given institutions and policies

Maximal change ("revolutionary") leadership; tending toward fundamental transformation of existing institutions and policies

As a conservative, the leader generally remains transactional and works within constitutional means to maintain the system; as a reformer, the leader does likewise but also concentrates on structural modifications which may be transformational. However, as a revolutionary (or reactionary), the leader is clearly transformational. Persuasive and coercive means may be pursued to achieve a new constitutional form or a return to an older one.

Again, we can recognize the three patterns in the leadership of industrial organizations:

Theodore Vail promoted a "conservative", safe, secure, well-regulated, service-oriented Bell System that lasted for almost three quarters of a century.

Alfred Sloan "reformed" General Motors into its divisional profit centers.

Henry Ford "revolutionized" industry by his offer of wages of $5 a day and his production of automobiles by the assembly line.

A Model for Transformational Leadership

To sum up, we see the transformational leader as one who motivates us to do more than we originally expected to do. This original performance expectation is based on our original level of confidence in reaching desired, designated outcomes by means of our performance.

Such a transformation can be achieved in any one of three inter-related ways:

1. By raising our level of awareness, our level of consciousness about the importance and value of designated outcomes, and ways of reaching them.
2. By getting us to transcend our own self-interest for the sake of the team, organization, or larger polity.
3. By altering our need level on Maslow's (or Alderfer's) hierarchy or expanding our portfolio of needs and wants.

Much of the above will be found in Burns (1978). Where we differ from Burns is in three respects. Firstly, we have added the "expansion of the followers' portfolio of needs and wants." Secondly, Burns saw the transformation as one that was necessarily elevating, furthering what was good rather than evil for the person and the polity. For Burns, Hitler was not a transformational leader, despite his sharp upward energization and mobilization of Germany for paranoid aggression at the expense of personal freedom, and persecution of dissenters and minorities. For us, Germany was still transformed, although the leadership itself was immoral, brutal, and extremely costly in life, liberty, property, and the pursuit of happiness to his victims, and in the long run, to his "Master Race." Forty years after his death, Hitler's malign influence still is felt in the existence of two Germanies and neo-Nazism.

Indirectly, the Holocaust transformed the remnants of European Jewry from scattered, powerless minorities to the most powerful national state in the Middle East.

Conceptually, we put the emphasis on the observed change in followers and argue that the same dynamics of the leaders' behavior can be of short- or long-term benefit *or cost* to the followers. In *March of Folly,* Barbara Tuchman (1984) provides a long list of transformations from the fall of Troy to the U.S. debacle in Vietnam which resulted from leadership against the best interests of the followers. For purposes of analysis, what matters is that followers' attitudes and behavior were transformed by the leader's performance. A dominant leader of high school dropouts can convert them into a gang of delinquents. Involved may be altered consciousness, transcendence of self-interest, and movement *downward* on Maslow's hierarchy of needs. The same leader could also transform the ex-students into a community-service group. Burns puts his emphasis on whether society ultimately benefits from the leader's actions. The actions are transformational only if society benefits from them. But from our point of view, transformational leadership is not necessarily beneficial leadership. The actions could be costly to all concerned rather than beneficial. Herbert Kitchener is a case in point.

Field Marshal Herbert Kitchener, Lord of Khartoum, played the charismatic role in Britain in World War I that Churchill played in World War II. Based on his earlier service on the frontiers of the British Empire, Kitchener inspired mass enthusiasm and confidence in the British in 1914–1915 and "lifted his reputation to a height previously unparalled in British annals. His word carried instant conviction" (Magnus, 1968, p. 291). The famous 1914 poster featuring Kitchener's face and pointing finger, with the message "Your country needs you," was an image of Britain-at-war graven on the memories of a generation.

Kitchener had most of the personal attributes of a classic charismatic. His tough and ruthless standards in Egypt and the Sudan inspired both fear and affection in his troops. He was revered almost as a god. He even had a universally publicized symbol of his masculinity, aggressive strength, and virility—his enormous mustache.

He was extremely ambitious, indefatigable, impulsive, courageous, and a great risk-taker. His ideals lay in a firm belief in Britain's imperialistic burden to civilize the less-developed world. In particular, he had a love–hate relationship with the Arab culture.

As he aged, his energy and aggressiveness were converted into obsessive–compulsive behavior to control every detail of the world around him. But he was like a bull in a china shop. His approach was to negate any system of administration, to centralize all authority in himself. He then performed

> miracles of improvisation and extracted [incredible efforts] from subordinates whom he trusted and occasionally loved much more than they or anyone else believed they had to give. [Magnus, 1968, p. 380]

Kitchener clearly could transform organizations. He destroyed one old military administration after another, in Africa, India, and Great Britain. But he replaced them with ones not necessarily better able to deal with the problems they faced, particularly more complex and intangible problems, requiring the pooling of expert judgment and diversity of information sources.

Burns and I differ in a third way. He sees transformational leadership as the opposite end of a single continuum from transactional leadership. Conceptually and empirically, we find that leaders will exhibit a variety of patterns of transformational and transactional leadership. *Most leaders do both but in different amounts.* Robert Moses was the *transactional* power-broker in New York State for 50 years whose personal vision of what parks, dams, roads, tunnels, and bridges were needed permanently *transformed* the landscape, economy, and living patterns of the state (Caro, 1974).

Figure 2 displays a model for transformational leadership starting with a current level of effort based on the subordinate's current level of confidence and desire for designated outcomes. In Figure 1 it was seen that the transactional leader would contribute to such confidence and desire by clarifying what performance was required and how needs would be satisfied as a result. The transformational leader induces additional effort by further sharply increasing subordinate confidence and by elevating the value of outcomes for the subordinate. This is done by expanding the subordinate's needs, by focus on transcendental interests, and/or by altering or widening the subordinate's level of needs on Maslow's hierarchy.

If disinhibition is what is most important, it may be that much of what can be accomplished by the transformational leader in the world of work in the United States is mainly a matter of serving as a trigger, guidance, or release mechanism for the motivation to work that already is to be found in the American worker. According to Yankelovich and Immerwahr (1983), their survey evidence indicates that the work ethic remains strong among American jobholders. More that 70 percent of

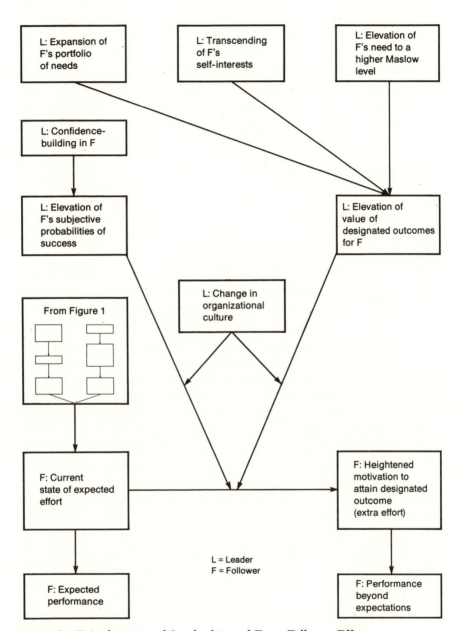

Figure 2 Transformational Leadership and Extra Follower Effort

the work-force endorses the work ethic, and 52 percent say that they have an inner need to do the best job possible, regardless of pay.

The current state of expected follower effort is based on what the transactional leader has accomplished as seen in Figure 1. This effort is heightened by the transformational process displayed in Figure 2 in which the value of the outcomes for the follower are elevated by expanding the follower's portfolio of needs, influencing the follower to transcend his own self-interests for higher goals and/or by altering the follower's needs on Maslow's hierarchy. Confidence-building by the leader elevates the follower's subjective probabilities of success in attaining the designated outcomes. The follower's probability estimates of success and his valuation of the outcomes are also affected by what the leader does to the organization's culture of shared norms and values.

Leadership and Organizational Culture

An organization's culture consists of its core values, its basic philosophy, and its technical, financial, and humanistic concerns. The forms of its culture can be seen in its jargon, stories, humor, role models, and ceremonies. The culture makes for a shared interpretation of events. It maintains the organization's boundaries, and provides members with a sense of community, loyalty, and committment (Siehl & Martin, 1982).

The transactional leader works within the organizational culture as it exists; the transformational leader changes the organizational culture. For Mitroff, Kilmann, and Saxton's (unpublished) conception of organizational culture, this means the transactional leader accepts what can be talked about; the transformational leader changes what can be talked about. The transactional leader accepts group and self-identities as currently defined; the transformational leader changes them. Other aspects of the organizational culture which the transactional leader accepts and the transformational leader changes include: who rules and by what means; the work-group norms, as well as ultimate beliefs about religion, ideology, morality, ethics, space, time, and human nature. The transactional leader accepts and uses the rituals, stories, and role models belonging to the organizational culture to communicate its values; the transformational leader invents, introduces, and advances the cultural forms. The transformational leader changes the social warp and woof of reality.

Nicholson, Ursell, and Blyton's (1981) study of British trade union leaders placed emphasis on their success in formulating and changing of organizational ideology. They found that the power of the trade union leaders was associated with their ability to mobilize and exploit shifting ideological themes. Hays and Thomas (1967) saw as effective military leaders those who could promote esprit de corps in their own units. Such esprit de corps means strong identification with the organization rather than or in addition to attraction to one's own unit. Otherwise, the norms of the unit can develop counter to the goals of the organization. This happened in Korea in front-line rifle units which developed strong cohesiveness within the units but weak identification with the cause of the total organization. Normative behavior in the individual units consistent with the organizations' goals depends considerably on the leadership (Zander & Curtis, 1965). The importance to the study of industrial leadership of organizational culture, particularly the development and change in its ideology, is illustrated by the observation by Peters and Waterman (1982) that well-managed companies had strong cultures and that these strong cultures were usually a consequence of leaders who had hammered away at particular sets of cultural beliefs in messages to their organization for many years (e.g., Thomas J. Watson at IBM or Rene McPherson at the Dana Corporation) (Kiechel, 1983). Company founders, such as William Paley of CBS or Steve Jobs of Apple Computer, often were transformational leaders shaping company policies, norms, and values that dominate its culture. The personality and talents of the founders are reflected in the organization that develops. The set of values the founders articulate, their personal assumptions and vision of the future, become embedded in the emerging corporate culture (Martin et al., 1984). But the transforming leader who firmly establishes the corporate culture can be far removed in time from the company founder. Alexander Graham Bell displayed his telephone by 1876 and started the Bell Telephone Company soon after, but Theodore N. Vail, starting 30 years later, endowed the Bell System with its organizational culture for the three quarters of a century which ended in 1984 with the breakup of AT&T into seven independent companies. His policy slogan which was at the heart of the system was, "One policy, one system, universal service." He sought government regulation for his company which he conceived to be a natural monopoly that must put the public interest ahead of profits. Public utilities giving good service at fair rates should not have to compete in the marketplace against unfair rates. The approach set into place everything in "Ma Bell" from secure managerial career planning to providing common and preferred stock for widows and orphans. The plan worked well into the 1960s until the rise of a new interconnect industry and the legitimization of competition by the courts and the Federal Communications Commission (Von Auw, 1984).

In all, it is not surprising that we often identify organizational cultures as mainly the product of one transformational leader—Wriston of Citicorp, Revson of Revlon, or Watson of IBM.

Great Men

The leadership of the great men (and great women) of history has usually been transformational, not transactional. These leaders have influenced their contemporaries in two ways: through their own personalities and through the ideas for which they stand. In either case, the influence was unlikely to be a matter of a simple cost–benefit transaction. Nor was it a two-way, cost–benefit exchange. For example, it was more difficult and less rewarding for the Hebrews led by Moses to move up to a higher level of spirituality and to dematerialize their god (Freud, 1922). Nor was it necessarily the easy and more beneficial path for the transformational leader, Moses, to promote change instead of accepting things as they were. For Erikson (1969), great men like Martin Luther and Mahatma Gandhi demonstrated "a grim willingness to do the dirty work of their ages." To be transactional is the easy way out; to be transformational is the more difficult path to pursue.

Leaders are Both Transactional and Transformational

As noted earlier, while conceptually distinct, transformational and transactional leadership are likely to be displayed by the same individuals in different amounts and intensities. Three world-class leaders, Charles de Gaulle, Franklin D. Roosevelt, and Lyndon Johnson, illustrate the variations in pattern. Charles de Gaulle represented an extreme transformationalist who had little time for transactional leadership. For de Gaulle,

> long range national goals, [and] dignity and greatness [were] worthier goals than mere material happiness. . . . [This] led him to brush aside or neglect values and concerns of crucial importance to many, hence the recurrent divorce between himself and the French. . . . As for the French, their willingness to give priority to France's greatness decrease[d] whenever the requirements of the latter cease[d] being the same [as] their own daily necessities. Once order [was] restored, independence insured, the threat of great crisis removed, [there was] mutual disenchantment, as in

the winter of 1945-1946, when the Frenchmen's obsession with the daily difficulties and deprivations conflicted with de Gaulle's ambitions, or in the years 1965-68. [A divorce occurred] whenever the French [did] not live up to the imperative of grandeur, but satisf[ied] themselves with what he deem[ed] mediocrity and, so to speak, [gave] the lie to his claim [of greatness for] France. [Hoffman & Hoffman, 1970, p. 292-293]

At the same time, de Gaulle found parliamentary politics repulsive. He unified the French, not by compromising or accommodating to their conflicting self-interests, but by rising above them. Opponents were despised. He was incapable of working with subordinates and colleagues who resisted him. Exchanges and political deals were not for him (Hoffman & Hoffman, 1970).

More balanced in respect to transformational and transactional leadership, Franklin D. Roosevelt could play the consummate transformational leader with his fireside chats, inspiring addresses, remaking of the American landscape, and encouragement of intellectual solutions to national problems. But he also could play the consummate transactional politician in the give-and-take of the balance of powers between executive, legislature, and court. He didn't believe in entering battles, no matter how good the cause, unless he felt he could win.

More extremely transactional was Lyndon Johnson, even though his Great Society did represent a considerable transformational effort. In his own quest for power, Lyndon Johnson was always engaged in exchange relationships. He toadied up to the older men and women of power and wealth to extract whatever favors he could eventually seek from them. He could convincingly appear as reactionary with reactionaries and radical with radicals since he had no principles of his own other than his own need "to be a somebody." His subordinates were expected to trade the dedication of their lives in his service (with complete obedience) in exchange for his "taking care of them" by giving them modest patronage positions. He couldn't have cared less about the substance of political processes; only the processes themselves, and the impact on his fame and power mattered to him (Caro, 1982).

Transformational Leadership in Complex Organizations

Numerous examples of transformational leadership can be cited which have occurred in modern industrial, educational, social, and military organizations. Thomas J. Watson transformed IBM; Robert Hutchins transformed the University of Chicago; Jane Addams transformed Hull House; George Patton transformed the Third Army.

But among these leaders of complex organizations who were transformational in their effects on their subordinates, their organizations, and their environment, much transactional behavior could also be seen. Henry Ford was illustrative of this. In 1914, he made a deal that workers found hard to resist. He offered them the unusually high wage for that time of $5 a day in exchange for their accepting rigid control of their behavior both inside and outside the plant. No idle time was to be tolerated. Internal spies were employed to enforce disciplinary rules. Yet, it was this same Henry Ford who revolutionized the automobile industry, making possible the mass production of the cheap, affordable automobile for the mass market.

This same Henry Ford hired the handicapped and illiterate and was a visionary who organized a Peace Ship in 1916 to visit the leaders of the Big Powers in World War I in an effort to halt World War I. However, he was also known for his antitheoretical, anti-Semitic, and anti-intellectual prejudices.

The questions remain whether transformational leadership is a rarity or whether it is commonplace in the complex organizations and whether it is usually productive or counterproductive when it appears. Thus, Zaleznik (1983) notes that would-be leaders embedded in a bureaucracy are likely to be downgraded for imaginative capacity or their ability to visualize purposes and generate new values. Nevertheless, based on intensive interviews with successful directors of organizations ranging from movie studios and symphony orchestras to businesses and industries, Bennis (1983) concluded that rather than being rare, many of the elements of transformational leadership are essential for success of these directors, particularly when their organizations are undergoing "times of agonizing doubts and uncertainties." Included in the essential characteristics for these directors were the ability to create, articulate, and communicate a compelling vision that induces commitment to it, clarity about it, and support for it. In the same way, Prahalad and Doz (1982) argued that the central task of top management in strategic redirection of a business is the management of mind sets and motivations. A new consensus, a new balance of power, and a changed allocation of the organization's resources is achieved by the transformation of cognitive maps of how and what is to be done.

Decision Styles and Leadership

Both transactional and transformational leaders display all the recognized leader decision styles but in varying amounts and intensities.

They can be directive, negotiative or persuasive, consultative, participative, or delegative. Thus, we may see the transactional leader telling subordinates the specific payoffs they are to be given for complying with directions; the transformational leader may identify the transcendental goals toward which he may direct followers to work. The transactional leader may bargain about what exchanges will be provided for services rendered; the transformational leader may provide persuasive symbols and images about what a renewed organization would look like. The transactional leader may consult on what the follower wants to receive in exchange for compliance; the transformational leader may consult followers on their awareness of the importance of the organization's ultimate objectives; the transactional leader may participate with subordinates in reaching consensus on how they each will fulfill an acceptable exchange; the transformational leader may search for a participative consensus for restructuring the organization. The transactional leader may delegate responsibility to subordinates in exchange for their fulfilling an agreement; the transformational leader may delegate to encourage subordinate development.

A Pilot Study

To see if the concept of transformational leadership made any sense in the context of the complex organization, an open-ended survey was completed with 70 male senior industrial executives as a preliminary pilot study. A transformational leader was described to the executives as someone who raised their awareness about issues of consequence, shifted them to higher-level needs, and influenced them to transcend their own self-interests for the good of the group or organization and to work harder than they originally had expected they would. The executives were asked to describe any person whom they had encountered in their own careers who fit all or part of this description. All respondents claimed to have known at least one such person. Most cited a former immediate superior or higher-up in the organization to which the respondents had belonged at the time. A few mentioned family members, consultants, or counselors.

In the aggregate, the transformational leader was seen to lead the respondents to work "ridiculous" hours and to do more than they ever expected to do. A common aim reported by the respondents was to try to satisfy the leader's expectations of them and to give the leader all the support asked for. Other reactions included: the desire to emulate the leader, increased awareness, higher quality of performance, greater innovativeness, readiness to extend oneself and to develop oneself further, total commitment, belief in the organization as a consequence of belief in the leader, and heightened self-confidence.

A number of subtle elements were discovered in this survey of 70 senior executives. Many of these individuals (all were men) indicated that the transformational leader they could identify in their own careers was like a benevolent father who remained friendly and treated the respondent as an equal despite the leader's greater knowledge and experience. The leader provided a model of integrity and fairness with people and also set clear and high standards of performance. He encouraged followers with advice, help, support, recognition, and openness. He gave followers a sense of confidence in his intellect, yet was a good listener. He gave autonomy to followers and encouraged their self-development. He was willing to share his greater knowledge and expertise with them. Yet he could be formal at work when and if necessary. He was seen to be firm and would reprimand subordinates when necessary. However, most respondents were inclined to see the transforming leader as informal and close. Such a leader could be counted on to stand up for his followers.

Along with the heightened and changed motivation and awareness, frequent reactions of followers to the transforming leader included trust, strong liking, admiration, loyalty, and respect.

This pilot inquiry led to speculation that while transactional leadership can provide satisfactory payoffs in the short term, transformational leadership is likely to generate more effort, creativity and productivity in the long run. Subordinate competence as an organization member will be developed further as a consequence of the transformational leader's nurturance and vision.

Transformational Leadership and Charisma

It was also concluded from this survey that the quantitative examination of the transformational leader must pay attention to the socioemotional elements of charisma—"devotion, awe, reverence, and blind faith." (Wilner, 1968, p. 6). Managers, officers, and administrators can be found to whom followers form deep emotional attachments and who in turn inspire their followers to transcend their own interests for superordinate goals, for goals higher in level than those previously recognized by the followers. Even in hardened bureaucracies, there are leaders whose knowledge of the system, coupled with good connections and the ability to mobilize and husband resources, enables them to keep their eyes on the bigger issues. They take the risks required for "creative administration." Such idiosyncratic leaders (Hollander, 1978) are able to arouse in their subordinates faith and trust in the leader's motives and competence. Subordinates become willing to strive for the higher goals set forth as challenges for the group by the leader.

The deep emotional attachment which characterizes the relationship of the charismatic leader to his followers may be present when transformational leadership occurs, but we can distinguish a class of charismatics who are not at all transformational in their influence. Celebrities may be identified as charismatic by a large segment of the public. Celebrities are held in awe and reverence by the masses who are devoted to them. People will be emotionally aroused in the presence of celebrities and identify with them in their fantasies but the celebrities may not be involved at all in any transformation of their public. On the other hand, with charisma, transformational leaders can play the role of teacher, mentor, coach, reformer, or revolutionary. Transformational leaders structure and articulate problems for followers, enabling the followers to more easily comprehend problems so that they can more effectively deal with them. Transformational leaders can also oversimplify problems so that their follows may make overly hasty responses to them, bolstering each other's positions or even evading the problems altogether. As we shall see in Chapter 3, charisma is a necessary ingredient of transformational leadership, but by itself is not sufficient to account for the transformational process.

Importance of Transformational Leadership

The need to better understand how leaders in business and industry can induce second-order increases in effort was evidenced in an in-depth interview survey of a representative national sample of 845 working Americans. The survey found that while most employees liked and respected their managers, they felt their managers really didn't know how to motivate employees to give their best. Only 23 percent said they were working as hard as they could in their jobs although 70 percent endorsed the work ethic. But only 9 percent would agree that it was simply a matter of connecting how much they earned to how hard they work. Most reported that there actually was little connection between the two (Yankelovich & Immerwahr, 1983). Similar conclusions could be reached, no doubt, about how hard students or military service personnel are trying to do their best.

If transformational leadership is as important to productive and service organizations as it is to political action, society, and history, then we will need to learn how to develop in managers the sensitivity and interpersonal competence required for them to function as transformational leaders. We will need to determine how to select potential transformational leaders who probably may not show up as well on many currently available predictive tests which primarily assess transactional leadership. We will need to overcome the parochialism which has focused empirical leadership research on the easier-to-study transactional leadership in which the leader succeeds in helping the followers to satisfy some need they hold (for example, see Hollander, 1978). The transactional leader induces performance among followers by negotiating an exchange relationship with them of reward for compliance. Transformational leadership arouses transcendental interests in followers and/or elevates their need and aspiration levels. In doing so, transformational leadership may result ultimately in a higher level of satisfaction and effectiveness among the led.

We need to improve our understanding of the short- and long-term motivation, commitment, involvement, satisfaction, creativity, and productivity of industrial, governmental, military, and educational personnel as a function of the extent to which their superiors are transactional or transformational. To begin to fulfill this need, we set out to determine the behavioral components of transactional and transformational leadership and their relation to performance outcomes of satisfaction and effectiveness—that is, to the achievement of both expected performance and performance beyond expectations.

In Chapters 11 and 12, we have described how we used what we had found in our pilot study to construct survey questionnaires which were administered to 176 senior U.S. Army officers who were asked to use them to describe their superiors. Emerging from our analyses were three transformational factors—charismatic leadership (including inspirational leadership), individual consideration, and intellectual stimulation; and two transactional factors—contingent reward and management-by-exception. As expected, and as we were able to replicate in subsequent exploratory studies with educational administrators, world class leaders, and business, government, and industrial employees, extra effort by subordinates, perceived unit effectiveness, and subordinate satisfaction were more highly correlated with the transformational factors than with the transactional factors.

We now turn to the first and most important of these factors—charismatic leadership.

Part II

The Emotional Component

AFTER THAT FIRST MEETING with the Director in his office, I knew I was going to accept his offer of a job with him if he made me one. He had that "command presence" which made you feel you would be pleased to work for him and what he stood for. You couldn't help but feel a strong sense of attraction to him and have confidence that you were joining a winning team if you became one of his subordinates. The earlier balance sheet of pros and cons, about whether or not to accept the job if it was offered to me, that I had completed to help me make up my mind was discarded. Now I simply felt "in my guts" that here was the guy I wanted to work for.

Chapter 3

Charisma

In the popular media, charisma has come to mean anything ranging from chutzpah to Pied Piperism, from celebrity to superman status. It has become an overworked cliche for strong, attractive, and inspiring personality. In social science and political science, charisma has been used to describe leaders who by the power of their person have profound and extraordinary effects on their followers. Charismatic leaders inspire in their followers unquestioning loyalty and devotion without regard to the followers' own self-interest. Such leaders can transform the established order.

Increasingly since Max Weber (1922/1947) borrowed the term from theology by way of Rudolph Sohn, charisma (Greek for gift) has become like the weather, something about which we can talk but not do much. Weber's charismatic was a religious savior, an innovative prophet with personal magnetism, promoting a specific doctrine. A mystical ascetic, he was like Superman in his narcissistic concern for himself rather than for others.

Charisma has been widely discussed by sociological, psychoanalytic, and political commentators, but shunned for the most part by experimental social and organizational psychologists and by organizational behaviorists. One exception was an essay by House (1977) on the possible conceptual value of charisma to the organizational sciences. But as of 1976, House could find no empirical efforts to study the phenomenon. This may be one reason critics complain that despite the thousands of empirical studies of leadership, this literature offers little guidance to the serious practitioners. Yet it is clear that behavioral appreciation of leadership must go beyond conceptualizing it in terms of initiation and consideration, or task and relations orientation, or direction and participation. Behavioral studies of leadership must deal empirically with such phenomena as charisma and inspiration.

Characteristics of Charisma

Charisma Depends on Followers As Well as Leaders

For Max Weber, charisma was also to be seen in the reactions of followers. It was their "devotion to the specific and exceptional sanctity, heroism or exemplary character of an individual person, and of the normative patterns or order revealed or ordained by him" (Weber, 1947, p. 328).

For political scientists, charisma packs an emotional wallop for followers above and beyond ordinary esteem, affection, admiration, and trust. It has an intense emotional component of "devotion, awe, reverence, and blind faith" (Wilner, 1968, p. 6). It is an unqualified belief in the "man and his mission" about what is, what should be, and what should be done." It is an absolute emotional and cognitive identification with the leader (p. 9). Thus, seven of nine successful utopian communities had ideologies that greatly encouraged their members to endow their leader with the extraordinary gift of charisma (Kanter, 1972).

The extent to which followers are ready to endow leaders with charisma depends on the personality of the followers as much as on their leaders. Psychological distress often precedes one's joining of a charismatic sect (Galanter, 1982). In comparison to control samples, the "Moonies," who ardently support their charismatic Reverend Moon, show greater feelings of helplessness, cynicism, distrust of political action, and less confidence in their own sexual identity, their own values and in the future (Lodahl, 1982).

For psychoanalytically oriented psychohistorians, charisma entails massive displacements of feelings onto the public stage by both leader and followers. The feelings are connected with a search for love that has remained unfulfilled in their own family life.

> It is only when the psychohistorian has a full realization of the overwhelming quantity of desperate clinging, inner emptiness and violent rage which

have been the sad result of the loveless atmosphere in most families throughout history, that they can begin to appreciate the full force of the displacement of the drama of unfulfilled love, disillusionment and hostility onto the public stage. [Demause, 1982, p. 173]

Furthermore, according to Demause (1973), psychosexual conflicts are displaced by shared group fantasies. These fantasies allow people to relieve shared private feelings, to act out and defend against their own repressed inhibitions using rationalization, reaction formation, and so on with materials provided by current public events and public discussion.

Situations Fostering Charisma

The charismatic is an idolized hero, a messiah and savior who appears in times of great distress. This salvation from distress is what therefore engenders the

special emotional intensity of the charismatic response . . . followers respond to the charismatic leader with passionate loyalty because the salvation, or promise of it, that he appears to embody represents the fulfillment of urgently felt needs. [Tucker, 1970, p. 81]

Acute and chronic crisis components are a necessary element in a theory about charisma. The Chrysler Corporation must be turning "belly up" for an Iacocca to make his appearance. The bigger the crisis, the more the emotional disturbance, the more such emotionality can be invested in the savior. But it is not only acute crisis that brings out the charismatic leader. Charismatic leadership arises when crisis is chronic such as when the ultimate values of a culture are being attacked (Hummel, 1972). Charisma carries with it a challenge to the old order, a break with continuity, a risky adventure, continual movement, ferment, and change. Organizational cultures in transition are ripe for charismatic leaders to appear in industry. Charisma arises when traditional authority and legal, rational, and bureaucratic means have failed. Don't look for charismatic leadership in the already old, highly structured, successful organizations but rather in those old ones that are failing or in new ones that are struggling to survive. Traditions are losing legitimacy in the older failing organizations; they have not become fully legitimatized in the new.

The competition between old and new systems of values where change to the new has not been legitimated is another beginning scenario for charismatics. The rise of chronic structural unemployment may be the nexus for the rise of new types of charismatic labor leaders. The change from smokestack industry to service and high technology may presage the rise of new charismatic industrial leaders.

According to Erikson (1958) people become "charisma hungry" in times of distress due to the decline of old values and rituals, shocks to the culture, growing fears, anxieties, and identity crises. For example, Mahatma Gandhi satisfied this public hunger by giving Indians a new collective identity and new rituals (Erikson, 1969). Hitler rose as savior in Germany under the dislocation and disappointments of military defeat and economic distress. The government was seen as weak and as unlikely to cope with the nation's problems. The rise of Mussolini to power in 1922 aptly illustrates the same theme.

> [Italy] had lost sight of its aims and will, lacked faith in itself and was affected by a mass inferiority complex. [It] suffered from both real and imaginary ills. The idea of a savior capable of bringing well-being to all by the sheer force of his will was not only appealing, it was a last hope. And Mussolini, savior and superman, promised law and order, a full appreciation of victory and its worth, an Italy cured of poverty, restored to its dignity, resuming its place among the great nations of Europe, and governed by youth and youthful energy. [Fermi, 1966, pp. 214–215]

Numerous other illustrations of the appeal of the charismatic leader as savior from distress can be provided. Martin Luther King and Jesse Jackson gave hope to the disadvantaged blacks that by their own personal efforts combined with collective action they could reshape American society to advance their place in it.

It is easier for charismatics to appear in societies that seek, expect, and/or encourage their appearance. Charismatic prophets and messiahs could arise in ancient Israel because they fit with a long prophetic tradition. They were being awaited. In the absence of tradition, as in ancient China, the emergence of such charismatics was much less possible (Hummel, 1972).

Originated by Americans, the Quality Circle Movement first flowered in Japan. Part of the reason was that the responsible leadership called for by its American originators was more in tune with Japanese rather than American norms at that time about leadership. Most accounts of the Quality Circle Movement, which played an important part in the Japanese postwar economic miracle, credit its inception to American industrial engineers, Edward Deming, Charles Protzman, and others who, starting in 1949, introduced statistical quality control methods to Japanese management. The consultants' approach required frequent consultation between management and employees. This fell on fertile ground since traditionally Japan with its Ringei method had emphasized the importance of full consultation among leader and subordinates.

In crediting the innovation to the Americans, what has been unappreciated was the prevailing leadership philosophy in Japan at the time as well as the leadership approach advocated by the engineers such as Protzman. He, for example, was unimpressed by the then nascent Human Relations Movement in the United States with its focus on informal and shared leadership. Protzman's emphasis was on the manager's charismalike, transformational responsibilities to ''secure the faith and respect of those under him by his being an example of high purpose, courage, honor and independence.'' This fit squarely with Japanese tradition which said that leaders were men of exemplary moral courage and self-sacrifice. Again, consistent with Japanese tradition, the Americans stressed management commitment to long-term continuity of purpose (Tsurumi, 1982).

In all, charismatic leader-follower relations are latent in a wide array of situations, not only appearing ''in extravagant forms and fleeting moments, but in an abiding, if combustible, aspect of social life that occasionally bursts into open flame'' (Geertz, 1977, p. 151). Trice and Beyer (1984) uncovered studies of charismatic relationships in such diverse organizations as suburban school systems, communes, utopian communities, colleges, Alcoholics Anonymous, the National Council on Alcoholism, the Chippewa Indian tribe, a maternity home, a British manufacturing firm, Tanganyikan labor unions, and the royal courts of England, Java, and Morocco.

The Charismatic Relationship

Theologically, charisma was an endowment of spiritual grace from God. For secular social science, it is an endowment of an extremely high degree of esteem, value, popularity, and/or celebrity-status attributed by others. This engenders in these other people strong emotional responses of love or hate. The leader with charisma attains a generalized influence which is transformational. It transcends the immediate situation and ordinary exchanges of compliance with promises of rational reward or threats of immediate punishment. Basking in the glory of the charismatic may be sufficient reward for the starstruck just as doing God's work is sufficient reward for the pious. Admiration for charismatic leaders and the desire to identify with them and to emulate them are powerful influences on followers. As an attribution, charisma is in the eye of the beholder. Therefore, it is relative to the beholder. But charismatics actively shape and enlarge audiences through their own energy, self-confidence, assertiveness, ambition, and seizing of opportunities. The dynamic process involved according to House (1977) is as follows: Imbued with self-confidence in their own competence, conviction in their own beliefs and ideals, and a strong need for power, charismatic leaders are highly motivated to influence their followers. Their self-confidence and strong convictions increase their followers' trust in their leaders' judgments. Charismatic leaders engage in impression management to bolster their image of competence, increasing subordinate compliance and faith in them. The charismatic leaders relate the work and mission of their group to strongly held values, ideals, and aspirations shared in common by their organization's culture. In organizational settings, they paint for their subordinate an attractive vision of what the outcomes of their efforts could be. This provides subordinates with more meaning for their work. It arouses enthusiasm, excitement, emotional involvement and commitment to group objectives. Roles are defined in ideological terms that appeal to the subordinates. Charismatic leaders use themselves to set examples for subordinates to follow.

Success as a leader flows from one's charisma. But equally so, the charismatic must continue to demonstrate effectiveness as a leader, that is, that the actions which can be attributed to him are continuing to benefit the community of followers. The effectiveness must be real or apparent. Often, the charismatic survives with more attention given the apparent than the real. Image of success and effectiveness is pursued. As long as the image of success and effectiveness as a leader can be sustained, the charismatic remains deified by his supporters (Gerth & Mills, 1946).

Television has both helped and complicated the image-building and image-maintaining aspects of the charismatic leader's efforts. The brevity and selective editing capabilities can be used to protect the image, but the live camera is also a force for bringing reality into the living room. Events favorable to the image can be staged, but events unfavorable to the image can also dramatically show up as if the leader was face-to-face with supporters.

Endurance of Charisma

Although the influence of charismatic leaders may be contingent on the situation, the attribute of charisma remains. After victory in World War II, the masses of French and British citizens were now more concerned with economic recovery. Both France and Britain turned de Gaulle and Churchill out to pasture. But these leaders' personal stature in the eyes of the world and much of their influence remained. De Gaulle was brought back stronger in power 12 years later in the Algerian confrontation, threat of revolution, and constitutional crisis. After removal as prime minister, Churchill went on to influence international realignments and to provide the Western democracies with the image of the Iron Curtain whose perception still influences Soviet–American relations.

The endurance of their transforming effect is a prime concern for the charismatics themselves. Some have succeeded in making a lasting impact; others have not. The transformations brought about by the charismatic leader are often seen to endure long after the charismatic has died. (Symbolic of the endurance of charisma is the continued public display 60 years after Lenin's death of his embalmed body.) The known world was remade socially, culturally, and politically by Alexander the Great in his own short career. Simon Bolivar's efforts had lasting political effects on much of Latin America. Mohammed's actions transformed societies stretching from North Africa to Indonesia and left lasting works on cultures from Spain to Central Asia. But the very opposite is just as likely. The death of a charismatic military commander is highly demoralizing and disruptive to his troops (Hays and Thomas, 1967). Hitler's projected thousand-year "New Order" died with him; the German salesman achieved an economic dominance in Europe for Germany which Hitler never could. Mao Zedung felt he would transcend his own death by living on in a permanent revolution. But his death brought an end to the "permanent revolution" and continuing turmoil in China. A more rational government eventually appeared.

Focused on the expressive, the emotional, and the non-rational, the relationship between the charismatic leader and the led is basically unstable. It must be routinized by the development of organizational rules and arrangements to achieve stability (Weber, 1947). The charismatic, revolutionary hero, Buonaparte, becomes the Emperor Napoleon.

The charismatic leader is a hard act to follow. Routine institutional practices and the cultural imperatives built by the charismatic leader must replace him after he is gone. Yet often these collapse with his demise. Tito of Yugoslavia planned carefully for the succession after his death but was not optimistic that any associate could accumulate the personal authority that his charisma had given Tito (Drachkovitch, 1964).

Trice and Beyer (1984) looked at four ways in which a leader's charisma is routinized. In the phenomenal growth of Alcoholics Anonymous and the National Council on Alcoholism, both begun by charismatic leaders, they were able to find to a considerable degree: (1) development of an administrative apparatus that puts the charismatic's program into practice; (2) transfer of charisma to others in the organization by rites and ceremonials; (3) incorporation of the charismatic's message and mission into organizational traditions; and (4) selection of a successor who resembled the charismatic with sufficiency of esteem to achieve the charismatic's personal influence.

Emergence of Charisma in Complex Organizations

For Max Weber, charismatic leaders were the inspiration for the birth and development of organizations which subsequently became traditionally or bureaucratically managed. Charismatic leaders were the innovative leaders responsible for the creation of organizations; managerial bureaucrats were required to run them. Charismatics made the rules for bureaucratic administrators to live by. According to Berger (1963), charismatics were also to be found at the center of institutional structures with the power to radicalize them.

We most often associate charisma with political and religious figures rather than with leaders in rationally organized business, industry, education, and government. In fact, a senior administrator at a large state university was heard to say at a faculty committee meeting planning the search for a new dean: "Deans cannot be leaders." What he meant was whoever was selected for the post primarily had to concentrate on seeing that his school conformed to the bureaucratic order and higher authority as given. Creativity, innovation, and motivation of the school's constituencies should remain of secondary concern.

Nevertheless, charisma is widely distributed as an interpersonal attribute in complex organizations and is not limited only to world-class leaders.[1] Furthermore, we see charisma as a component—probably the

---

[1] A number of commentators such as Blau & Scott (1962), Dow (1969), Etzioni (1961), House (1976), Oberg (1972), Shils (1965), and Tucker (1968) have reached the same conclusion.

most general and important component—of the larger concept of transformational leadership. In this regard, we see charisma is to be found to a considerable degree in industrial, educational, governmental, and military leaders. Support for this position comes from the quantitative analyses in Chapters 11 and 12 where we find that many followers described their organizational superior as someone who made everyone enthusiastic about assignments, who inspired loyalty to the organization, who commanded respect from everyone, who had a special gift of seeing what was really important, and who had a sense of mission. The entranced subordinates had complete faith in leaders with charisma and felt good to be near them. Subordinates said they were proud to be associated with charismatic leaders and trusted such leaders' capacity to overcome any obstacle. Charismatic leaders served as symbols of success and accomplishment for their followers.

It may be true that charismatics are more likely to appear in political and religious movements than in business or industry (Katz & Kahn, 1966). We have paid more attention to charisma in political and religious movements, but we suggest that it is not necessarily uncommon in the complex organizations of business executives, educational administrators, military officers, and industrial managers. For Zaleznik (1983), charisma is one of the elements separating ordinary managers from true leaders in organizational settings. True leaders attract intense feelings of love (and sometimes hate) from their subordinates. Subordinates want to identify with the leaders. Feelings about ordinary managers are bland but relations are smoother and more steady. Like most intimate relationships, the relations between charismatic leaders and their followers tend to be more turbulent. For Berlew (1979), the charismatic leader generates excitement by creating a common vision, making supporters feel stronger and originating valued opportunities that are meaningful to the supporters.

Smith (1982) discriminated between 60 charismatic and noncharismatic business leaders. Charismatic leaders were described by their subordinates as significantly more dynamic. Subordinates also said they worked harder (longer work weeks) under charismatic leaders and were more confident and trusting.

According to Handy (1976), ''commando leaders'' turn up when challenging and exhilarating tasks need to be undertaken in an organization. But they tend to be regarded as ''glamorous nuisances'' even though they are highly effective. (Presumably they would be less of a nuisance in an organic, flexible organization.) At the same time, Hollander (1978) believed that charismatic leadership is less likely to emerge in any continuing complex organization because of the close contact of superior and subordinate preventing the maintenance of the magical properties of charisma. But charismatics, like Lenin and Kitchener, for example, had immediate lifelong subordinates who worshiped them with intense devotion. Social distance between leader and follower may help the magic of charisma but is not essential for it. Furthermore, intimacy may take many forms. It can be enacting learned role expectations involving power and control of one person over the other. It can be spiritual, transpersonal, and built on a sense of universal consciousness that all men are brothers. It can be mature interdependence.

Yukl (1981) thinks the presumed scarcity of charismatic leaders in business and industry may be due to the lack of managers with the necessary skills. However, Berlew (1974) feels that many managers have the skills but don't recognize the opportunities available. It may be that those who choose to work in business and industry are less willing to risk what is required to stand out so visibly among their peers. Being a conforming organizational member may be more important for success than standing up for one's convictions.

For House (1977), charismatics can be found locally. Signs of their existence include: followers' trust in the correctness of the leader's beliefs, similarity of followers' beliefs to the leader's beliefs, unquestioning acceptance of the leader by followers, followers' affection for the leader, willing obedience to the leader by followers, emotional involvement of followers in the mission of the organization, heightened performance goals of followers, and belief by followers that they are able to contribute to the success of the group's mission.

Charisma and Types of Organization

Weber (1947) had noted that charismatic leadership was a substitute for providing order and direction in complex organizations which were not in the bureaucratic mold nor operated according to tradition. Today we see the rise of the *ad hoc,* flexible organization in high-technology industry whose organizational forms of processes avoid bureaucratic and traditional rigidities by recourse to temporary systems and organic forms of organization (Robbins, 1983). Elaborate formal coordination and planning is likely to be replaced by teamwork and devoted, intense effort by members. The prime movers display a lot of the characteristics of charismatic leadership (Quinn and Cameron, 1983).

Following study of 80 chief executive officers and 10 innovative organizational leaders, Bennis (1982) concluded that common to them was "the capacity to create and communicate a compelling vision of a desired state of affairs" (p. 55). They could communicate their vision to clarify it and induce the commitment of their multiple constituencies to maintaining the organization's course. These leaders also revealed the self-determination and persistence of the charismatic "especially when the going gets rough." Yet they emphasized adaptability of themselves and their organizations to new conditions and new problems. These successful top managers concentrated on the purposes of their organizations and on "paradigms of action." They made extensive use of metaphor, symbolism, ceremonial, and insignia as ways of concretizing and transmitting their visions of what could be and committing their organizations to them. They defined what is right, good, and important for their organization, thus were instrumental in developing and maintaining their organization's culture of shared norms and values.

Based on his observations of successful leaders in participative systems, Lawler (1982) concluded that leadership occurs "through a combination of factors that can be captured by words like vision, communication, symbols, and charisma." Such leaders are more concerned with doing the right things than with doing things right.

Requisite Abilities, Interests, and Personality of the Charismatic Leader

Self-Confidence

A universal trait of the charismatic leader is his own self-confidence and self-esteem. Charles de Gaulle epitomized this feature of complete confidence in the correctness of his position and in his capabilities to solve whatever was troubling France. Charismatics make this a clear aspect of their public image. Even when personally discouraged and facing failure, they are unlikely to make public such feelings (Tucker, 1970). Such self-esteem helps charismatics to avoid defensiveness in conflicting interpersonal situations and to maintain the confidence that their subordinates have in them (Hill, 1976). Presumably, charismatic leaders project on to like-minded loyal followers their continuing confident opinions of themselves. Driven out of Jordan in 1970, defeated in Lebanon in 1976, driven out of Beirut, then from Damascus and then again from

Tripoli in 1984, Yasir Arafat continued to show a smiling face to the public and continued to command the support of a majority of Palestinians.

Self-Determination

For Weber (1947), charisma was firstly a personal characteristic of some leaders which set them apart from ordinary people as a consequence of their transcendental purposes and their endowment with extraordinary determination, power and capability. Nietzsche's superman had much of the same character: inner-direction, originality, self-determination, sense of duty, and responsibility to his unique self. For Nietzsche, ordinary men conformed to the expectations of others. Nietzsche's superman could free himself from the expected. He was a point of contact with the future who created new values and goals. He was the master, not the slave of organizations. He struggled for power to free himself and became master of his own fate. Although Nietzche's superman, determined and inner-directed, had much in common with the charismatic, some elements of the superman are counter to transformational leadership. While the transformational leader is concerned with successful organizational change, the Nietzchian superman is seeking freedom for himself. While the transformational leader is concerned about development of others as well as himself, the superman is narcissistic and extremely self-oriented (Nietzche, 1885/1974).

Abilities Required to Be Transformational

Charismatic leaders are transformational in that they, themselves, have much to do with the further arousal and articulation of such feelings of need among followers. Charismatic leaders have insight into the needs, values, and hopes of their followers. They have the ability to build on these needs, values, and hopes through dramatic and persuasive words and actions (e.g., Martin Luther King's "I Have a Dream" speech and his March on Selma, Alabama). Identical with what we have said before about transformational leaders, charismatics, according to Gardner (1961), have the ability to "both conceive and articulate goals that lift people out of their petty preoccupations." Such leaders can unite people to seek objectives "worthy of their best efforts." Charismatic leaders are great actors. They are always "on stage." They are always projecting to their followers their extreme self-confidence and convictions so that they become larger than life. They must be able to present themselves as miracle workers likely to succeed where others would fail (House, 1977).

As Yukl (1981) notes, charismatic leaders can say things publicly that followers feel privately but cannot express. Then these public utterances become slogans for the movement; for example, King's "We shall overcome" and Lenin's "Land, Peace, Bread." In the 1984 Presidential campaign, Gary Hart's "New Ideas" expressed a yearning among better-educated voters for a problem-solving focus on the future rather than a continuation of the policies of the Right or the Left.

Additional Transformational Tendencies

Charismatics take advantage of the Pygmalion effect (about which more will be said in the next chapter) and reciprocate in their confidence in their followers and in their optimistic expectations about their followers' performance. Follower self-esteem and enthusiasm are raised as a consequence, and the effort is increased among followers to fulfill the leaders' expressed expectations.

Charismatic leaders arouse achievement, affiliation, and power motives among their subordinates linked to the mission of their group. "You can do more than you thought possible," "One for all, and all for one," and "Nice guys finish last" illustrate respectively charismatic leadership appeals to followers' achievement, affiliation, and power motives.

Charismatic leaders can generate a frame of reference and an image of reality for followers (Smircich & Morgan, 1982). Although this can be an interactive, consultative process, it is a particularly strongly sensed and felt image when associated with charisma. Charismatic leaders influence what is figure and what is ground and thus define the situation for followers. This freedom may be due to the charismatics' ability to resolve these conflicts outside of themselves. Luther and Gandhi are illustrative (Erikson, 1969).

Resolution of Internal Conflict

Psychoanalysts suggest that the unusual vision of charismatic leaders that makes it possible for them "to see around corners" stems from their greater freedom from internal conflict. Ordinary managers and leaders lacking charisma are more likely to experience such conflict between the emotions, impressions, feelings, and associations emerging from the id and the strong, controlling, conscience of the superego. Freedom from the id–superego conflict makes possible strong ego ideals. The charismatic leader can be more assured that what he values is right and important. He can articulate purposes for the organization such as to ''be the best in the business'' for which enthusiasm among colleagues can be aroused. Under such leadership, colleagues can find meaning and satisfaction transcending their own self-interest. Another consequence of his strong ego ideal is that the charismatic leader, convinced of the goodness and rightness of his own point of view, is likely to be more forthright and candid in his reprimands of subordinates. He can replace subordinates with a clear conscience (Keichel, 1983).

On the other hand, the ego of the ordinary manager—particularly the middle manager who is expected to fill a role of cooperativeness and conformity—is kept busy with his inner id–superego struggles and constraints. His concerns are bundled metaphorically into the body of a man in a Grey Flannel Suit, fitting into the mold, not making waves, defending his turf, making the right moves for his career. The ordinary manager is a continuing victim of his self-doubts and personal traumas regardless of his extensive career success (Levinson et al. 1978).

Korman et al. (1981) found the consequences of this inner turmoil in the experience of many managers. They suffered from their unfulfilled expectations and from their sense of a lack of control over fate. Even highly successful male executives in midlife reported doubts and conflicts about themselves, their values, their careers, and about the meaning of success (Henry, 1961). Again, Tarnowieski (1973) discovered a great deal of personal and social alienation among several thousand managers. Their careers no longer met their personal needs and they felt alienated from the organizations for which they worked. In the same way, successful young executives and their wives revealed strong feelings of stress, a loss of personal alertness, an increasing sense of meaninglessness in everyday activities (Bartoleme, 1972), and a loss of emotional feeling (Maccoby, 1976). Approximately 80 percent of another sample of middle-aged managers reported undergoing periods of intense frustrations as early as their late 30's; 15 percent never really recovered (Schultz, 1974).

As the extreme antithesis of the transforming, charismatic leader, the inhibited and defensive bureaucrat struggling with his own id versus superego conflicts

> has a conscience that's always keeping score and just may be poisoning the wellspring of self-confidence with guilt. All het up with nowhere to go—no

very bright ideal to pursue—his aggressive energies will be sluiced into attacks on himself and on those around him: he'll distrust his own competence and theirs. The result is corporate politics at its least productive: turf battles, a boss rivalrous toward subordinates and unwilling to help them along, demoralization in all its senses. [Kiechel, 1983, p. 140]

Success Without Charisma

A charismatic personality makes success as a leader more likely, but it is not essential for such success. Just as celebrity status alone does not make a charismatic leader, so we can identify successful leaders such as George Washington, who had few of the personal characteristics of a charismatic. He showed little confidence in his ability to lead the Continental Army against Britain. He actually tried to avoid the appointment as commander and failed to achieve many momentous military or political triumphs. He did not create new beliefs. He was committed to maintaining the existing institutions and to protecting them from the excesses of British Parliament and the Crown. As a military officer and government bureaucrat, he followed the accepted practices of his day and avoided biases and favoritism to further his efforts. Nevertheless, Washington was a most successful military and political leader worshipped by his supporters because he embodied the values of his society (Schwartz, 1983).

Again, leaders can be successful in many other ways without the attributes of charisma. Leaders may succeed by negotiating satisfactory agreements among conflicting interest groups, by providing contingent rewards for compliance, and by arranging for encouraging participative solutions among those who will have to live with the decisions reached (Zaleznik & Kets de Vries, 1975).

When Charismatic Leaders Fail

Charismatic leaders are not all necessarily effective in the positions of influence they achieve. John F. Kennedy was one of our most charismatic Presidents who did arouse national fervour for domestic change and American power abroad, but he was unable in his two years in office to effect much domestic reform and to achieve much success in his foreign endeavors. Fidel Castro is another highly charismatic leader. He did successfully transform Cuba, but generally he has been somewhat less successful in his rather costly efforts to export his revolution to elsewhere in Latin America and Africa.

Despite their self-confidence, self-determination, and freedom from inner conflicts, some charismatic leaders will fail partly or fully in their endeavors as a consequence of particular deficiencies or exaggerated tendencies. Sometimes they may fail due to the overwhelming constraints they face and how they try to cope with them. Thus, how leaders with a sense of mission, self-confidence, ambition, and other attributes of charisma handle the organizational constraints that frustrate their aims also makes a difference in whether they succeed in transforming organization managements, or fail in a dissatisfying standoff to reconcile what they want to see done with what can be done. John Connor was a successful business executive who accepted office as U.S. Secretary of Commerce. There he was frustrated by his inability to have much influence over the Department of Commerce. He stayed in office for a while, displaying an uncomplaining sense of optimism, then resigned (Zaleznik, 1967). U.S. Senator and Vice-President Hubert Humphrey similarly had the sense of mission, self-confidence, and immense ambition, but he talked too much, thought too little, and after finding that his idealism was getting in the way of his political success learned that politics was the art of compromise. Unfortunately, he compromised his liberalism, agreed to become Lyndon Johnson's Vice-President, and submerged his own liberal ideals to become a loud public spokesman for Johnson's Vietnamese war despite his own private aversion to it (Solberg, 1984).

McCall and Lombardo (1983) uncovered clues that may help point to what may make it possible for junior executives with some of the characteristics of charismatics to appear and thrive in organizational settings or to fall by the wayside. They completed an interview study of 20 executives who had begun their careers seemingly able to work miracles in their organizations but who had been "derailed" in their careers. These were compared with 20 executives who had successfully climbed to the top of the ladder.

Certain personal flaws made a difference. Self-determination could be too strong. One interviewee gave as an example: "he wouldn't negotiate; there was no room for countervailing views. He could follow a bull through a china shop and still break the china." This stubborn insensitivity to others could not be overcome by an executive's outstanding past. It was a frequent cause of derailment.

Additional flaws mentioned were coldness and arrogance, betrayal of trust, and failure to delegate, to staff effectively, and to build a team.

While any of these flaws might be fatal to a charismatic in an organizational hierarchy, the charismatic political leader might be able to get away with any of these shortcomings by appeals to his larger, more distant constituencies. But for the industrial executive, part way up the organizational ladder, too many such flaws create among his more powerful colleagues strong antipathies to his subsequent promotion.

"Natural leaders," promising young executives, also stumbled and fell on their way up the corporate ladder because of their inconsistencies and unpredictability. They became sources of confusion in the corporate network. Those who reached the top were more likely to establish reputations embodied in the formula, "I will do exactly what I say I will do when I say I will do it. If I change my mind, I will tell you well in advance so you will not be harmed by my actions" (McCall and Lombardo, 1983, p. 11).

As these executives with initial promise moved up, the same strengths that had led to their early promotions became weaknesses. Loyalty to colleagues became overdependence or cronyism; excessive ambition alienated their supporters; superior expertise caused them to bog down in detail. Continued success at lower levels which led some promising junior executives to become cold and arrogant, resulted in the subsequent refusal of colleagues to want to continue working with them.

Thus, some of the important elements in many successful political charismatics such as their inner directedness, self-confidence, ambition, and sense of mission, if not tempered by the constraints of the organization, are likely to get the rising charismatic junior executive in trouble. Also, exploratory studies (Chapter 12) suggest that in complex organizations charismatic leaders play a less important role in the effectiveness of the organizational unit they supervise than in the effectiveness of the organization as a whole. Nevertheless, despite this, some highly self-determined, self-confident charismatic leaders have managed to rise or stay on the top of even the most hardened bureaucracies. Witness the long tenure of Admiral Hyman Rickover, charismatic head of the Navy's nuclear submarine program. Like many a political charismatic, with a power base in Congress rather than the Navy, he was able to remain in his position despite his unpopularity among many of his Navy colleagues (Polmar & Allen, 1982).

Charismatic Leaders Who Do Not Transform Followers

Even when successful as leaders, charismatics may fail to have a transforming or inspirational influence on followers. It will depend on how their charisma combines with the other transformational factors of individualized consideration and intellectual stimulation in specific leaders. Charismatic mentors will guide and support the personal growth of their disciples. Equally charismatic patrons will exchange support, protection, and security for loyalty and service, keeping their clients in the same continued state of dependency. Charismatic, inspirational teachers will provide intellectual stimulation; charismatic celebrities who lack the intellect will not. Charismatic junior Army officers with their cry of "follow me," will provide inspiration to take action; charismatic ascetics or mystics may foster escapism and lethargy.

The charismatic who is a successful transformational leader (followers are influenced) and an effective transformational leader (followers benefit from the transformation) can be distinguished from the charismatic who is not. The successful and effective transformational leader is engaged with authentic rather than false needs of followers and with mutual enhancement of effort. Individualized consideration is more likely to be displayed. Relatively speaking, the charismatic transformational leader dealing with authentic needs will rely somewhat more on rational, intellectual persuasion; the false messiah who fails to have transforming effects will rely more on emotional appeals. We expect to find a greater discrepancy between the actual and perceived competence of the charismatic leader who fails to display transformational leadership with the charismatic who does. While both inspire followers, the charismatic transformational leader more often will appear in the role of teacher, mentor, or coach; the charismatic who is not transforming will appear in the role of celebrity, shaman, miracle worker, or mystic. The charismatic transformational leader structures problems for followers providing for their easier comprehension so that followers can more effectively deal with them; the charismatic leader who fails to uplift followers oversimplifies problems for them so that the followers readily make impetuous responses to them, blindly support each other's positions, or evade the problems altogether.

Charisma and the Transformation of Organizations

Interest has increased in leadership that brings about organizational renewal, that changes the course of organizational events, and that engages the full persons of subordinates and colleagues in a transcendental organizational purpose. Charismalike gifts of vision and mission are seen as not only possible in organizational settings but necessary for leadership in the more successful ones. For Peters (1980), the transformation of organizations is largely associated with charismalike chief executive officers. He reported on 20 companies that had "executed major shifts in directions with notable skill and efficiency." Showing the evidence of strong ego ideals, their chief executive officers [CEOs] chose a single theme "and almost unfailingly . . . never miss[ed] an opportunity to hammer it home." The CEOs were characterized by such charismatic behaviors as:

> Consistency in support of the theme, usually over a period of years. Orchestration of all management systems, formal and informal, to achieve noticeable shifts of organizational attention. Conscious use of symbolic behavior, often regarded by outsiders as transparent hokum. [p. 23]

George F. Johnson of Endicott-Johnson shoes, Thomas J. Watson, Sr. of IBM, and Alfred P. Sloan of General Motors are prime examples of charismatic chief executive officers who transformed their respective firms, according to analyses of their biographies described in Chapter 12. In the same way, the transformation of Antioch College in 1919 and of Swarthmore College in 1920 could be readily attributed to the dynamic personalities and enthusiasms of their new presidents.

A Model of Charismatic Leadership in Complex Organizations

House (1977) offered seven propositions about the more overt aspects of charismatic leadership in complex organizations that fit with social and organizational psychology.

1. "Characteristics that differentiate leaders who have charismatic effects on subordinates from leaders who do not have such charismatic effects are dominance and self-confidence, need for influence, and a strong conviction in the moral righteousness of their beliefs" (p. 194).

2. "The more favorable (attractive, nurturant, successful, or competent) the perceptions of the potential follower toward a leader the more the follower will model: (a) the [values] of the leader; (b) the expectations of the leader that effective performance will result in desired or undesired outcomes for the follower; (c) the emotional responses of the leader to work-related stimuli; (d) the attitudes of the leader toward work and toward the organization" (p. 196).

3. "Leaders who have charismatic effects are more likely to engage in behaviors designed to create the impression of competence and success than leaders who do not have such effects" (p. 197).

4. "Leaders who have charismatic effects are more likely to articulate ideological goals than leaders who do not have such effects" (p. 198).

5. "Leaders who simultaneously communicate high expectations of, and confidence in followers are more likely to have followers who accept the goals of the leader and believe that they can contribute to goal accomplishment and are more likely to have followers who strive to meet specific and challenging performance standards" (p. 201).

6. "Leaders who have charismatic effects are more likely to engage in behaviors that arouse motives relevant to the accomplishment of the mission than are leaders who do not have charismatic effects" (p. 203).

7. "A necessary condition for a leader to have charismatic effects is that the role of the followers be definable in ideological terms that appeal to the follower" (p. 205).

Figure 3 is the House model which shows the linkages among the variables of these seven propositions.

Expansion of the Model

The seven propositions deal with charismatic leaders' personality, their value as a role model for followers, their use of impression management, their stimulation of high expectations, and their articulation of appealing ideological and transcendental goals and roles.

A number of additional propositions can be added. Although the seven propositions cover the more observable, rational aspects of charisma, they fail to capture the full flavor of the less-explicable emotional elements and antecedent conditions of consequence so well delineated by Schiffer (1973):

> From time to time in history . . . a phenomenon with the unique ingredients of mob psychology . . . springs up as if from nowhere and proceeds on a broad sweeping course through a group, with each passing day gaining the reinforcement of a citizenry involuntarily caught up in the process like the victims of a strange disease. The earliest symptoms of such epidemics are often far from clear. . . . Commonly, the provocative agent is . . . some specific individual, whose unique personality is supposedly the true source of the process . . . [or] a standard-bearer for a new and exciting ideology . . . for stirring up the communal empathy of a people. As the wave gains momentum, the media of communication—once bards, now TV cameras and commentators— . . . lend lustre and dimension to the whole happening; a strange hypnoid state begins to infiltrate the most

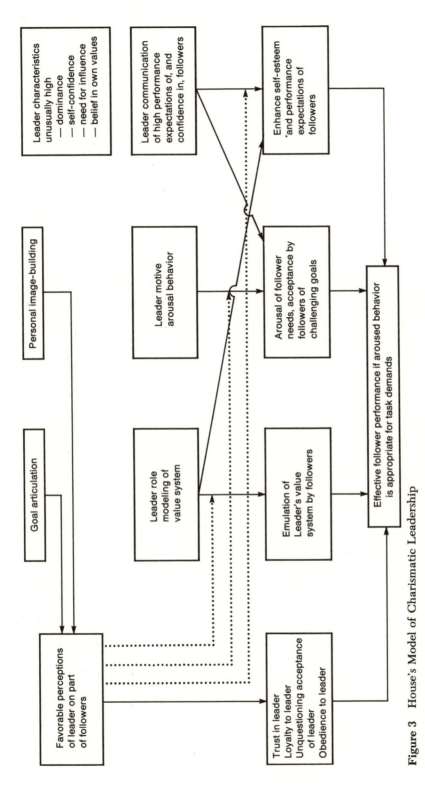

Figure 3   House's Model of Charismatic Leadership

Note: Dotted lines indicate that favorable perceptions moderate the relationship between leader and follower responses.

Source: From House, 1977, p. 206.

55

vulnerable minds. . . . the social scientist looks for economic and cultural factors . . . to explain the new 'miracle'; the intelligentsia dissect the personal mystique of the hero; avant-garde theories and sophisticated cliches bombard the mind, already softened by the media's propaganda. Like a rash in a communicable disease, the first reaction develops into a deeper and fevered agitation gripping the body politic. The disease takes full hold, and many parts of society succumb to a strange and crippling affliction: charisma. [Schiffer, 1973, p. 3]

This agitation, this lustre, this excitement is not fully captured by House's propositions. Nevertheless it shows up within complex organizations: Lee Iacocca at Chrysler convincing workers, suppliers, congressmen, and customers that Chrysler could be turned around and doing it; the young Robert Hutchins recasting the prestigious University of Chicago in his own image; Hyman Rickover taking on the whole Navy Department with an idea, the nuclear submarine, whose time had come. It is our argument that the agitation, lustre, and excitement and much of what the Iacoccas, Hutchinses, and Rickovers can do at the top of the organization, can occur in varying amounts and degrees all through complex organizations. Such charismatic effects can be studied and found or developed in leaders at all levels of the complex organization. Proposition 8 is a formulation which attempts to capture the above.

Proposition 8: The charismatic leader reduces resistance to attitude change in followers and disinhibitions of behavioral responses by arousing emotional responses toward the leader and a sense of excitement and adventure which may produce restricted judgments and reduced inhibitions.

The mystical and the fantasy aspects of charisma need to be more fully considered in theory. Charismatics are not merely dominating, self-confident, and convinced of their own beliefs. They believe they have supernatural missions and purposes. Martin Luther King really had a waking dream of what he was to accomplish. Followers don't merely have favorable perceptions of the leader. For them the leaders are supermen, act like mesmerists, and are larger than life. Followers' critical judgements may be suspended. The sense of reality of the charismatic leaders and their followers are inordinately affected by psychodynamic mechanisms such as projection, repression, and disassociation. Followers' own processes and needs are projected onto the charismatic personality. John F. Kennedy ushered in a new Camelot complete with his Queen Guinevere and knights ready to do battle in Cuba, Berlin, and Vietnam with the villainous foes of freedom, the Cuban devils and Soviet dragons. The depth of the public depression resulting from Kennedy's assassination can only be explained by the strong, emotional, idolization of the image of Kennedy as dragonslayer, savior, and creator of a new life on earth for the disadvantaged. In reality, he was an astute politician who changed a fictitious Soviet superiority in missiles—the so-called missile gap—into the beginning of a new arms race led by the United States. He did not lead but was led into supporting the civil rights movement. His statesmanlike qualities grew with his experience in office. But for the mass of the U.S. public, his image was that of the youthful world leader who was lifting the United States out of the stodgy Eisenhower years with the focus of a future of U.S. leadership among the nations of the world and in space.

In some instances, their very lack of talent may make some popular actors and politicians charismatic in that it is easier for the uncritical followers to identify with them and gain vicarious satisfaction for their own frustrated ambitions. Logic-tight compartments repress what is not wanted in the leader and enhance what is. Charisma depends on a regression to imagery. The childlike image of the faultless leader replaces a realistic appraisal (Schiffer, 1973). This connects with the fact that when evaluating their superiors often subordinates do not rate their superior as they have been asked to do, but rather they rate prototypes they carry around in their heads of a generalized leader. Reactions to charismatic leaders are likely to obey similar psychometric principles. These conclusions are summed up in Proposition 9.

Proposition 9: The larger-than-life status of charismatic leaders make them useful targets of their followers' projections and catalysts for rationalization, repression, regression, and disassociation.

There has to be among the followers shared norms for the charismatic leader to resort to particular psychological mechanisms in his appeals (Hummel, 1972). Sinfulness is a shared norm in the Judeo-Christian world; the Western charismatic leader can stimulate guilt among his followers. The importance of ''face'' is a shared norm in the Orient; the Oriental charismatic leader can focus on shame. The use of rationalization and denial again requires that the followers share norms and group fantasies. This leads us to Proposition 10.

Proposition 10: Shared norms and group fantasies among followers facilitate the emergence and success of the charismatic leader.

Again, unquestioning acceptance of the leader is not an absolute essential consequence of charismatic leadership. It may be true for some followers but:

Followers can be under the spell of a leader and can accept him as supremely authoritative without necessarily agreeing with him on all occasions or refraining from argument with him. In the highly argumentative atmosphere of a modern radical party, for example, a leader can be both charismatic and contested on specific points, as Lenin often was by his close followers. Indeed, he can even manifest some of his charisma in the inspired way in which he conquers dissent by the sheer power of his political discourse. Immense persuasiveness in argument may, in other words, be one of the extraordinary qualities by virtue of which a leader acquires charisma in his follower's eyes. We should not, therefore, envisage the charismatic authority-relation as one that necessarily involves automatic acquiescence of the followers in the leader's views or excludes the possibility of their disagreeing with him on occasion and up to a point. . . . As an innovator the charismatic leader tends at times to break with established ways of thinking and acting, and thus to take positions which diverge from his followers' expectations and consequently raise disturbed questions in their minds. [Tucker, 1970, p. 74]

In high-technology industry, strong substantive argumentation may be characteristic of charismatic leaders and their immediate technical subordinates. Unquestioning acceptance may be completely absent.

Proposition 11: The charismatic leader may make extensive use of successful argumentation in influencing others and justifying his position. The charismatic leader may display superior debating skills, technical expertise, and ability to appropriately muster persuasive appeals.

Another element in charisma which needs to be captured is what Tucker (1970) regarded as universally true. The charismatic leader inspires hatred in those who strongly favor the old order of things. Franklin D. Roosevelt was "That Man!" to U.S. conservatives of the 1930s; Lenin was Antichrist for the members of the Russian Old Regime; Fidel Castro is the Devil to Cuba's middle-class exiles. At the very same time that Yasir Arafat still commanded the allegiance, reverence, and loyalty of most Palestinians, other Palestinians, who believed that he was becoming too flexible about negotiating with Israel, had launched a mutiny to destroy him and his military force. We should also be looking for signs of this hatred of the charismatic leader in industry. Charles Revson, who built the Revlon cosmetics and fashion empire, was hated and reviled by many of those who had to stand his abuse if they worked for him. Yet, he also had lifelong loyal supporters who saw him in an opposite light (Tobias, 1976). This hatred of the charismatic leader also argues strongly for dyadic rather than group analyses of supervisor–subordinate relationships. One can see the subordinates of a single charismatic superior divided in the extent to which they love him or fear and hate him.

Proposition 12: Analogous to thesis and antithesis, the very behaviors and qualities that transport supporters into extremes of love, veneration, and admiration of the charismatic personality, send opponents into extremes of hatred, animosity, and detestation.

We need theoretical elucidation of the extent to which different charismatic leaders have displayed quite different styles to achieve their impact. On the one hand, de Gaulle was always more concerned about being right than achieving immediate results. He spoke of his "contempt for contingencies." His attitude was unbending (Hoffman & Hoffman, 1970). Other inflexible charismatic leaders of our time include Qaddafi and Khomeini. On the other hand, John F. Kennedy and Franklin D. Roosevelt avoided speaking out to risk political battles which they felt they might lose. Lenin also was a practical activist and a pragmatic organizer (Tucker, 1970). Yet Kennedy, Roosevelt, and Lenin had the universal charismatic sense of mission, strong ideologies, and devoted followers. We sum up this in Proposition 13.

Proposition 13: Charismatic leaders vary greatly in their pragmatism, flexibility, and opportunism.

Finally, we need a proposition 14 to sum up the extent that the appearance of charismatic leaders is contingent on the situation in which the followers find themselves. To some extent, whether leaders will be able to be transforming depends on whether their group of followers are ready to be transformed. (More will be presented about this in Chapter 10.)

Proposition 14: Charismatic leadership is more likely to be seen when groups, organizations, cultures, and societies are in a state of stress and transition.

Figure 4 attempts to show how the charismatic leader accomplishes the confidence-building and value enhancement of the transformational process from Figure 2. Given the personality and intellect required, the charismatic leader articulates an ideology that enhances goal clarity, focus, and value. With the increased follower attention also come biases in judgement and exaggerated confidence in process. The leader engages in impression management directly or through the mass media and mass rallies (if a political leader) or employee rallies and house organs (if a leader of a complex organization). Either directly or by mass communication, reverence and blind trust are generated by the followers in the leader resulting in exaggerated follower energization. An unintended consequence of ideological articulation is the polarization of antifollowers who reject the leader as strongly as followers accept him.

Just as charisma may be found in modestly located leaders, so it may be present or absent in world-class leaders. Lee Iacocca stands out today in industry for his charisma for those within his firm as well as for the

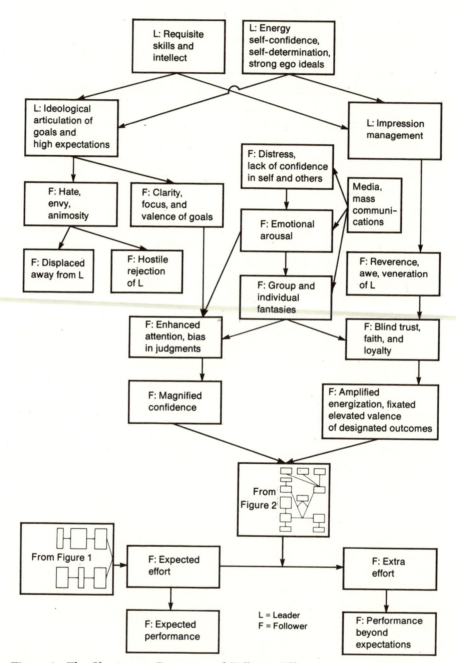

Figure 4   The Charismatic Processes and Follower Effort

world outside (Anonymous, 1981A). There was unusual agreement among Wall Street analysts and assembly line workers that the charismatic Iacocca could save Chrysler, if anyone could. And he did. Traits attributed to him include personal magnetism, shrewdness, enthusiasm, energy, temperament, determination, courage, and foresight. All of this is coupled with an extremely strong desire to overcome challenges and motivate his subordinates to do as well.

Equally dynamic was Louis B. Mayer, a czar of the movie industry, who was celebrated as a larger-than-life mogul. He was a consummate salesman and showman among those from whom he sought help, such as the New York financial community. At the same time, he was seen by those whom he exploited as tyrannical, vain, temperamental, semiliterate, and reactionary. He used mass meetings with his studio workers to try to inspire them, yet his long speeches were laced with sarcasm and threats. Illustrative of the extent to which charismatic leaders generate hatred as well as love, Samuel Goldwyn was quoted as saying when Mayer died that the reason so many people showed up to his funeral was because they wanted to make sure he was dead (Johnston, 1937).

There were numerous world-class leaders who were not charismatic. Henry R. Luce was an ideologue who wielded great influence through his *Time–Life–Fortune* publications (Jessup, 1969). General George C. Marshall was one of the most important and influential of our military leaders, yet he remained cold and impersonal and repressed his own feelings. His influence was based on his intelligence, concentration, and willingness to accept influence from his subordinates in searching or creating the best solutions to problems (Payne, 1951). Although a strong ideology and intellect are to be found in many charismatic leaders, we need to look elsewhere to fully understand their ability to inspire their followers.

Chapter 4

Inspirational Leadership

INSPIRATIONAL LEADERSHIP IS a subfactor within charismatic leadership behavior. (Chapter 12 will show that while inspiration of loyalty has some association with individualized consideration and intellectual stimulation, inspirational leadership is most highly correlated with charismatic leadership.) Charismatic leadership clearly is inspirational: emotionally arousing, animating, enlivening, and even exalting to followers and their efforts. But inspiration, as such, can be self-generated and does not have to stem from charisma. It doesn't even have to result from leadership at all. We can be inspired to come to the aid of others by seeing their distress; we can be inspired by the collective attitudes of our colleagues and fellow citizens; we can be inspired through conditioning by symbols and rituals of cultural pride and patriotism; we can be inspired by our mass media and by our institutions. We can be inspired by reading the Preamble to the U.S. Constitution, or the Bible.

However, here we should like to focus on the inspirational leadership process—the arousal and heightening of motivation among followers that occurs primarily from charismatic leadership. We recognize that leaders do not need be charismatic to be inspirational; they can make use of institutional means or inspire by identifying with a charismatic movement. Nevertheless, most but not all charismatics are inspirational. An exemplary inspirational leader was General George S. Patton, who generated extraordinary efforts in the forces under him. He felt that "80 percent of his mission" was to arouse the morale of his men (Ayer, 1971).

Samuel Goldwyn was at the other end of the continuum. A publicity seeker, he was extremely difficult to work with and seldom had much good to say about others. He had to be free of any higher authority. His influence and success were attributed to salesmanship and willingness to risk large sums of money on blockbuster movies rather than to the inspiration of others (Johnston, 1937).

Emotional Versus Intellectual Stimulation

We can be inspired by a cold, calculating, intellectual discourse, the brilliance of a breakthrough, or the beauty of an argument. Yet, it is our emotions that ultimately have been aroused by the brilliance or beauty. We may hold an intellectual genius in awe and reverence. The inspirational influence on us is emotional. We differentiate this emotional arousal from intellectual stimulation, a separate factor of leadership behavior, to be discussed in Chapter 6, which moves us to look at old problems in new ways or to follow a rational chain of arguments to their logical conclusion. A charismatic savant inspires us by arousing our emotions. The savant, without reference to the reverence in which he or she is held, may equally stimulate us intellectually to work through an elegant logical sequence. We restrict inspirational leadership to leadership that employs or adds nonintellectual, emotional qualities to the influence process and reserve the factor of intellectual stimulation to influence processes emphasizing convincing argument, logic, and rationality without appeals to feelings, sentiments, and emotions. Consider the specific leadership behaviors Yukl (1981) used to illustrate what he meant by inspirational leadership:

> My supervisor held a meeting to talk about how vital the new contract is for the company and said he was confident we could handle it if we all did our part. . . . My boss told us we were the best design group he had ever worked with and he was sure that this new product was going to break every sales record in the company. [p. 121]

The inspiring supervisor was not dispassionate. On the contrary, the biased emotional qualities can be seen throughout.

The supervisor talked about how *vital* the new contract was. He said he was *confident in us*. He told us we were the *best* group he had *ever* worked with. He was *sure* the product would *break every record*.

In sum, as a consequence of their self-confidence, absence of inner conflict, self-determination, and requisite abilities, leaders will be held in high esteem by their followers, particularly in times of troubles and challenges. They can generally inspire their followers by emotional supports and appeals which will transform their level of motivation beyond original expectations. They can generally inspire their followers also by means of intellectual stimulation—as will be discussed in Chapter 6. Charismatic leaders can do one or the other, or both.

Charisma and Inspiration

Inspirational talks and emotional appeals are used by charismatic leaders to arouse motivations to transcend self-interests for the good of the team. As Yukl (1981) notes, follower effort on various types of tasks will be stimulated by the charismatic leader in this way to accomplish the group's mission. The arousal process may focus on followers' achievement, power or affiliation motives.

> Arousal of achievement motivation is relevant for complex, challenging tasks requiring initiative, calculated risk taking, personal responsibility, and persistence. Arousal of power motivation is relevant for tasks requiring subordinates to be competitive, persuasive, and aggressive. Arousal of affiliation motivation is relevant for tasks requiring cooperation, teamwork, and mutual support among subordinates. [p. 61]

Although both Lenin and Trotsky were charismatic leaders, Lenin was a man of intellect and organization, while Trotsky played on mass appeal. "Lenin needed an office; Trotsky needed a stage" (Fischer, 1965, p. 51). Intellectual stimulation emphasizes logic and analysis; inspirational leadership appeals to sensation and intuition. Ordinarily charisma is likely to be associated with a mix of intellectual stimulation and inspirational leadership. As Tucker (1970) indicates:

> a charismatic leader does not acquire charisma exclusively because of his inspirational sense of mission . . . his personality per se independently of the content of his message, is not sufficient explanation for his impact upon his followers. [p. 88]

The full-blown charismatic leader identifies and articulates the serious threats faced by his followers, increases their conscious awareness and concern about the threats, and also intellectually stimulates them to pursue how to be saved from them. Churchill aroused the British repeatedly to make them aware of the Nazi menace. He was an overflowing fountain of ideas on how to meet the Nazi threat. At the same time, he inspired confidence in ultimate victory which did not waver despite fearsome odds.

Inspirational Appeals of Charismatic Leaders

We are most familiar with this kind of leadership. Sales managers do it at motivation meetings with their salespeople. Coaches give their team rip-rousing pep talks. It is now even being used to promote academic objectives.

> [Educators] support anything to remove anxiety about [a standardized] test and make students think positively about the experience. . . . At an academic pep rally . . . eighth graders chant[ed] 'beat the test'. . . . [Following the middle school's] first academic pep rally. . . . they improved in all three categories on [Florida's] standardized test of basic skills: reading, writing and mathematics. [*New York Times,* 1983, p. A19]

Team competitions, fun, and exciting games were stressed.

> "We boost and hype the kids all day to learn, to study, to be successful", said Kelly Kilpatrick, principal of Jefferson County High School [in Florida]. . . . Last year, 12 students at Jefferson took the Scholastic Aptitude Test. This year, Mr. Kilpatrick said he expected more than 100 to sign up. In 1977, when Florida's literacy test was introduced, only 49 percent of Jefferson's students passed the mathematics section. Last spring, the school's rate of passing was 94 percent, tied for second in the state. [*New York Times,* 1983, p. A19]

As with charisma, empirical research on inspirational leadership has been sparse. But this scarcity does not reflect its importance. There is a time and place where a lot of persuasive talent can be most usefully engaged in telling and selling. An important need can be served by envisioning what real benefits are involved, clarifying what goals can be reached and why, and building a sense of confidence in success. Bennis (1983) sees as most important source of success for a firm, a chief executive officer who can create and communicate a compelling vision of what is desired and who can energize and transform subordinates into commitment to make a stronger effort.

Inspirational leadership has been most applauded by the masses and most derided by skeptical intellectuals who equated it with demagoguery, manipulation, exploitation, and mob psychology. Its emphasis on persuasive appeals to faith rather than to reason, to the emotions rather than to the intellect, and to various mechanisms of social reinforcement rather than to logical discourse has made it seem fit only for the immature and the undereducated. Nevertheless, Vaill (1978) sees "high performing systems" involving members who "report peak experiences in connection with their participation. They will enthuse, bubble and communicate joy and exultation" (p. 110). When elated by inspiring leaders, subordinates are willing to accept increased risk.

The Arousal Process

A familiar stock situation for Americans is the half-time scene in the football locker room. Our team is behind and the coach appeals, cajoles, and threatens. The team must do-or-die for victory. A well-known master of this art was Vince Lombardi, who felt his approach could be transferred to arousing greater performance from salesmen and workers, in general (Kramer, 1970). Certainly, it remains a common practice in the world of marketing. The weekly pep rallies are commonplace in sales organizations. Firms such as Mary Kay and Amway have made the rousing rally of salespeople the key to their success, the former by building emotional appeal around its successful salespeople, the latter by convincing prospects of the workability of a pyramid scheme.

Also familiar are the stirring preachers of evangelism, the lectern-pounding political orators, and the rousing after-dinner speakers. Jesse Jackson is most extreme in this regard among current politicans, particularly when he addresses black audiences. Nowadays, of course, much of this arousal has been institutionalized in anonymous media messages. Social and political movements ranging from equal rights for women to reducing property taxes depend heavily in transforming a passive, inactive constituency into an aroused, alarmed, active one.

For the charismatic, transformational leader, the arousal process is not a matter of a leader helping subordinates to meet their expectations; it is a matter of a leader influencing subordinates to exert themselves beyond their own expectations and self-interest. That extra effort is inspired by the appeal of the leader's symbols, images, and vision of a better state of affairs along with his persuasive language. It is stimulated by increased feelings of identity with the leader, hence with the leader's goals. It can also be supported by various institutional reinforcements and peer pressures. Peters and Waterman (1982) enumerated a number of ways successful managements stimulate the performance of their employees. At Tupperware, for example, the key management task is seen to be motivating its over 80,000 salespeople. Every Monday night all salespeople attend a rally for their distributorships. A "count-up" is held in which everyone marches onto the stage according to their previous week's sales. High sellers are last. Their peers give them standing ovations. Almost everyone receives one or more pins and badges. Such reinforcing identification of each salesperson's weekly performance promotes competition between salespeople, although not necessarily conflict. More important, it arouses effort to compete better against one's own prior performance.

Inspirational Leader Behavior

Yukl and Van Fleet (1982) defined as *inspirational,* leader behavior that:

> stimulates enthusiasm among subordinates for the work of the group and says things to build their confidence in their ability to successfully perform assignments and attain group objectives. [p. 90]

Such inspirational leadership was mentioned fairly often in 1511 critical incidents of effective leadership in the Reserve Officer Training Corps (ROTC) and 129 incidents of effective leadership behavior by U.S. Air Force officers in the Korean War. In contrast to 18 other types of leader behavior, only *problem-solving* (intellectual stimulation?) was mentioned more often in the ROTC study and only *consideration* was mentioned more often to interviewers in the Air Force study.

Examples of inspirational leadership in the ROTC study were as follows:

1. Instills pride in individuals.
2. Uses pep talks to build morale.
3. Sets an example by his own behavior of what is expected.
4. Provides personal encouragement to a subordinate to build his confidence.
5. Makes cadets feel proud of their unit by complimenting their good performance. [p. 98]

Examples of inspirational leadership reported for Air Force officers were:

1. Inspires enthusiasm and self-confidence (e.g., by showing subordinates that they can accomplish a difficult task, persuading them that their task

or mission is important, giving a pep talk when the group is discouraged).

2. Sets an example of courage and dedication (e.g., by risking his own life to save a subordinate, leading subordinates on a dangerous mission rather than staying behind, sharing in the hardships imposed on subordinates during a difficult mission). [p. 98]

Inspirational leadership, according to subordinates' ratings, correlated with objective measures of effectiveness as a leader. Among ROTC cadet first sergeants, effectiveness was based on measurement of performance of the units led. Effectiveness as an ROTC platoon leader was assessed in a realistic combat exercise by a team of military observers.

Action Orientation

Leaders arouse followers to extra effort with an action orientation opposite to the bureaucrat's initial proclivities focused on constraints, prerogatives, precedents, and formalisms. Most extreme in this regard was Theodore Roosevelt and most illustrative was what he did as a crisis was building between the United States and Spain over Cuba. As an Assistant Secretary, he became Acting Secretary of the Navy for just three or four hours when the Secretary went home early on February 25, 1898 to take a half-day's rest. Roosevelt sent a "momentous" cable to George Dewey commanding the Asiatic squadron to move on Manila Bay. He issued instructions where our European and South Atlantic squadrons were to rendezvous if President McKinley changed his mind and war was declared with Spain. He ordered all naval commanders all over the world to keep their ships filled with the best possible coal and bought all the coal he could buy in the Far East. No doubt, his actions contributed to the decisive American victories in Manila Bay and Santiago when war came. The next morning, Secretary Long returned to his office never again to leave Roosevelt in charge, even for part of a day. What Long felt was Roosevelt's impulsiveness was carefully planned action by Roosevelt to prepare the United States for war with Spain. As soon as he could, Roosevelt seized his chance to act (Beal, 1956). Theodore Roosevelt inspired a generation of Americans as the man of action who charged up San Juan Hill as quickly and precipitously with his Rough Riders as he charged into the powerful industrial monopolies and despoilers of the American West.

Confidence-Building

For Yukl (1981, p. 121), confidence-building is the major element in being an inspirational leader. Inspirational leadership occurs when "the leader stimulates enthusiasm among subordinates for the work of the group and says things to build subordinate confidence in their ability to perform assignments successfully and attain group objectives." Thus, when soldiers are faced in the immediacy of combat with the threats of death or being wounded, neither adding to the soldiers' fears through disciplinary threats nor appealing to high ideals, great causes and long-term objectives are as likely to encourage extra effort and exertion as building a sense of confidence. What will be most encouraging is the soldier's confidence in his leadership, in his buddies, in his equipment, and in himself.

> Confidence is perhaps the greatest source of emotional strength that a soldier can draw upon. With it, he willingly faces the enemy and withstands deprivations, minor setbacks, and extreme stresses, knowing that he and his unit are capable of succeeding. . . . The soldier must be given confidence in the weapons of war that are employed against the enemy. This includes not only his rifle and other personal weapons, but the entire war strength of the nation. It is satisfying to know that one's rifle is more effective than the enemy soldier's . . . that there will not be a shortage of ammunition for that rifle or for the supporting artillery; that our country is producing more and better weapons; that our ships control the seas and our planes the skies. . . . The soldier's confidence that his leaders are tactically proficient and combat-wise, makes it much easier for him to advance toward the unknown. He is strengthened by the knowledge that, if he should become a casualty, his friends and leaders will come to his rescue; and that, once removed from the scene of battle, he will receive proper medical attention. . . . Belief in his own abilities contributes to the confidence of the combat soldier. . . . [He] must be made aware of [his] successes. If [he does] not believe [he has] done well in one fight, [his] confidence for winning the next is at a minimum. Expectations of failure destroy morale. Confidence in victory ensures it. [Hayes & Thomas, 1967, pp. 244–245]

The key to military performance stimulation thus lies in building and maintaining confidence in self, peers, leadership, and national strength and purpose. One can see these themes appearing in the leaders' exhortations to their troops again and again down through history:

Henry V before Agincourt in 1415; Dwight Eisenhower before the landings in Normandy in 1944.

Obviously, there must be substantive reality and truth in the confidence-building messages or the disconfirmation will destroy credibility of the leadership as well as prove disastrous. The French and European heavily armored nobility that charged the small band of English archers at Agincourt were extremely confident, too confident, in fact, as well as ignorant and unrealistic about the penetrating power of the long bow.

Inspiring Belief in the "Cause"

Along with instilling confidence, belief in the greater causes also remains extremely important. To sacrifice one's life or risk being seriously wounded without purpose is intolerable. For the mercenary, financial reward may be enough; for the career soldier, career advancement may be enough, but the ordinary soldier has to believe that "the causes he is fighting for are morally right and worth sacrificing for" (Hayes & Thomas, 1967, p. 245). The Vietnam tragedy for the United States was seen by one chief of staff as due to the failure to establish a national consensus about the correctness of its course. Another chief of staff argued strongly against any U.S. military intervention in Central America without such a consensus.

History is replete with examples of how the combination of confidence in one's capabilities and the belief in the correctness of one's cause produced extraordinary effort and success. Cromwell's New Model Army was built with both confidence in its arms and beliefs bolstered by anti-establishment religious convictions in the righteousness of its cause. Strengthened by their beliefs in Islam and in the Jihad, the Arabs swept out of Arabia in the seventh century and defeated the often more heavily armed forces sent against them in a band of countries stretching from Spain to India.

In the world of work, people who come to believe they are working for the best company with the best products and resources are most likely to be committed, involved, loyal, and ready to exert extra effort.

Again, it is obvious that where beliefs are misguided, the extraordinary effort also produces disaster. In World War I, French doctrinaire belief in the importance of their élan to victory resulted in continued slaughter of their men in frontal charges against entrenched German machine guns.

Making Use of the Pygmalion Effect

In the myth of Pygmalion, the sculptor fell in love with his beautiful creation. As a consequence, Aphrodite was moved to turn the statue he had created into a lovely woman. In George Bernard Shaw's modern version, Professor Higgins falls in love with the duchess whom he has created out of a cockney flower girl.

The Pygmalion effect was first experimentally induced in the elementary classroom. Teachers were led to believe they were working with better pupils. They unwittingly fulfilled the prophesies. The pupils, indeed, did better as a consequence of the induced expectations about them held by their teachers (Rosenthal & Jacobson, 1968). When teachers expected better performance from pupils, they demonstrably attended more to those pupils, expressed more satisfaction, encouragement and praise to them, called on them more frequently, and communicated more frequently with them in a positive, accepting supportive manner.

Adult military instructors in the Israeli Army were led to believe without any basis in fact that a portion of their trainees had more command potential than other trainees. The effect was to produce better performance on paper-and-pencil tests of learning in those trainees believed by their instructors to be of high command potential. Better trainee attitudes were also produced. The trainees themselves who were supposedly of high potential, in turn, credited their instructors with better leadership (Eden & Shani, 1982).

In its most general form, the Pygmalion effort is a performance-stimulating effect. People who are led to expect that they will do well, will be better than those who expect to do poorly or do not have any expectations about how well or poorly they will do. People tend to try to confirm rather than disconfirm positive beliefs that others have about them. They try to validate such beliefs by behaving in a way that is consistent with the beliefs. The leader who arouses in subordinates confidence in their own capabilities and confidence in those with whom they work, all things being equal, by raising expectations about the success of their efforts, will increase such efforts to succeed.

Additional Inspirational Practices

Inspirational leadership in complex organizations makes use of a variety of other individual and institutional practices to emotionally arouse subordinates. Peters and Waterman (1982) call attention to introducing new projects, volunteering, experimentation and a culture and climate that are inspiring. These tend to be featured in excellently managed firms.

New Projects

Extra effort can be generated by a leader who continues to introduce new projects and new challenges in a highly flexible organization. The chief executive officer of TRAK, a sporting goods company, keeps his stars "turned on" by coming up with new projects for his valuable people. Organizational flexibility, continual reorganization, as needed, and task teams are permanent features of TRAK's strategy for stimulating performance.

Volunteerism

Another common practice is for the leadership to encourage volunteerism. When ad hoc task forces are set up, the relevant experts can decide whether or not they wish to be placed on it. The short-lived, temporary ad hoc task force enables the excellently managed firms to have the right experts, in the right place, at the right time, spurred on by self-selection and new challenges. The task force is exciting and likely to spur practical action.

Experimentation and Incrementalism

Another spur to action in most of the excellently managed companies is their leaders' willingness to experiment. Testing and learning is the favored process rather than analysis and debate. Performance is stimulated by policies that encourage experimentation, and testing to learn about whether an idea will work rather than just talking and thinking about it. Action is valued above planning. Taking small risks in small incremental steps with small-scale tryouts is encouraged. Incrementation is the favored decision-making process.

Organizational Climate and Communications

Managements stimulate performance and extra effort with the culture and climate of openness and trust they create. The network of communications is vast, open, and informal. Peer pressure keeps it from becoming anarchic. At Walt Disney Productions, everyone including the president wears a name tag with only his first name on it. The Chairman of the Board of IBM answers any complaint that comes to him from any employee.

Many firms stress "management-by-walking around" to meet employees—whatever their level in the organization—as they perform their tasks. Brief memoranda rather than lengthy reports serve as attention-grabbers and effort stimulators. Admiral Elmo Zumwalt provided this with his famous Z-grams to the various units under his command.

The Moral Question

Black-Hatted Practices

Emotional arousal practices can be moral or immoral. So far, we have focused on the moral. But leaders can wear black hats as well as white hats. The sales manager who rouses his salespeople to reaching new highs in sales of a legitimate, useful product makes a useful contribution to his organization, his salespeople, and society. This is distinctly different ethically and morally from the sales manager who rouses his salespeople with false promises and unobtainable goals, or who encourages conflict of the salespeople with each other in order to keep them all weak relative to the manager.

Arousing Competitive Feelings

Promoting competition among subordinates which stirs rivalry, anxiety about losing, and inability to trust associates is a favorite black-hatted approach to stimulate subordinates by pitting them against each other. The emotions of severe competition are aroused. Mao Zedung created factions and worked around legitimate office holders. He encouraged their subordinates to come to him but not to tell their bosses. Mutual distrust and competitive cliques resulted. Nance (1979) described a company president for whom he had worked who

> would play one man against another by frequently moving his department managers to test one against the other on each job. His practice was to call in a former manager in the presence of the current manager and ask his opinion of a proposal or recommendation made by the current manager. It was brutal! . . . such a system creates an ineffective organization by turning it into an armed camp instead of a team effort. [p. 19]

Coercion

The coercive, bullying, stemwinding, browbeating, aggressive, combative leader can sometimes obtain remarkable transformations in the amount of energy followers are willing to expend for him, particularly in the short run and particularly if he has gained control over the necessary resources, and is inventive, manipulative, exploitative, and politically astute. Lyndon Johnson was exemplary in displaying this as one side of his complex leadership style with his immediate subordinates (Caro, 1982). Woodrow Wilson was emotionally attracted to abstractions about justice and democracy but he could not manage his competitiveness and aggressiveness in working with colleagues. He only could work well with colleagues who flattered and adored him or with those with whom there was a mutual relationship of hate (Zaleznik, 1967).

Contingent Considerations

Inspirational appeals may fall on deaf ears or they may fall on ears whose owners are impatiently waiting to hear the message.

Receptivity

The inspirational appeal is seen by Yukl (1981) to occur when someone is led to carry out some action which will express his ideals and values. A subordinate may accept a special assignment following an appeal to his loyalty to the organization; a soldier may volunteer for a hazardous mission following an appeal to his patriotism. The transformational character of inspirational leadership is clear. The follower must be moved to feel that what is wanted of him can be justified, not by receipt of a tangible reward (as in transactional leadership) but by the prospect of contributing to a better world, doing one's duty to God and country, making one's organization the marketplace leader, and so forth. Self-interests are transcended for the good of the group, the organization, the nation, or the world. But inspirational appeals will fall on deaf ears if fundamental beliefs and values are not already present in followers, such as patriotism, obedience to authority, reverence for tradition, commitment, and loyalty to the organization. The American soldier in Vietnam in 1965 was much more ready to accept dangerous assignments for the Cause and inspired by his leadership than he was in 1970. He could be inspired in 1965 by his leaders' messages about bringing the war to a successful conclusion. By 1970, he was disillusioned and strongly resistant to the same appeals. Furthermore, institutional and group supports may be important. Conversion through group pressure to conform as practiced in fundamentalist revival meetings or cultist brainwashing may bring about these fundamental changes in beliefs and values, reducing the resistance to inspirational appeals to join the revolution or take the pledge to be born again.

Relevance

Inspirational activities by the transformational leader become of particular importance:

> When subordinate commitment (e.g., enthusiastic effort, self-sacrifice, initiative) is essential for effective unit performance.
> When the work is difficult and frustrating, and subordinates are likely to become discouraged by temporary setbacks and lack of progress.
> When the work is dangerous, and subordinates are anxious or fearful.
> When subordinates have ideals and values that are relevant to the activities of the group and will serve as the basis for inspirational appeals.
> When the leader's unit is in competition with other units or organizations. [Yukl, 1981, p. 193]

Further Considerations

A caveat was issued by Lundberg (1978). Leaders can be too stimulating. This may be particularly true for groups faced with complex tasks, no experience, or a high degree of stress.

The appeals used to stimulate performance range from altruism to greed. If Maslow's (1954) figures have any validity, leaders (in the

United States) are likely to be more successful when they appeal to
higher-level needs such as those for recognition, achievement and self-
actualization, as these are much less likely to have been met satisfactorily than lower-level needs, for example, safety and security. Of course,
if you are an unemployed older worker living in an inner city consuming
much of your free time watching murder and mayhem on television, appeals to your safety and security are likely to get more of your attention
and extra effort than appeals to your self-actualization. When you are
faced with continuing threats to your economic and physical well-being,
leaders with the most appeal for you will be those offering more jobs and
more police protection.

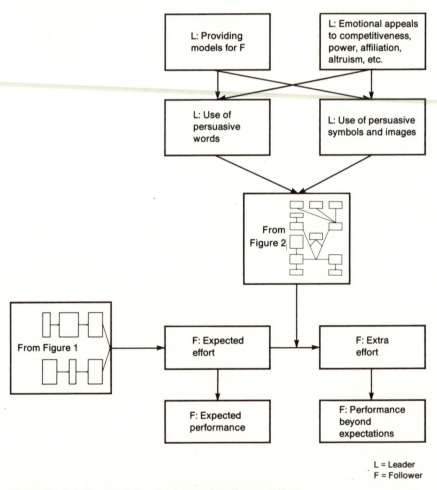

Figure 5   Inspirational Leadership and Follower Effort

A Model of Inspirational Leadership

Figure 5 shows an attempt to model the major elements in an inspiring leader's transformation of ordinary into extraordinary effort by followers.

The inspirational leadership of the charismatic leader is laid out in Figure 5 in terms of the extent the leader provides examples and patterns for the follower. These prototypes are simplified to increase salience, clarity, and understanding by use of vivid, colorful persuasive language and by use of meaningful symbols and imagery. The leader's emotional appeals are simplified in the same way, thus contributing to the transformational process shown in Figure 2 which brings about enhanced confidence and broadened and elevated goals.

Part III

Individualizing and Intellectualizing

ELEANOR SAMUELS HAD an "A" list and a "B" list of assistants. Those on the "A" list were the first to know what was happening, to be consulted about changes, to be delegated special assignments and responsibilities, and to be given merit raises. Those on the "B" list were tolerated as "second-class citizens." She was considerate of the welfare of those on the "B" list but only if they took the initiative to complain to her about their problems. She would go out of her way to promote the interests of those on the "A" list. Not so for those on the "B" list. Those on the "A" list were brighter, more energetic, and more dedicated to the organization. Their performance was superior. One could not say whether the lower commitment, involvement, and loyalty of the "B" group came about as a consequence of their being on the "B" list, or whether it resulted in their being cast there and was subsequently sensed by them.

Chapter 5

Individualized Consideration

Some Famous Examples

Andrew Carnegie exemplified individualized consideration. He gave as much responsibility to employees at all levels in management to make the most of whatever talents they had at a time when autocratic management was the rule. His own experience as a child laborer made him empathetic to the needs of the blue-collar worker (Wall, 1970). J. Paul Getty was another magnate who placed a premium on careful, accurate differential selection of subordinates who then had to take as much responsibility as they could handle. Also, Getty would personally help individual employees in need, regardless if the need was business-related or not. At the same time, he did not hesitate to fire a highly regarded manager who he felt was wasting time (Hewins, 1961).

Although seemingly considerate to outsiders, many famous leaders were affable to their peers on the outside of their institutions but ruthless, inconsiderate tyrants on the inside. Joseph Stalin could be good old "Uncle Joe" to American diplomats and a murderous and cruel despot inside Russia. Armand Hammer's patience, politeness, generosity, and friendliness to business and political contacts outside his organization were paralleled by his dictatorial dominance over everyone inside his firm, the Occidental Petroleum Corporation, in which he was unable to tolerate disagreement with his point of view (Considine, 1975).

Consideration for others has emerged as a consistently important aspect of leader–subordinate relations. Generally, it has been found to contribute to subordinate satisfaction with the leader and in many circumstances to subordinates' productivity. It is central to participative management to the extent that it focuses on the employee's needs for growth and participation in decisions affecting his work and career. Our open-ended survey of executives suggested that transformational leaders frequently were benevolent fathers to their subordinates. They tended to be friendly, informal, and close and treated subordinates as equals although they (the leaders) had more expertise. They gave advice, help and support and encouraged their subordinates' self-development.

In Chapter 12 our factor analytic study of U.S. Army officers reveals a factor of individualized consideration. The officers are seen by their subordinates to display such behavior as giving special attention to neglected members, treating each of their subordinates individually, and expressing appreciation for well done work. Conversely, lack of such consideration (meddling, dictating, interfering, overcontrolling) was found by Fiedler and Leister (1977) to impair what a subordinate's intelligence could have contributed to the work to be done. Only experienced subordinates could deal effectively with such inconsiderate superiors.

Consideration and Individualizing

But, as Miller (1973) found, consideration can break into two factors. On the one hand, there is consideration revealed in regular group meetings, in consultation with subordinates as a group, in treating all subordinates alike, and in consensual decision-making. On the other hand, consideration can be individualized. Each subordinate will be treated differently according to each subordinate's needs and capabilities. Descriptive of this, as seen in our quantitative explorations (Chapter 12), was giving personal attention to members who seem neglected and treating each subordinate individually.

Individualized consideration can take many forms. Expression of appreciation for a job well done will be most important. But superiors can also point out weaknesses of subordinates constructively. They can assign special projects that will promote subordinate self-confidence, utilize the subordinate's special talents, and provide opportunities for learning.

Both consideration and individualization are featured in *leader-member exchange,* a process in which a supervisor consults with each of his subordinates individually. Each subordinate is asked to discuss his concerns and expectations about his own job, his superior's job, and their working relationship. Then the superior shares some of his expectations about his own job, his subordinate's job, and their relationship. Reciprocal understanding is improved between superior and subordinate (Graen et al., 1982).

Superiors can critique subordinate reports to help improve their writing and their oral presentations. They can advise subordinates about new programs and invite subordinates to accompany them on visits to plants and clients. Subordinates can be sent to meetings or assigned to critique reports as a substitute for the superior. Outside interests can be discussed. What seems to emerge here when we take into account both our qualitative and our quantitative surveys is that transformational leadership involves individualized attention and a developmental or mentoring orientation toward subordinates. Transformational leaders practice delegation consistent with their judgments of their individual subordinates, current levels of competence and need for growth opportunities.

It should be clear that all transformational leaders do not necessarily display consideration, individual or otherwise. They can depend on their charisma and/or intellectual stimulation. For example, although a world-class charismatic leader, Lord Herbert Kitchener, Britain's turn-of-the-century and World War I military hero, was generally inconsiderate toward others. He found it difficult to delegate anything, or to engage in teamwork with fellow officers, and was unwilling to listen, to care about the opinions of others, or to try to persuade them to his point of view. He had little use for organizational channels of communication which he bypassed, as needed. He actually wanted to be seen as cold, ruthless, and inconsiderate (Magnus, 1968).

A majority of those executives who worked for him saw Charles Revson, founder of a cosmetics empire, as extremely inconsiderate, and more often than not found themselves fired by him or quitting his employ despite their high salaries. Yet, a few around him saw him as generous to a fault (Tobias, 1976).

Illustrative of the variations is how considerate or inconsiderate recent U.S. Presidents were of their immediate assistants in the White House.

Presidents and Their Assistants

While serving as assistant to the President of the United States has usually been a great career opportunity in politics, law, and business, the

Presidents themselves have varied greatly in the extent they have exhibited individualized or general consideration of their staff assistants and given them opportunities for career development by enlarging their responsibilities. President Reagan delegated a great deal of authority to his immediate staff subordinates, Baker, Clark, Deaver, and Meese, yet avoided getting them together on a regular basis to deal with their differences. Eisenhower had all the differences among his immediate subordinates funneled into a one-page memorandum by his Chief of Staff, Sherman Adams, on the basis of which Eisenhower would reach a decision. Franklin D. Roosevelt was known for his tendency to delight in playing off one subordinate against another. Jimmy Carter brought his advisors together and tried to work through the details with them to iron out the disagreements among them.

Harry Truman came closest to giving his subordinates what we see as individualized consideration.

> President Truman didn't believe in the single chief of staff system. He had six principal advisers, with whom he met every morning for up to an hour, had a little bourbon and branch water with one of them in the Oval Office to sum up the day, and then took a bundle of papers upstairs, put on his green eyeshade and read and studied reports until late in the night. [Reston, April 26, 1983]

According to Sorensen (1966), John F. Kennedy was like Truman except that his four principal subordinates were not each as restricted to their own assigned areas. He saw himself at the center of a wheel-like network of staff relationships and encouraged the peripheral staff members to contact him directly. He was in attendance at all staff meetings.

At the other extreme were Lyndon Johnson and Richard Nixon. Johnson bullied his immediate principal subordinates into compliance with whatever he had decided. He did not invite criticism from them nor permit disagreements among them to surface. Nixon "ran his staff by stealth. . . . He delegated vast powers to Bob Haldeman and John Ehrlichman in an atmosphere of Byzantine secrecy and intrigue" (Reston, April 26, 1983).

A Developmental Orientation

Elements of this developmental component in consideration are to be found in the Confucian concept of the leader as moral example and Plato's image of the leader as physician, shepherd, or ship's captain

(Paige, 1977). It is the transforming leader who has a developmental orientation toward his subordinates. The potential of all subordinates are "evaluated both for fulfillment of their present job and for future positions of greater responsibility" (Hays & Thomas, 1967, p. 196). The leader sets examples to be followed and assigns tasks on an individual basis to subordinates to help to significantly alter their abilities and motivations as well as to further immediate organizational needs.

The transforming leader will consciously or unconsciously serve as a role model for subordinates. Margerison (1980) found that 208 senior executives attributed their own successful development as managers to having had a manager early in their careers who acted as a role model and from whom much could be learned.

For Quinn and Hall (1983), to build teams and organizations leaders require an existential orientation (concerned about the "here-and-now"). They need to be considerate, empathic, concerned, caring, and supportive. Such consideration will reduce the role ambiguity of subordinates, particularly if the leaders are experts (Podsakoff, Todor, and Schuler, 1983).

Developmentally Oriented Behavior

A factor analysis by Morse and Wagner (1978) of items of managerial behavior, originally organized around Mintzberg's (1974) ten management roles, yielded as a factor, "providing for growth and development." Like the other factors which emerged, managers seen to actively fill this and the other roles were also likely to be rated high in effectiveness. Developmentally oriented leader behaviors reported by subordinates included career counseling, careful observation and recording of the progress of subordinates' performance, and encouraging subordinates to attend technical courses.

Delegation

Practicing delegation to provide challenging work and increasing subordinate responsibilities seem particularly important. Successful CEO's were found by Peters (1980) to encourage such delegation and autonomy "far down the line." General Omar Bradley (1951) pointed out that "There is no better way to develop leadership than to give an individual a job involving responsibility and let him work it out." Margerison's (1980) survey of 208 chief executives and senior officers reported that important influences on the development of their successful careers as managers prior to age 35 were: "being stretched" by immediate bosses, and being given leadership experience, overall responsibility for important tasks, and wide experience in many functions.

Individualized Orientation

Zaleznik (1977) concluded that personal influence and the one-to-one, superior–subordinate relationship were of prime importance to the development of leaders. He argued that an organizational culture of individualism should be encouraged, even an elitism focused on the early identification of prospective leaders among one's subordinates.

Individualized attention is seen as especially important to the new military commander of a unit. The commander must learn the names of all in the unit at least two levels below and become familiar with their jobs.

> The platoon leader should know well all the men in the platoon as early as possible. Even the company commander should attempt to know all the men in the entire company. [Hays & Thomas, 1967, p. 196]

Promoting Familiarity and Contact

Similarly, Peters (1980) found that successful chief executive officers (CEOs) characteristically established and maintained extensive contacts with managers down-the-line. The CEOs did not hesitate to circumvent the official chain of command. This all required them to spend an extraordinary amount of time in the field. They increased the motivation of their managers through surprisingly large grants of autonomy far down the line. Thus, Thomas V. Jones, chairman and president of Northrop, built an aircraft manufacturing organization which avoided formal hierarchical reporting channels. Easy communicating across managerial levels was the norm. As CEO, he involved himself at all levels of operation. Such freedom of interaction was seen as due to the nonthreatening climate which was promoted. It was also fostered by emphasizing the need for individual managers' understanding at all levels unconstrained by organizational barriers.

Individualized consideration implies seniors maintaining face-to-face contact, or at least frequent telephone contact with juniors. The

Intel Corporation accepted the fact that recently graduated engineers are more up-to-date on the latest advances in technology compared to experienced executives of greater power and status in the firm. Therefore, the firm has consciously encouraged frequent contact and open communication between the recent college graduates and the senior executives by leveling arrangements. Senior executives and junior professionals are all housed in small, unpretentious, accessible offices sharing common facilities. Stressed in the organization's culture is influence on decisions based on what one knows rather than how much power one has. In other firms, "walk-around-management" promotes individual contact and communication between those low and those high in the hierarchy.

Informal Versus Formal Communication

Klauss and Bass (1982) expected that the planning of project engineers would depend heavily on formal management information systems. But they found that the 400 engineers were most influenced and gained most of their decision-relevant information from informal contact and individual discussions rather than from written documentation. Consistent with this, Mintzberg (1975) saw as a myth that mangement information systems with their aggregated information are the basic data inputs for management decision-making. Rather, he noted that two thirds to three quarters of the total work time of managers is spent in oral communication. It is the immediate, timely, tidbits of gossip, speculation, opinion, and relevant facts which are most influential, not generalized reports reviewing conditions over a recent period of time. Individualized attention of superior to subordinate provides this opportunity for inputs of current and timely information. However, Klauss and Bass (1982) found that managers were most likely to make such contact face-to-face with colleagues at their same organizational level (or by telephone for such colleagues at a distance physically). For superiors and subordinates, despite the implications for consideration, written memoranda were more frequently used. Nevertheless, Mintzberg (1975) concluded that regular face-to-face debriefing sessions by superiors with subordinates to disseminate important information to them will provide a better basis for organizational decision-making and reduce the superior's superficiality in dealing with the erratic flow of demands on his time, his overload of work, and the abruptness of his decision-making. Yet, unless it becomes a matter of policy such as is seen in "walk-around management," communications from superior to subordinate are more likely to be on paper rather than by face-to-face contact.

Walk-around management collapses the barriers of distance and hierarchical levels that block open, immediate, face-to-face communications. It is illustrated by Jerry Lewis, the Plant Manager of Steuben Glass Company, who starts his day at 6 A.M. walking around among his craftsmen discussing whatever may arise when meeting each of them. By the time he reaches his desk, he may have already helped clarify a number of matters with individual glassblowers as well as unearthed several problems for him to remedy. Moreover, a continuing contribution is being made to employee commitment, involvement, and loyalty.

Fulfilling the Individual Subordinate's Desire for Information

Individualized consideration is seen in the superior keeping each subordinate fully informed about what is happening and why—preferably by face-to-face or telephone rather than by memorandum so that a two-way conversation takes place rather than a one-way transmission from superior to subordinate. Changes of plan don't occur to the surprise of subordinates. Subordinates come to feel that they are on the inside of developments and do not remain bystanders. If the interaction is two-way, subordinates have the opportunity to ask questions to clarify understanding. At the same time, superiors learn firsthand their subordinates' reactions and concerns about the matter.

Attention to Differences Among Subordinates

Meyer (1980) emphasized the importance for military leaders of individuation in consideration. Leaders need to avoid treating all subordinates alike. Rather, they must discover what best motivates each individual soldier and how to employ him most effectively. They must be generous in the use of their time for this. Their interest must be genuine. For Meyer (1980), consideration is revealed in an authentic respect for subordinates which is likely to be reciprocated as a consequence.

Individual Counseling

Military leaders are expected to be counselors. They should be able to help their subordinates to make adjustments to their problems. In doing so, they may themselves have to cope with the conflict in roles as commanders and as counselors (Hays & Thomas, 1967). In the military, emphasis on individual counseling skills for leaders is seen to be greatest for leaders at the lowest levels in the organization although some focus on the individual is required at all levels. Personal counseling skills are at a premium for these leaders (Ayres, 1978).

> Personal counseling skills rely heavily upon listening skills and are oriented to problem identification . . . these skills are needed most for those leaders who have a great amount of interaction with their subordinates, i.e., . . . corporals, sergeants, lieutenants, and captains. Leaders at these levels can be highly effective in getting the individual or soldier to express feelings so as to explore the problem enough to clarify it. [p. 45]

Skillful attention and appropriate responding to personal needs are most important at these lower levels. Nevertheless, individualized consideration is still important at the middle levels of noncommissioned officers, and for the senior captain, major, and junior lieutenant colonel, but the focus changes.

> What personal counseling is done will probably relate to a need to reinforce subordinates' identification with the Army; therefore, leaders may find that they have to counsel those individuals who are expressing or manifesting difficulty in conforming to the organization's behavioral norms regarding both on- and off-the-job-conduct. At this level it is crucial to keep an eye open to signs of stress or distress; probing soldiers about these signals will promote a leader's understanding of the relationship between job demands and individual motivations and needs. This point in the career sequence is also a career crossroad for many, a time when they may be contemplating retirement and a new career, or a time when they may actually be transitioning into civilian life. [p. 45–48]

Even at the top levels of noncommissioned officers, colonels, and generals, "errant" subordinates with problems may surface who require immediate attention.

In the case of the industrial foreman, such individualized consideration through individual counseling was seen by Kaplan and Cowen (1981) in a survey of 97 first-line supervisors regarding the problems they discussed with individual subordinates. The most important of these problems included: difficulties with fellow workers, concerns about promotion opportunities, job dissatisfaction, financial problems, family problems, and concerns about job security. To help, the foremen were most likely to just listen or to offer support and sympathy. They became more active by asking questions to draw the subordinate out, getting the subordinate to come up with alternatives, sharing personal experiences, suggesting another person with whom to consult, and giving advice. Listening to and helping with the personal problems of subordinates was seen to be an important part of the supervisor's job.

Mentoring

Individualized consideration is seen when the senior executive or professional takes time to serve as individual counselor for the junior executive or professional. The mentor is a trusted counselor who accepts a guiding role in the development of a younger or less-experienced member of the organization. Mentors use their greater knowledge, experience, and status to help develop their protégés, not to simply pull the protégés up the organization ladder on the mentors' coattails. This relationship makes mentoring unique among various kinds of superior–subordinate relationships. For example, it contrasts with merely being supportive or providing advice when asked (Shapiro et al., 1978). Compared to the formal, distant relationship most likely to be seen between a high-level executive and a junior somewhere down the line, the mentor is paternalistic, a father-figure, and perhaps a role model for the subordinate (Levinson et al., 1978).

A follow-up of 122 recently promoted persons in business mentioned by Johnson (1980) indicated that two thirds had had mentors. This popularity of mentoring in business, government, and industry reflects current interest both of individual employees as well as their organizations in the career development of the individual employee.

The Mentoring Arrangement

The mentor is not necessarily the immediate superior of the junior. Juniors often select as mentors someone higher up in the organization, frequently in a completely different organizational sector than the protégé. Lyndon Johnson was particularly adept at becoming the protégé of important, powerful, older politicians such as Sam Rayburn who were much further advanced in their careers (Caro, 1982). Sometimes the mentors are outside the organization., They may be relatives, friends, or former teachers. But most mentors are one's immediate supervisors or higher executives in one's organization (Johnson, 1980). We value positive feedback we receive from those we esteem much more than the same feedback we might receive from those we do not value (Bass et al.,

1961). It follows that we will place a premium on such feedback from mentors higher in authority in the system and seen by us to be experienced, knowledgeable, and esteemed.

If, indeed, "people who feel good about themselves, produce good results" (Blanchard & Johnson, 1982, p. 19), mentors can more readily make this happen. Mentoring is neither new nor unusual. (Mentor was the friend of Odysseus to whom was entrusted the education of his son, Telemachus. Mentor served as Telemachus' counselor, guide, coach, and teacher.) Mentoring may be a consequence of a senior or a junior's initiatives or it may be a matter of organizational policy or culture. At Jewel Companies, for example, vice-presidents are assigned as mentors and as "first assistants" to their apprentices. Emphasized in the mentor's role is teaching, listening, and consensual decision-making. Many other organizations such as Bell Laboratories have also set up formal mentoring programs (Shapiro et al., 1978).

Objectives

Formal mentoring programs, Zaleznik (1983) concluded, can usefully focus attention on individualized, senior–junior relations.

> Experimenting with one-to-one relationships, such as apprenticing junior executives to senior mentors, could inject a healthy elixir into the marginal culture. [p. 39]

A mentoring program can develop an organization in which protégés are less ready to quit and are more satisfied with their work and with their career progress. Mentoring can help protégés to be more ready, willing, and able to cooperate in joint efforts (Hunt & Michael, 1983).

Who Can Mentor?

Many executives cannot make good mentors. For example, some executives do prefer to work with people rather than spend their time in solitary activity, but they usually want to avoid emotional involvements. They do this be seeing themselves as role players in a process, less concerned with the substance of an issue compared to compromising and reconciling differences. But mentoring requires executives who can tolerate emotional interchanges. They need to be able to accept conflict as a dispute over substance, not as a personal attack. Personal attack and personal defense in interpersonal dynamics need to be avoided as such (Zaleznik, 1967).

Many seniors lack sufficient empathy which is particularly important to mentoring. This means more than merely paying attention to juniors, but being able to sense emotional signals and "make them mean something in a relationship with an individual" (Levinson et al., 1978, p. 73).

Levinson et al. concluded that mentors needed to be older and more experienced by about 8 to 15 years than their protégés. A greater disparity in image results in an interfering generation gap. Less disparity results in a peer relation rather than a mentoring relation. (Peer mentoring is possible but its different dynamics are not relevant to our discussion here.) Levinson et al. also suggest that mentors need to be of the same sex. Hunt and Michael (1983) add that mentors need to be highly placed, powerful, and knowledgeable, and that they need to be executives who will not be threatened by their protégé's potential to equal or surpass them.

Subordinates are more likely to model their own leadership style according to that of their superiors if they perceive their supervisors to be successful and competent. They parallel their supervisor's occupational values if the superior is seen by them to be considerate (Weiss, 1978). Presumably, mentors who are successful, competent, and considerate are more likely to serve as role models and sources of values for their protégés.

Differences Among Protégés

Field-dependent protégés compared to field-independent protégés are probably more likely to show the influence of their mentors as models and sources of value (Weiss & Shaw, 1979). In addition, the protégé's self-esteem will be of importance. Based on studies of leader–subordinare modeling (Korman, 1976; Adler, 1982), we infer that protégés with a strong sense of self-esteem will model themselves after competent mentors if they regard the mentors as competent, and if they believe their mentors to be in control of their paths to valued rewards and to organizational advancement. On the other hand, protégés low in self-esteem may try to model the leadership styles of mentors if the mentors are easy to identify with and are personally attractive to the protégés.

Benefits to Mentor

Mentoring protégés and developing subordinates are seen as important and valuable roles for an executive (Morse & Wagner, 1978). The executives' own promotion is facilitated if their replacement is seen as already adequately prepared to step into their shoes. Mentors accumulate respect, power, and future access to information from those individuals they have helped to develop. Mentors spread their influence into other parts of the organization through their former protégés. Performance in developing subordinates may be used as a criterion for evaluation and reward by the mentors' superiors (Jennings, 1967). Successful mentors also gain esteem among their peers (Kram, 1980). The longtime general manager of the Baton Rouge Refinery of Exxon had an almost unique reputation in the corporation as the developer of future Exxon executives who eventually were promoted above and beyond him.

Mentoring is a creative, satisfying, rejuvenating experience (Levinson et al., 1978). It also has payoff in the extent subordinates can fully use their intelligence to make a contribution to the organization's success (Fiedler & Leister, 1977).

Benefits to Protégé

Subordinates, as apprentices, learn firsthand about the uses of power, of integrity, and of the artistic and craftsmanlike elements in effective management (Zaleznik, 1967). Mentoring helps subordinates in the mentor/protégé dyad to develop positive and secure self-images.

Mentoring helps women subordinates, in particular, to integrate career and family responsibilities (Kram, 1980). Mentors are particularly important for the career success of women managers without family connections in the firm (Missirian, 1980).

Protégés learn from mentors how the organization works; mentors enhance the protégé's visibility in the organization by informing higher-ups about how good a job the protege is doing (Johnson, 1980). [According to Margerison (1980), becoming visible to top management was seen by 208 senior managers and chief executives as an important influence in their successful career development as managers.] Finally, for whatever the reason, those two thirds of executives with mentors in Roche's (1979) study earned higher overall compensation than the one third of executives who did not have mentors.

Conditions Promoting Mentoring

Some situations tend to bring out the mentoring in superiors and their attention to the development of their protégés. For example, company policy may encourage mentoring by making successful development of subordinates an important criterion for reward and promotion of managers. Yukl (1981) offers the following additional conditions as conducive to the occurrence of training and coaching by the leader which is also applicable to the mentor who is not necessarily the immediate superior of his protégé.

> When the work is complex and highly technical, and a long period of learning and experience is necessary for a subordinate to master all aspects of the job.
>   When the nature of the work and/or technology is changing, and subordinates need to learn new skills and procedures. When some subordinates have skill deficiencies and need additional coaching and instruction to overcome performance problems.
>   When it is frequently necessary to train new subordinates, due to a high turnover rate or to rapid expansion of the leader's unit.
>   When some subordinates need special training to prepare them to assume new responsibilities and advance to higher positions of authority. [p. 195]

The subordinates themselves contribute to this individualized developmental aspect of leadership. Zaleznik (1967) notes that often rather than rational and purposive effort by two separate persons— leader and subordinate—what is seen are subordinates who "position themselves around the leader as reflected images" (p. 66). The circumstance becomes one in which occur dramatic reenactments of fantasies that restore the self-esteem of the subordinates during their early experiences with disappointment.

Problems with Individuation

When leaders enter into individualized relationships with particular members of a group, such as we described in the case of Eleanor Samuels at the beginning of Part III, they show more closeness with those members who form an inner subgroup. Those in the inner circle accept more responsibilities and obtain more assistance from the leader. There is greater mutual support, sensitivity, and trust between the leader and his inner circle. In a large department of 60 members investigated over a nine-month period, while it underwent reorganization, inner circle members received "greater amounts of all resources . . . and more supportive and sensitive treatment" than did outer circle members. Inner circle members received more latitude in developing their own roles along with more inside information. They had greater influence on decision-making, and received more support for their actions and more consideration for their feelings than did outer circle members. Inner circle members were more involved and active in organizational affairs than were outer circle members. Inner circle members acted more consistently with their superior's expectations; outer circle members became more deviant from what their superior wanted and expected. Outer circle members reported they had more severe problems with their superior. Inner circle members were more satisfied with their jobs, its rewards, the work itself, and supervision. Clearly, this individualization of consideration strongly suggests the need to focus research attention on the individual leader–subordinate relationship rather than the leader–group relation (Graen, 1975; Graen & Cashman, 1975).

This differential treatment for those subordinates given special attention, the leader's "inner circle," and those not so favored who are cast into an outer circle, create problems for both. Those members in the leader's "inner circle" may bear greater costs as well as greater benefits than those on the outside. For example, their own reputations may hinge on the success or failure of their leader. They may suffer "guilt by their close association." More effort may be expected from them. Those on the outside may feel less commitment to the leader, less equity in the situation, and a loss of the leader's affection. The cliques of "ins" and "outs" may set up barriers between the cliques resulting in restricted communications, support and cooperation between them. In short, while providing individualized attention according to the differential abilities and needs of their subordinates, transformational leaders have to take care that they do not crystallize an "in-group" and an "out-group" within the larger group of their subordinates. They can avoid this by providing different attention at different times to their various subordinates. They can focus on different subordinates as different overall group needs occur. They can remain mindful of the superordinate group and organizational goals of consequence. They can keep their various subordinates aware of the subordinates' needs to integrate their needs for personal growth with the needs of their group and organization. In the aggregate, transforming leaders must balance out their attention to their various subordinates. Individualized consideration

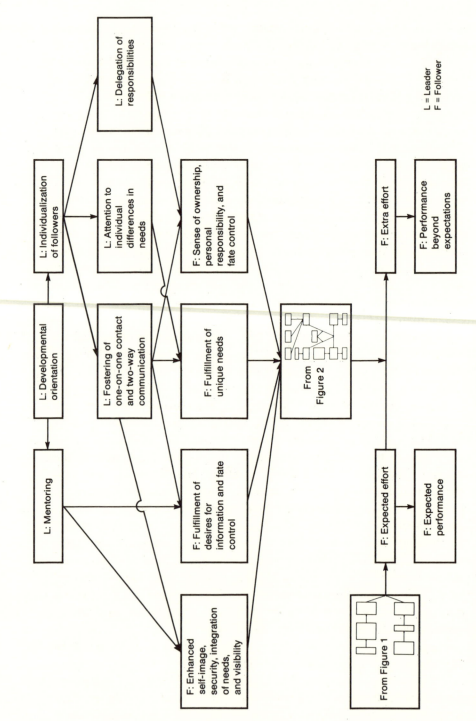

Figure 6 Individualized Consideration by Leader and Follower Effort

L = Leader
F = Follower

should not mean overall long-run inequities in leader–subordinate relationships.

A Model of Individualized Consideration

Figure 6 shows individualized consideration as a matter of mentoring and individuation by the leader. Mentoring increases confidence, and fulfills some of the follower's "need to know." Individuation means one-to-one contact and two-way communication. Such contact is expected to enhance the follower's self-image, desire for information, fulfillment of needs that are very special or unique to that follower, and the follower's sense of some "ownership" of decisions of consequence to him. When the leader treats each follower individually this furthers these follower reactions, all of which contribute to the transforming process seen in Figure 2.

Chapter 6

Intellectual Stimulation

THROUGH THEIR CHARISMA and/or individualized consideration, transformational leaders stimulate extra effort among their followers. They also evoke such heightened effort by means of their intellectual stimulation. Thomas Jefferson, polymath, prided himself on his reasoned judgment and intellectually based principles which he expounded and shared and which made him a man of great continuing influence in the transformation of 13 colonies into the United States.

Edwin Land, founder of Polaroid and its main driving force, illustrates the industrial leader whose intellectual brilliance combined scientific achievements in chemistry and physics with innovative success in business. He also needed the self-confidence and self-determination of the charismatic to persevere in his efforts despite rejection of his plans for instant photography by Kodak and other firms to whom he first offered his ideas. Land transformed U.S. industry with an appreciation of how new products create their own markets (Olshaker, 1978).

Another industrial leader with a strong intellectual base is Armand Hammer, M.D., of Occidental Petroleum. His business interests and activities range from ownership of an art gallery to whiskey distilling and from gold mining to multibillion dollar ammonia deals with the Soviets (Considine, 1975).

But there were plenty of intellectual lightweights who nevertheless were able to remain highly influential. Louis B. Mayer was described as almost an illiterate. History "was bunk" for Henry Ford, who castigated intellectual prowess.

The Intellectual Component

Intellectuals and Their Success as Leaders

By the transformational leader's intellectual stimulation, we mean the arousal and change in followers of problem awareness and problem solving, of thought and imagination, and of beliefs and values, rather than arousal and change in immediate action. The intellectual stimulation of the transformational leader is seen in the discrete jump in the followers' conceptualization, comprehension, and discernment of the nature of the problems they face and their solutions. This is in contrast to the arousal in followers of immediate increases in action rather than in ideas, contemplation, and thought prior to taking such actions. Intellectual in the sense of scholarly is not necessarily implied.

Instead of their focus on short-term operations, Wortman (1982) argues that executives at and near the top of the organization must increase their concentration on strategic thinking and on intellectual activities engaging themselves and their subordinates in the tasks of analysis, formulation, implementation, interpretation, and evaluation. In this way, executives will play a role as transforming leaders to the degree they can discern, comprehend, visualize, conceptualize, and articulate to their colleagues the opportunities and threats facing the organization and the organization's strengths, weaknesses, and comparative advantages. Leading in the locating and innovating of alternative strategies and their evaluation also may contribute to the transformation of the organization and its management. Luis Munoz Marin, Puerto Rican governor, sums up the intellectual contribution to political leadership as: "the ability to imagine nonexisting states of affairs combined with the ability to influence other people to bring them about" (Paige, 1977, p. 65). Kolb (1982) similarly sees leadership in complex organizations as: "the ability to manage the problem solving process in such a way that important problems are identified and solutions of high quality are found and carried out with the full commitment of organization members" (pp. 1-2).

Although both Marx and Lenin were intellectuals, Marx, who was the source of the ideas, received mixed receptions from his socialist audiences. But Lenin epitomized the leader who could transform such audiences with his intellectual discourse. According to many Russian Marxist delegates to a 1906 conference, "The logic of Lenin's speeches is like a mighty tentacle which twines all around you and holds you, from whose grip you are powerless to tear yourself away" (Tucker, 1970). It is this intellectual stimulation that has the transforming potential. But merely being a person with ideas is not enough in itself. The writings of Voltaire, Rousseau, and d'Alembert certainly contributed to the intellectual ferment leading to the French Revolution, but it was Mirabeau, Danton, and Robespierre who gave it its transforming leadership from parliamentary democratic reform to radical dictatorship.

Teachers as Transformational Leaders

Many have noted the extent to which leaders may have to serve as teachers. The rabbi leads because he is a teacher. As a profession, teachers often play the role of transformational leader, sharply changing the beliefs and values of at least some of their students (Burns, 1978). Revolutionaries, often from center or right backgrounds, are transformed by contact with a liberal intellectual establishment of educators. Similarly, students from working class, peasant, or petit bourgeois backgrounds may be shaped into reactionary leaders by conservative and reactionary teachers.

Importance to Transformational Leadership

"His ideas have forced me to rethink some of my own ideas which I had never questioned before" sums up the intellectual stimulation that can be provided by the transformational leader relatively independently of his charisma, as such, as will be noted in the quantitative analyses of Chapter 12. Other leadership influences we will identify as intellectual are: "He enables me to think about old problems in new ways." "He provides me with new ways of looking at things which used to be a puzzle for me."

The intellectual component may be obscured by surface considerations. Accused of making snap decisions, General George Patton commented:

> I've been studying the art of war for forty-odd years . . . a surgeon who decides in the course of an operation to change its objective is not making a snap decision but one based on knowledge, experience and training. So am I. [Puryear, 1971, p. 382]

Many scholars feel that the importance of a leader's technical expertise and intellectual power, particularly, in high performing systems, has been ignored and underrated in comparison to his or her interpersonal competence (Vaill, 1978). But this need to consider technical compared to interpersonal competence is not new. British naval commanders in Nelson's time were strict disciplinarians. Nevertheless, whether they were praised or reviled by the ordinary seaman depended to a considerable degree on their commander's technical competence.

> HMS Goliah, at the Battle of Cape St. Vincent, [was] sore beset as she . . . broke through among the enemy fleet in the action of February 14, 1797. The ship was handled by Captain Sir C. H. Knowles as if the eyes of all England were upon him . . . but Captain Knowles was tried for not lending assistance, when he needed it himself. The court-martial honourably acquitted him. . . . We were told not to cheer when he came on board; but we loved our captain too well to be restrained. . . . We manned the yards, and gave three hearty cheers. Not a man on board but would have bled for Sir C. H. Knowles. To our regret, we lost him to our ship at this very time. He was as good a captain as I ever sailed with. He was made admiral, and went home in the Britannia. [Nicol, 1983, pp. 44–45]

Even acknowledged tyrants can offset all their deleterious interpersonal relations by their sheer mastery of their trade. McCall and Lombardo (1978) quote the description of a head chef who

> (1) ruled with an iron rod, (2) did not tolerate mistakes, (3) flaunted his inequitable income, (4) inspected every single dish, and (5) seldom praised anyone. Nevertheless, the "esprit de corps" of his kitchen "would have done credit to the marines." A key factor in this tyrant's leadership? "He was the best cook in the whole brigade, and we knew it" [p. 159]

Relation to Charisma

Although intellectual stimulation emerged as a distinct factor, both our item correlations in Chapter 11 and the literature on charisma note the overlap and the lack of independence of one with the other. Charismatic prophets have extraordinary powers of vision about ways of dealing with what is troubling their followers and the ability to communicate the vision. From 1933 until he was called to be prime minister in 1940, Churchill kept in front of the British Parliament and public the dangers to Europe of a belligerent, rearming Germany. Charles de Gaulle's charisma among the French was earned from his vision and faith in the ultimate victory of the allies over Hitler.

On the other hand, one can find leaders whose charisma was based more on their practicality and interpersonal skills. Franklin D. Roosevelt is often cited as illustrative of the nonintellectual charismatic. He was seen by some of his contempories to have "a second-rate mind." Nevertheless, he was astute enough to recruit a "brain trust" of intellectuals who provided him with the ideas and plans for needed economic reforms which he was able to institute rapidly. Ronald Reagan clearly is another nonintellectual charismatic leader.

Kemal Ataturk, the transformational modernizer of Turkey, did not have

> infallible foresight, but a sheer inexhaustible resourcefulness. No sooner had one plan run into difficulty than he came up with another that by-passed the obstacle. When unexpected opportunities appeared, he stood ready to seize them. The long-range goal of independence was fixed, but to reach it Kemal was tacking with every changing wind.
>
> When it came to setting up a new institution, Kemal deliberately used vague terms that would veil its novelty and preserve his freedom of action. [Rustow, 1970, p. 218]

Just as with Roosevelt, few of his reforms were original with Ataturk. He was not conservative, but "composed new clarifying, messages about the desired reforms to westernize Turkey" (Rustow, 1970).

Marx was mainly an intellectual prophet although he did organize revolutionary movements; Lenin was an ideologue and visionary but even more a practical politician. Hitler was both. He illustrated the overlap of charisma and intellectual leadership. He was a "conspiracy theorist" who produced a set of pseudo-intellectual arguments to justify his barbarous solutions to stressful problems which earned him charismatic status among his followers. The conspiracy fitted the Germans' own paranoid projections about Jewish conspiracies against them and about being betrayed in 1918 by their own government. (Tucker, 1970).

When Intellectual Stimulation by the Leader Is Needed

Almost by definition, the intellectual contribution of a leader is particularly important when groups and organizations face ill-structured rather than well-structured problems (Mitroff, 1978). Yukl (1981) gives some examples of contingencies in which the leader's problem-solving contributions, per se, can result in the needed transformation of his group or organization.

When the group exists in a hostile environment, and its survival is endangered by competitors and external opponents who cause periodic crises.

When there are serious problems that reduce the unit's effectiveness, such as inadequate equipment, inappropriate procedures, delays, excessive costs, and so on.

When disruptions of the work are likely, due to equipment breakdowns, supply shortages, absent subordinates, and so on.

When the leader has sufficient authority to make changes and initiate actions that will solve serious problems facing the work unit. [p. 196]

Yet, if Mintzberg's (1975) observations are the norm, managers have little opportunity to concentrate on intensive problem-solving. According to these observations, managers are forced to jump from one issue to another, continually responding to the interruptions due to a constant stream of callers and mail. They spend very little time on any single issue, much less engage in any serious long-term problem-solving. It would seem that managers who would engage themselves and their subordinates in prolonged intellectual effort on one issue as many of the best chief executive officers (CEO's) do (Peters, 1980) have to consciously and deliberately have the authority to close their doors to callers and switch off all telephone calls. But, this, in turn, may create havoc with the managers' need to serve as transactional leaders who provide the guidance and contingent rewards for day-to-day operating performance.

As a solution, some organizations deal with this pressure of daily events by moving managers from line positions to special task forces whose only responsibility is for long-range planning. Staffs are created whose primary effort can be devoted to planning and problem-solving rather than to immediate line issues. But this separation of functions of line and staff generates all kinds of new problems in commitment, communication, and understanding (Fisch, 1961).

Another solution lies in the ability, resources, and willingness of managers to delegate effectively. Plenty of managers do free themselves by delegation for sufficient amounts of time to concentrate on various aspects of organizational problems. Drenth and Koopman (1984) found that among Dutch managers, as an organizational problem is identified, solutions searched for, and choices made and implemented, it works best when, top managers' first, are heavily involved in diagnosing the problem. They then delegate to middle managers the search for a solution. Finally, First-line supervisors detail its implementation.

Kilmann (1979) represents the other extreme from Mintzberg,

managers have often been considered as generic decision makers rather than as problem solvers. Perhaps decision making is more akin to solving well-structured problems where the nature of the problem is so obvious that one can already begin the process of deciding among clear cut alternatives. However, decisions cannot be made effectively if the problem is not yet defined and if it is not at all clear what the alternatives are, can, or should be. [1979, pp. 214–215]

More of an intellectual component is needed for effective management even if it seems that managers are too busy being transactional.

Relative to Subordinate Intellect

The intellectual contribution of a leader to helping subordinates must be considered in light of the subordinates' abilities. The leader (transformational or transactional) must be superior in ability to other members in one or more characteristics relevant to the problems facing the group, but not so superior that communications break down between leader and led. The leader must be able to make his ideas understood. Leadership potential, in general, goes with being "smart, but not too smart" (Riley & Flowerman, 1951).

A number of factors may militate against the overly intelligent member as a leader in addition to communication difficulties. If vastly superior in intellect, the would-be leader may no longer appreciate subordinates' problems or be interested or concerned with helping solve them. Also, the creative, original, and novel ideas of the overly capable individual may call for too great a change in behavior by subordinates who will become resistant to such proposed change (Bass, 1960).

Evidence that the overly intelligent manager (according to intelligence test scores) often fails to do as well as the manager who scores somewhat lower was presented by Ghiselli (1963). Again, Kraut (1969) found that managers with high scores on a test of intellectual ability were rated more favorably by their peers but did not advance in their careers any faster than others.

Gill (1982) has speculated about the reasons. He discovered that when inexperienced students were given training in prioritizing, those in the middle range in intelligence test scores profited the most in subsequent prioritizing and decision-making with an in-basket test. He suggested that the very bright spent too much time "intellectualizing" about the issue, were too rational, and tried to emulate a rational model of decision-making in their thought processes.

Those somewhat less gifted in intelligence were more pragmatic. They were more content to be satisfied with less than optimum solutions, to accept that they were faced with a situation in which their possibilities for rationality and search were limited. Their decision-making behavior was closer to the normal that had been described by Simon (1960).

Difference from Transactional Leadership

In this intellectual sphere, we see systematic differences between transformational and transactional leaders. The transformational leader may be less willing to be satisfied with partial solutions, or to accept the status quo, or to carry on as before. He is more likely to be seeking new ways, change for its own sake, taking maximum advantages of opportunities despite the higher risks. Gill's successful manager is more likely to remain transactional, focusing on what can clearly work, keeping time constraints in mind, doing what seems to be most efficient and free of risk.

What may separate transformational from transactional leaders is the transformational leaders are more likely to be proactive than reactive in their thinking; more creative, novel, and innovative in their ideas; more radical or reactionary than reforming or conservative in ideology; and less inhibited in their ideational search for solutions. Transactional leaders may be equally bright but their focus is on how to best keep the system running for which they are responsible—reacting to problems generated by observed deviances, looking to modify conditions as needed and remaining ever mindful of the organizational constraints within which they must operate.

An indirect suggestion that a different type of intellectual functioning is associated with successful transformational leadership is seen in data from Rusmore (1984). He tested 208 male public utility managers on seven measures of intellectual ability. Two factors emerged: (1) general intelligence (based on tests of verbal, quantitative, and abstract reasoning) and (2) cognitive creativity (based on tests of obvious consequences, remote consequences, and unusual uses). As expected, each factor correlated with superiors' ratings of the managers' performance.

Rusmore's managers were classified as supervisors and salaried foremen, mid-level executives, and high-level executives. Analyses were repeated for each of the three levels of executives and supervisors. Mean factor scores ($\times 100$) on general intelligence increased from -34

to 11 to 29 with increasing level in the organization. They increased as well on cognitive creativity from −34 to 17 to 24 with increasing organizational level. There was also some corresponding change in the correlations of each of the factors with performance as one looked at the data about supervisors, middle managers, and higher-level executives. General intelligence contributed more to the performance ratings of first-line supervisors than to that of high-level executives. Middle managers were in between in this regard. Conversely, cognitive creativity was more important to the performance ratings of the high-level utility company executives than to first-level supervisors. Again, results for the middle managers were in between. These findings were above and beyond the fact that, as would be expected, both general intelligence and cognitive creativity were higher among those managers at higher levels. It would seem that successful transformational leadership would be more dependent on general intelligence at lower organizational levels and on cognitive creativity at higher levels. It is not unreasonable to assume that more opportunity for creativity exists at higher levels.

The results, implying the importance of cognitive creativity to performance at higher levels of management, argue for the broad educational approach to preparation of business managers. This was a reason for abandoning the undergraduate curricula of the 1950s which stressed learning about current business practices. Encouraged instead was undergraduate education in the humanities, economics, mathematics, science, and social science, preparatory for graduate education in management which was to provide prospective managers with the necessary broad background to enable them to effectively keep up with new developments in business, society, and technology. Unfortunately, again business education seems to be falling back to learning about current business practices upgraded to the 1980s with the addition of computers and mathematical models.

Experience and Conflict with One's Superiors

For Fiedler and Leister (1977), whether the intellectual ability of leaders makes a difference depends on their experience and how much they are in conflict with higher authority. Experienced managers can apply their intelligence better to managing and guiding their bosses. Bright young managers may be handicapped by their lack of experience.

Stress occurs when superiors are interfering, meddling, and dictatorial and/or when they induce role ambiguity in their subordinates and a sense of disorganized management. Generalizing from the fact that stress tends to reduce intellectual functioning, Fiedler and Leister argue that faced with stressful conflict with one's boss, a manager's intellectual functioning will be impaired. But we can cope with stress through falling back to previously learned habits. Hence, experience should help.

Fiedler and Leister (1977) suggested that leaders with greater intelligence will produce more task effective groups if the leaders are motivated to lead, are experienced, encounter little stress with their superior, and believe they have good relations with their subordinates. In a field study of 158 Army infantry squad leaders, leader intelligence was found to correlate positively with squad performance among experienced squad leaders but much less so among inexperienced ones; more with motivated leaders and less with unmotivated ones; more with leaders unstressed by their boss and not at all with squad leaders stressed by their boss; more with those having good relations with their own subordinates; and less with those having poor relations.

Particularly important in the equation, Fiedler and Leister (1977) reported, were the intellectual demands of the tasks involved. For leadership tasks like policy advising, intelligence was positively predictive of performance for military leaders in little conflict with their superiors, but it was negatively predictive for leaders in stressful relations with their boss. Intelligence was less help but remained detrimental on tasks with little intellectual demand such as routine paperwork. The effects of experience, on the other hand, were not altered by the nature of the task; experience correlated positively with performance on intellectual tasks and on nonintellectual tasks. Thus, overcontrolling superiors, who indulged in interfering, meddling, autocratic, and dictatorial behavior, and superiors who created uncertainty evidenced by role ambiguity and disorganized management tended to stifle the intellectual contribution of Army officers to their performance as leaders. Another way of seeing this is that inconsiderate leaders at one level reduce the intellectual contribution of their subordinates. The effect is magnified by the rank of superior and subordinate; it is much greater with commanding and executive officers than with noncommissioned officers.

Symbols and Images

Symbol Manipulation

Transformational leaders concerned with ideas can project these ideas as images which excite subordinates and colleagues. With these images, they are able to send clear rather than ambiguous messages.

The intellectual contribution of the transformational leader is seen in the leader's creation, interpretation, and elaboration of symbols. The symbols are representations of chunks of information or signs representing sets of cognitions related by overlapping functional associations (Eoyang, 1983).

The U.S. flag symbolizes a set of cognitions—parades, ball games, holidays, military events, national patriotism, ceremony, and devotion. The crown serves similarly for the British. Eoyang agrees with Burns (1978) that transformational leaders alter not only motivational levels, values and beliefs, but also provide acceptable symbolic solutions to problems. Transformational leaders can reconcile psychological contradictions between various cognitions and experiences "by providing a coherent symbolic context which incorporates the separate elements into a meaningful and consistent gestalt." Thus, a considerable portion of an originally indifferent American public can be convinced that the U.S. must support unpopular governments in Guatamala, Honduras, and El Salvador against insurgents but support the insurgents against the government of Nicaragua, because Nicaragua represents Cuban and therefore Soviet expansionism into Central America whereas the governments of El Salvador, Honduras, and Guatamala symbolize opposition to such Cuban and Soviet opportunism.

For those who already are primarily convinced in a Soviet world domination theory, Central America symbolizes a closer-than-ever threat to our North American homeland. For others, images of floods of refugees pouring over our Southern borders are brought into play along with domino theories. Every U.S. President from Harry Truman to Richard Nixon explained U.S. policy toward Vietnam as a need to prevent a domino from falling, thus endangering a stack of such dominoes from Burma to Australia.

> Belief systems cannot be complete and self-contained on the basis of logic alone . . . transforming leadership may provide an external symbolic framework which permits the psychological resolution of confused or ill understood cognitions and experiences. [Eoyang, 1983, p. 12]

Transforming symbols can directly modify cognitions and beliefs. The case of Marlboro cigarettes is illustrative. Marlboro was primarily a woman's cigarette. At the time, the men's market was larger and untapped. A cowboy with a tattoo on his wrist smoking a Marlboro cigarette became the symbol of masculine virility which massive advertising attached to Marlboro. Marlboro was thereby transformed into a "man's" cigarette.

New Symbols and Images

Transforming symbols such as the Nazi swastika or the Communist hammer and sickle can ''affect the value and importance attributed to established beliefs by introducing new ideas which take on comparable if not superior importance relative to previous notions'' (Eoyang, 1983). Consider how Roman troops, notoriously superstitious and mainly Mitra-worshippers, reacted to the rumor just before the battle at Milvian Bridge in 312 A.D. that a cross was seen in the sky, a cross symbolizing salvation and eternal life. Constantine's victory over pagan Maximilian and the subsequent triumph of Christianity were often attributed in naive theories to the appearance of this cross in the sky (a projection onto the sun-and-cloud configuration?).

Symbols substitute for real values. In the process of secondary reinforcement, the secondary reward which is in symbolic form comes to substitute for the primary reward. In chimpanzee research, chips come to substitute for food. Chips become money symbols as long as they can be exchanged subsequently for grapes. Followers attach symbolic value to their transforming leaders' intentions and visions of what might be.

The transformational leader uses a set of symbolic forms such as ceremonies and insignia to show that they are, in fact, leading. These ''crowns and coronations, limousines and conferences'' circumscribe the arena in which followers can focus their attention, the arena in which leading ideas come together with leading institutions. The important events within the arena are seen by followers as what ''translates intentions into reality'' (Bennis, 1982, p. 56).

Eoyang (1983) suggests that it is usually a difficult process to introduce transforming symbols representing new ideas counter to old beliefs. The transactional leader has an easier time of it. He uses old, already available, symbols and ideas fit with old belief systems. For instance, the national budget can be presented as merely a larger version of one's household budget. People know what it is to live beyond their incomes so deficit spending is easily but superficially understood as excessive government spending which results in confiscatory taxes symbolized by the taxpayer stripped of all of his possessions and left with only a barrel to wear to hide his nakedness.

Relation to Transformational Leadership

Introducing and establishing a new and enduring stable system of values, beliefs and associations is the epitome of effective transformational leadership. The enduring aspects captured by the new symbols that are substituted for the old symbols and images are an important component in intellectual stimulation of followers. They help to articulate, propagate, and recall the new ideas and beliefs as well as to attach emotional value to them.

Change in symbolism is a universal element in the armamentorium of the transformational leader. Kemal Ataturk's law banning the peakless fez which permitted touching the ground in prayer symbolized "an ostentatious break" with Islam for Turkey (Rustow, 1970). Franklin D. Roosevelt's "New Deal" reflected a completely new concept of massive Federal intervention in the health and well-being of the U.S. citizenry, previously relegated to the status of a local issue to be settled locally. The cross symbolized the promise of salvation, a new way of life and afterlife. Ghandi's spinning wheel symbolized the rejection of the British Raj and the self-reliant drive for Indian independence. De Gaulle's Cross of Lorraine symbolized the old French virtues of honor, dignity, and glory. Thomas Watson's conservative dress code for IBM employees was intended to impress customers and the employees themselves. The code symbolized dedication to service, uniform high quality, and seriousness of purpose.

Types of Intellectual Stimulation

The contrast between two political leaders in the effort to be intellectually stimulating was seen in the 1960 U.S. Presidential campaign. While Nixon stuck to the same themes in his speeches, John F. Kennedy brought up new subjects or new combinations of them in each new speech (Sorenson, 1966). Quinn and Hall (1983) suggested that leaders can provide intellectual stimulation in four different ways depending on their own personal preferences for rationality, existentialism, empiricism, or idealism. These four types of leaders differ in the extent to which their intellectual efforts are transformational and transactional. The existentialist's focus on creativity and the idealist's orientation toward growth are transformational, while the rationalist and the empiricist may use their intellect to maintain the status quo as transactional leaders as well as to adequately structure conditions for the future as transformational leaders.

Rationally Oriented Intellectual Stimulation

Rationally oriented leaders are likely to be strong in achievement motivation. They emphasize competence, independence, and industry.

They rely heavily on formal structure and a priori logic. Such leaders are decisive in that they require only a small amount of information to generate specific solutions. Their decisions are final. They emphasize speed and efficiency. They are directive, goal-oriented, and strong on initiation of structure in their intellectual stimulation.

Existentially Oriented Intellectual Stimulation

Existential leaders are more concerned about increasing security and trust and in building teams. They rely on informal processes and the belief that intellectual understanding can only emerge in the human process of interacting with the environment. Existentialists are integrative decision-makers who in their intellectual efforts use a great deal of information and generate many solutions for implementation. They favor creative synthesis over pure logic. They use their intellect to support others' ideas as well as their own.

Empirically Oriented Intellectual Stimulation

Empirical experts are oriented toward improving security, protection, safety, and continuity. Favoring empiricism, there is a tendency to rely on externally generated data. A "hierarchic" decision style is observed in which a great deal of information is used to carefully generate one "best" answer. Rigor, precision, and long-range planning are followed to implement solutions with elaborate contingency plans. Such leaders are conservative and cautious in their intellectual stimulation of subordinates. They also excel as transactional leaders in doing a good job in maintaining structure, providing information, monitoring, and coordinating.

Idealistically Oriented Intellectual Stimulation

Idealistic prime movers are oriented toward growth, adaptation, learning, cognitive goals, variety, and creativity. They place heavy reliance on internally generated, intuitive data. Their decision style is flexible. Idealistic leaders use a minimal amount of information to reach a conclusion, but are constantly gathering additional information and generating new solutions as necessary. They value speed, adaptability, intuition, and compromise. Such transformational leaders do particularly well in envisioning change (like charismatics) and acquiring resources. A high degree of inventiveness and risk-taking are often observed in idealistic leaders.

Intellectual and Emotional Stimulation

Intellectual stimulation becomes extreme in effect, particularly if it is coupled with emotional stimulation. Combined with emotional arousal, intellectual stimulation can turn into consciousness-raising, thought reform, and brainwashing. Chinese Communist conversion practices are an organized application of intellectual and emotional stimulation to transform values, beliefs, and performance en masse.

Chinese Conversion Practices

In January 1928, when the Communist general, Chu Teh, learned that six companies of young students recently conscripted by Chiang Kai-shek were about to attack the Communists at Ichang, Chu Teh decided to both capture the students and to convert them. The six Kuomintang companies were ambushed, captured, and disarmed. One of Chu's staff, a scholar, spoke to the captives as friends. A young officer told them that he, also, had been a student like them and that two of his brothers and a sister had been killed for their revolutionary efforts. A peasant soldier described the fate of his family victimized by their landlord. The accounts were so emotional that some of the speakers and listeners wept. The captives were then offered the choice of joining the rebel army or receiving travel money and passes to return to their homes. All but a few of the captives joined the revolutionary army.

This procedure became standard policy and practice for the next 20 years. Talks were given to the captured soldiers about the privations suffered by those who had joined the revolution. The evils of Chiang Kai-shek's government were discussed. In addition, the captured soldiers were encouraged to discuss their dissatisfactions with their officers, government, and landlords.

Consciousness Raising

The approach was then extended to "consciousness raising" efforts during land reform campaigns in the villages and in the factories in the

1950's when "democratic reform" and "production reform" were begun. Such consciousness raising became part of what Mao Zedung termed "mass line leadership." The Communist Party was to take the scattered and unsystematic ideas of the masses and through study to turn them into concentrated and systematic ideas. The Party would then disseminate these ideas back to the masses until the ideas were embraced by the masses as their own (Mao, 1967). Through this intellectual endeavor, the Party was to serve as the nexus of the transformational process.

In practice, of course, many of the ideas did not originate with the masses. What was supposed to be consultative leadership turned coercive, directive, and manipulative. Nevertheless, China did see considerable modification of originally top-down transformational policies as a consequence of mass reactions to them. Compromises were reached about marriage law reform, land reform, and simplifying the written language, for example (Barlow, 1981). The Chinese were converted rather than conquered.

Thought Reform

The intellectual process of mass line leadership coupled with the use of group discussion, peer group pressure, public confession, public praise, and public reproof forms the basis of continuing Chinese Communist "thought reform."

> The basic political and social constituents of post-1949 China are study groups of 10–20 persons. It is in these groups that . . . the Chinese people have been transformed or reformed. They are "voluntary" gatherings. It is said that one must choose to join a group and that no one is forced to do so. . . . These study groups are not a part of the Chinese government at any level. They are a sort of "grass roots" political organization and make up the new basic social element of Chinese society. The procedures used in these study groups are the means for mass line leadership consciousness raising, study/thought revealing, and self-criticism/criticism. . . . A group usually elects its own head (subject to designated criteria and to approval of the choice by higher authorities) and meets regularly for study. The amount of time spent in group study seems staggering. It varies greatly, but as much as four hours daily is sometimes required during a particular campaign. Materials for study might include selections from Marxist–Leninist writings or the writings of Mao Tse-tung; party policies or directives; materials concerning national issues or current national or local cam-

paigns; or items related to the specific work or neighborhood of study group members. The usual procedure is for some of the material to be read and then for everyone to discuss it. Everyone is expected to participate, and in various ways everyone is encouraged to do so (in effect, everyone must participate at least some of the time). [Barlow, 1981, pp. 304–305]

Coercive aspects are seen in the weight of peer pressure accentuated in a "shame" culture, the use of public confession and self-criticism and the extent that membership and attendence are forced rather than voluntary. When applied to foreign prisoners, these coercive aspects become extremely coercive and manipulative through the use of contingent physical and psychological rewards and punishments. Thought reform becomes brainwashing (Barlow, 1981).

A Model of Intellectual Stimulation

Figure 7 displays a model of intellectual arousal of followers by their leader. The leader's intellectual competence and orientation determines his approach and success in problem solving of ill-structured problems with and for followers. The leader's performance in this endeavor is moderated by his time to think and freedom from conflict with superiors. The interacting of the leader's alertness to problems, diagnosis, and the generation of solutions are communicated to followers symbolically, by means of vivid imagery and simplified, articulate language for easier comprehension and heightened attention. These in turn enhance follower role clarity and acceptance to contribute to the transformational process shown in Figure 2.

The Transformational Factors: Charismatic Leadership, Individualized Consideration, and Intellectual Stimulation

In reality, the intellectual stimulation provided by the transformational leader is unlikely to stand alone. Rather, the transformational leader is likely to display some combination of intellectual stimulation, charismatic leadership, and/or individualized consideration. As we will show in Chapter 12, these transformational factors tend to be intercorrelated rather than completely independent of each other. Generally, transformational leaders are likely to be higher rather than lower on all three factors.

To illustrate, the industrialist, Lorenz Iversen, was a transforma-

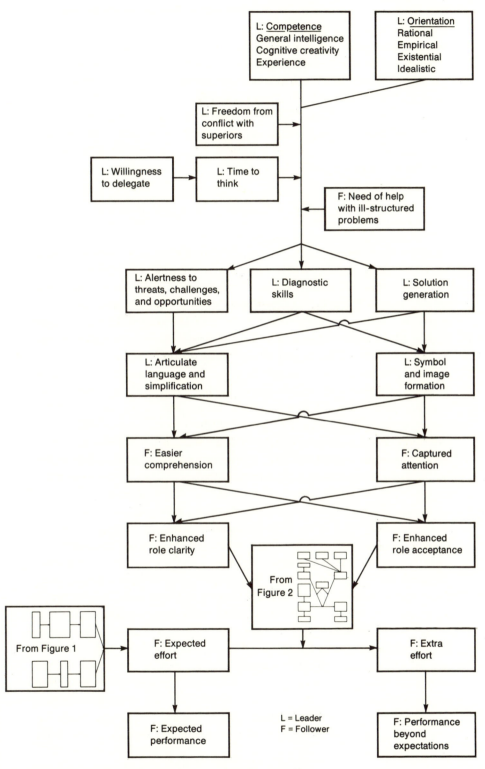

Figure 7 Intellectual Stimulation and Follower Effort

tional leader who exhibited continued strength on all three factors: charisma, individualized consideration, and intellectual stimulation.

Starting in 1902, Iverson rose through the staff ranks of the Mesta Machine Company to become its president in 1930. Inspirational leadership was seen regularly. He would bellow from a platform on the shop floor, "We got this job because you're the best mechanics in the world." The charismatic effect is still remembered by a worker in 1984 who joined the company in 1933.

> I get goose bumps just thinking about it. He really knew how to instill pride. We had then what the Japanese are bragging about now. [O'Boyle, 1984, p. 31]

His individual consideration was expressed in many ways. Layoffs were rare. When there were downturns in demand, workers took salary cuts and worked four-day weeks. He practiced "walk-around management" on the shop floor for face-to-face talks with employees about their work and family problems, not only with the day shift, but also on nights, weekends, and holidays. But he was a perfectionist and needed to be involved and in control of all details of the business.

His intellectual stimulation gave rise to many patented inventions on the equipment used by Mesta and led to heated arguments with associates on the best ways for tasks to be accomplished (O'Boyle, 1984).

Roberts (1984) completed a case study of transformational leadership over a two-year period involving a superintendent of schools and her constituencies. Roberts' study was another illustration of the importance to the transformational leader of the three factors. Her information came from observation of meetings, available documents, and 45 intensive interviews with principals, support staff, parents, and pupils. A transformation was seen to take place in stages during which the superintendent was the intellectual and motivational catalyst for innovation as well as the person who was instrumental in developing a supportive climate for change. First came a crisis—in this instance, there was a severe cut in the budget. With appropriate skill and determination, the superintendent responded to the crisis by providing those who must be mobilized to confront the crisis with a sense of mission; she used the budgetary crisis, not to retrench, but to galvanize people into action. The school district's mission statement was set forth "to treat the learner or the child as a unique individual with unique potential." She constantly reminded others of the statement and helped to operationalize it. She used the statement as the basis of a strategic vision incorporating expected trends in society and education—more democratic

society, self-reliance, accountability, computer technology, individualized learning, and so forth—for which the district had to prepare itself.

At the outset, the superintendent engaged in ''walk-around'' management to build a constituency of teachers who would support the
change effort. She engaged in one-on-one private discussions with ''an-
tis.'' She identified key personnel who appeared most ready to change
and rewarded them individually with public praise for their participation in the change efforts. She also made use of coaching as well as seeking out the people in the district with power as the ones ''to court first.''
The superintendent initiated the required structure to tackle the problem at hand, reorganizing the district office, reassigning persons, and
redesigning positions to reflect changes in the district and competencies
available. Further, she engaged administrative staff, teachers, and community in a participative process to gain wide commitment for change.
The consequences were an inpouring of innovative ideas for new projects and programs, a feeling that individual and organizational purposes were in alignment, and a sense of mutual support, respect, and
caring.

After two years in office, the superintendent was seen to have a
''cult-like'' following in the district, to be able to do almost anything she
wanted—to be an extraordinary ''mover and shaker,'' a visionary who
had had an inspirational impact on her district. She was an exemplary
case of transformational leadership bringing forth performance beyond
expectations.

Many transformational leaders also can be found who were low on
at least one of the three transformational factors. Ronald Reagan is a
case in point. Charismatic Ronald Reagan, who gave continued support and consideration to subordinates such as James Watt and Edward
Meese long after they had become political liabilities to him, repeatedly
displayed absence of intellectual rigor.

Ronald Reagan's charismatic charm gave him the great influence to
produce in 1981 massive increases in defense spending and massive
decreases in taxes coupled with sharp reversals in support for many
domestic programs. But intellectually, Reagan has been described by
the experienced Washington observer David Broder as ''heavily responsive to symbol and almost immune to logic.'' There is in Reagan a separation of cause and effect, a denial of logic, and a substitution of symbol
for substance. Nevertheless, the self-conviction and inspirational aspects of the transforming leader remain strong in him. Reagan remained effective in persuading the public because he was being true to
his own convictions. ''The script made sense to him.'' He was able to

convey this romantic meaningfulness to the public despite its unreality, lack of logic, and words that are contrary to deeds and results. His abilities centered on selection and delivery of plain speech using the words which best convey the emotional content (Broder, 1984).

One of Reagan's election campaign directors, John Sears, noted that Reagan has repeatedly been able to walk away from "more political car crashes than anyone else. . . . He just could walk away and not look back" (Glass, 1984). For most of his first four years in office,

> His policies . . . helped produce the worst recession since the 1930s . . . a trillion-dollar ocean of federal red ink, a deep-freeze with the Russians and corrosive little non-wars in the Middle East and Central America. And yet he remained the outlaw of gravity, floating serenely above the issues by some alchemy his own mystified handlers called "the Reagan magic." [p. 22]

Despite this, a majority of a national representative sample in early 1984 had personal confidence in him to do the right thing and liked him personally. Four out of five "liked the way he stands up for America." He does not need to work hard. He is the nice guy in a world of good guys and bad guys who disarms his enemies. He is the "quintessential American." He has "crinkly-eyed, apple-cheeked, next-door-neighborly warmth." He is decent, down-to-earth, and too old to be seen as an ambitious politician. The result was a landslide reelection in 1984. Despite much less support for the ideology and policies he espoused, the American public had great faith and trust in him to do the right thing (DeFrank et al., 1984). Transforming consequences included a strong revival in the United States of political and social conservatism, a new optimism among the better-off economically, a weakening of organized labor, a strengthening of big business, and a surge of economic growth in 1984 despite federal deficits and high interest rates.

Part IV

Transactional Leadership

O NCE YOU BECAME a member of Carla's group, you found out that she was a firm believer in behavior modification. She broke up your assignments into tasks from the simplest to the most complex and made it clear to you how each was to be done. You were expected to master the simpler tasks first. She always had a good word to say to you when you finally succeeded in achieving errorless performance on a new task. She was available to explain what you were doing wrong if you ran into trouble and to encourage you to try again. This was much different from my previous experience as a salesman where I met with my sales supervisor, Barry Barton, once every six months for a day to review my sales success for the previous six months and to set targets for the six months ahead. We looked at where I had succeeded and where I had failed and why. This helped us to plan ahead. As long as my daily reports to Barton indicated that I was following the planning, I was unlikely to hear much from him again until we met again in six months time. He only was likely to call or write to me if he failed to get a report from me, if he received a customer complaint, or if we suddenly suffered a loss of business in my territory.

Carla and Barry both are transactional leaders. Carla concentrates on contingent reward which we will see works reasonably well, although in practice its effects often are more modest than our theories about it would suggest. Barry practices management-by-exception which we are finding to be counterproductive despite its popularity with many managers.

Chapter 7

Contingent Reward

TRANSACTIONAL LEADERSHIP IS contingent reinforcement. The leader and follower agree on what the follower needs to do to be rewarded or to avoid punishment. If the follower does as agreed, the leader arranges to reward the follower or the leader does not impose aversive reinforcement such as correction, reproof, penalization, or withdrawal of authorization to continue. In the U.S. world of work, most of the reward or punishment is nonmaterial. It is feedback that things are or are not going as agreed. Ordinarily, it does not appear to be a matter of gain or loss of monetary reward. Seventy-three percent of a 1983 survey of U.S. workers felt that people frequently receive the same increases in pay regardless of how hard they work. But this is not to say that workers are uninterested in material benefits. Sixty-one percent wanted to see closer links between their performance and their pay (Yankelovich & Immerwahr, 1983).

Some of the feedback comes from the work itself, from co-workers and from elsewhere inside and outside the organization. But that portion that comes from one's leaders along with the material benefits they can provide is transactional leadership.

The Leader as Agent of Reinforcement

A bargain is struck. A contract is signed. An exchange is agreed upon. Leader and subordinate accept interconnected roles and responsibilities to reach designated goals. Directly or indirectly, leaders can provide rewards for progress toward such goals or for reaching them. Or, they can impose penalties for failure ranging from negative feedback to dismissal. Such positive and aversive contingent reinforcement are seen as the two ways managers in organized settings engage in transactional leadership to motivate employees. Contingent positive reinforcement, reward if agreed-upon performance is achieved, reinforces the effort to maintain the desired speed and accuracy of employee performance. Contingent aversive reinforcement is a manager's reaction to an employee's failure to achieve the agreed-upon performance. The manager's reaction signals the need to halt the decline in speed or accuracy of the employee's performance, to modify or change the employee's behavior. It signals the need for a reclarification of what needs to be done and how.

Ordinarily, in service and production, contingent reward takes two forms: praise for work well done and recommendations for pay increases, bonuses, and promotion (Sims, 1977). In addition, we may see commendations for meritorious effort including public recognition and honors for outstanding service.

Contingent punishment also may take several forms when an employee fails to live up to the manager's expectations. Thus, a deviance from norms may occur. Production may fall below agreed-upon standards; quality may fall unacceptably low. The manager may be required merely to call attention to the deviation. Being told of one's failure to meet standards may be sufficient aversive reinforcement for what was done wrong. Being told why can be helpful particularly to the inexperienced or inexpert subordinate, especially if the negative feedback is coupled with further clarification of what performance is desired. While other penalties may be levied, such as fines, suspension without pay, loss of leader support, or discharge, these are less frequent and less likely to promote effectiveness. When managers, for one reason or another, choose to intervene only when failures, breakdowns, and deviations occur, they are practicing management-by-exception. The general admonition to those practicing management-by-exception is, "If it ain't broken, don't fix it!"

Both contingent reward and contingent penalization are characteristic of transaction-oriented managers because such managers, unlike transforming leaders, are more concerned with efficient processes than with substantive ideas. They are more interested in what will work rather than in what is true. They display their flexible tactics by suitable use of their power to reward or punish to maintain or improve what they see are satisfactory processes and organizational arrangements (Zaleznik, 1967).

Contingent Reinforcement as a Transactional Process

The succinct, pithy statements in the *One Minute Manager* (Blanchard & Johnson, 1982) abstract current wisdom about the mainly transactional process of contingent reward in a few words whose essence is as follows:

> Set goals with subordinates.
> Clarify what performance is needed to reach the goals.
> Tell inexperienced subordinates what they did right, how you feel about it, and encourage more of the same.
> Tell experienced subordinates, when necessary, what they specifically are doing wrong and how you feel about it but reassure them you still value them as persons.

The exchange should not be a cold transaction of reward for compliance with agreements reached or punishment for failure to comply. Leaders must give reassurance of their continuing esteem for their subordinate regardless of what happens. The reassurance is sort of a base, overall, continuing reward for the subordinate for continuing to associate with the leaders and for trying to comply. The transaction also can be warmed by a transformational concern by the leaders for the development of the subordinate. Each goal–performance–reward cycle is a step toward the development of the subordinate to take increasing responsibility for his own actions so that experienced subordinates will become self-reinforcing. The leaders will almost have worked themselves out of their job with the fully developed subordinate for whom, as Ralph Waldo Emerson put it, the reward of a thing well done is to have done it.

Supervisors should not wait until the periodic performance appraisal interview to praise subordinates. Rather, goals (no more than three to six) should have been set which could be described on one sheet of paper. Brief praise for reaching such goals should be given as close to the time of reaching the goals as possible. Sincere encouragement should be provided for subsequent performance.

As much as possible, subordinates should be able to monitor their own progress by the clarity of the gap between their performance and the agreed-upon goals. The goals need to be reasonably achievable and therefore should represent incremental, small steps of progress. Positive feedback does not have to await 100 percent achievement of longer-term goals, nor should negative feedback be delayed until mistakes have reached disastrous proportions.

Some Evidence

Numerous experiments and field studies attest to the efficacy of leadership-by-contingent reinforcement. In a laboratory experiment, Spector and Suttell (1957) contrasted what they called reinforcement leadership with authoritarian and democratic leadership. The reinforcement leader maximized positive reinforcement for correct plans produced by teams of subjects. He specifically expressed approval every time good problem solutions were reached by them. When incorrect planning performance appeared, the reinforcement leader suggested how it could be improved. He also encouraged subjects to keep trying. The authoritarian leader made the group's decisions and did its planning. Under the democratic leader, responsibility was shared for planning and decision-making. The teams under reinforcement leadership did best. Members of low ability appeared to profit most from such leadership.

Praise and recognition as well as material rewards contingent on acceptable performance were observed to promote better performance and effectiveness by Hunt and Schuler (1976) and Oldham (1976). A field study by Reitz (1971) came to similar conclusions. Subordinate satisfaction was most enhanced when supervisors praised and rewarded subordinates for their acceptable performance as well as reproved them for unacceptable work. In the same way, Luthans and Krietner (1975) found that contingent penalization for unacceptable actions worked to improve performance when it was coupled with contingent reward for acceptable performance.

Giving rewards such as praise, recognition, and pay recommendations for acceptable performance not only helped improve such performance (Keller & Szilagyi, 1976) but also enhanced subordinates' expectations. The influence of the leader in the situation was also seen to be strengthened (Sims, 1977).

Podsakoff et al. (in press) found that hospital pharmacists were more satisfied with their situation if their leaders provided them with rewards (positive feedback) contingent on their performance. Such satisfaction was not present if rewards were not contingent on their performance. Particularly dissatisfying was noncontingent negative feedback, that is, not really being able to link reprimands with the behaviors that elicited them.

Loss of a supervisor's ability to provide rewards to subordinates contingent on the subordinates' performance was seen to have a variety of deleterious effects. According to his subordinates, not only is there an obvious loss of the supervisor's power to reward, but he also loses their desire to identify with him as well as organizationally sanctioned legitimacy and influence (Green & Podsakoff, 1981).

Cross-lagged causal analyses[1] by Greene (1976) confirmed the fact that it was supervisory reward behavior contingent on subordinate performance that subsequently resulted in improved subordinate performance and satisfaction among those whose performance merited reward. The effect had some permanency and was not just observable only in concurrent correlations of supervisory behavior and subordinate performance.

According to Peters and Waterman (1982, p. 123), better companies such as Tupperware put a good deal of effort into providing positive reinforcement for successful completion of tasks. Tupperware management makes a very conscious effort to "honor with all sorts of positive reinforcement" any valuable action completed by people at every level in the organization. The management also continuously searches for opportunities "to swap good news."

These management practices fit squarely with cognitive and behavioral theories and research in goal setting, motivation, learning, reinforcement, and reward. There is empirical data to support their efficacy. It is not surprising that leadership by means of contingent reward is most popular with research psychologists.

Factor-Analytic Description of Contingent Reward

Sims (1977) discovered that two factors could account for positive contingent reinforcement behavior by supervisors according to their subordinates. The first positive reward behavior factor explained 37 percent

---

[1] In a cross-lagged correlation analysis, two variables, X and Y, are measured twice within some period of time, say, three months in between. In addition to the *concurrent* correlations of X and Y at Time 1 and again at Time 2, also obtained are correlations of X_1Y_2 and Y_1X_2 to see which is larger. If X_1Y_2 is larger than Y_1X_2, it is inferred that X had more of an effect on Y than Y on X. These results need to be adjusted if the reliabilities and variances of X and Y are different.

of the variance among the supervisors. Items most highly correlated with this first factor included:

> Your supervisor would show a great deal of interest if you suggested a new and better way of doing things.
> Your supervisor would give you special recognition if your work performance was especially good.
> Your supervisor would personally pay you a compliment if you did outstanding work. [p. 126]

The second factor, accounting for 18 percent of the variance, dealt with recommendations for promotion and advancement. Items highly correlated with the second factor included:

> Your supervisor would see that you will eventually go as far as you would like to go in this organization, if your work is consistently above average.
> Your supervisor would recommend that you be promoted if your work was better than others who were otherwise equally qualified.
> Your supervisor would help you get a transfer if you asked for one. [p. 126]

Both these factors appeared thus to contain elements of what we saw as individualized consideration as well as contingent reinforcement. As will be noted in our quantitative analyses in Chapter 12, a factor emerged for us which included transactional exchanges and establishment of such exchanges by leader and subordinate. Contingent reward items of leadership behavior in our factorial studies include:

> Tells me what to do if I want to be rewarded for my efforts.
> Talks a lot about special commendations and promotions for good work.
> Assures me I can get what I personally want in exchange for my efforts.

Subordinate–leader interactions that involve prospective exchanges of reward contingent on acceptable performance also include:

> Whenever I feel like it, I can negotiate with him/her about what I can get from what I accomplish.
> There is close agreement between what I am expected to put into the group effort and what I can get out of it.
> Gives me what I want in exchange for showing my support for him/her.
> I decide what I want; he/she shows me how to get it.

This negotiation was the essence of the dynamics of leadership for Hollander (1978) who felt that leader and follower enter into an exchange beginning with a process of negotiation to establish what is being exchanged and whether it is satisfactory.

Structuring reward contingencies was one of Yukl's (1981) categories of leader behavior. It was "the extent to which a leader rewards effective subordinate performance with tangible benefits such as a pay increase, promotion, more desirable assignments, a better work schedule, more time off, and so on. Examples of behavior were 'My supervisor established a new policy that any subordinate who brought in a new client would earn 10 percent of the contracted fee.' [and] 'My supervisor recommended a promotion for a subordinate with the best performance record in the group' " (p. 122).

What we saw as part of the transactional contract between leader and subordinate, Yukl categorized as *goal setting*, "the extent to which a leader emphasizes the importance of setting specific performance goals for each important aspect of a subordinates's job, measures progress toward the goals, and provides concrete feedback. Examples were: 'The supervisor held a meeting to discuss the sales quota for next month.' [and] 'My supervisor met with me for two hours to establish performance goals for the coming year and develop action plans' " (p. 123).

Such goal setting is central to path–goal theory.

Path–Goal Theory

Path–goal theory attempts to explain why contingent reward works, and how it influences the motivation and satisfaction of subordinates. In its earliest version by Georgopolous et al. (1957), it focused on the need for leaders to "point out the paths to successful effort" (Bass, 1965, p. 150). Leaders do this by:

> Increasing personal payoffs to subordinates for work-goal attainment, and making the path to these pay-offs easier to travel by clarifying it, reducing roadblocks and pitfalls, and increasing the opportunities for personal satisfaction en route. [House, 1971, p. 324]

Evans (1970) noted the several ways that the leaders can serve in the path-goal process to affect a subordinate's effort. They can clarify the subordinate's role, that is, what they expect the subordinate to do. They can make the rewards more dependent on satisfactory performance. They can increase the size and value of the rewards. Quickly it was seen by House and Mitchell (1974) that such leadership was only needed and useful in certain circumstances.

It was needed only if the goal clarity, guidance, and contingent rewarding was not already provided by the organization, the work-group, or the situation itself. Whether the subordinates were personally

motivated for autonomy, or achievement, or affection made a difference. How much self-esteem subordinates had (so they can reinforce
themselves) was likewise an important consideration. Blanchard and
Johnson (1982) suggested that for the inexperienced, inexpert, subordinate, less clear about how and what to do, contingent praise (as well as
contingent reprimand), timely and frequent, is likely to be most efficacious. As the subordinate becomes experienced and expert, the
schedule of such reinforcement can be stretched further and further, as
knowing now how and what to do, a subordinate can become self-
reinforcing.

So guidance and direction from the leader is seen as more necessary
if subordinates are inexperienced or if the tasks to be performed are
complex and help is really needed. On the other hand, if subordinates
are faced with simple but boring or dangerous tasks, rather than being
directive, a leader may do better to be supportive and considerate. Too
high motivation, evidenced by a state of high anxiety, may call for calm-
ing support from the leader rather than any talk about contingent (i.e.,
uncertain) rewards to increase such anxiety. Confidence-building may
be required rather than more motivation (Yukl, 1981).

Whether the leader really knows what needs to be done obviously
will be particularly important.

Leadership Behaviors Involved and Effects on Subordinates

A more finely tuned examination of the elements in the contingent-
reward process was completed by Klimoski and Hayes (1980). The six
supervisor behaviors they identified were: supervisor explicitness in giving instructions (explicitness), frequency of communication about job-
related matters (communication), allowing the involvement of subordinates in determining performance standards (involvement), support
for efforts to perform effectively (support), frequency of performance
reviews (reviews), and consistency toward the subordinate (consistency).

The detailed assessments of their supervisors' contingent-reward
behaviors by 231 professional subordinates were correlated with the
subordinates' motivation and satisfaction. Only when the supervisors
were seen by the subordinates to be more explicit, to involve subordinates in determining standards, to provide support, and to maintain
consistency, did the subordinates expect that their effort would lead to

successful performance and that their successful performance would generate commensurate rewards. Frequency of communications and frequency of review by supervisors were irrelevant to subordinate expectations.

Effects of the supervisors on subordinates' satisfaction were more complicated. Particularly strong associations were found between subordinate satisfaction with their supervisors and the supervisors' explicitness, support, and consistency. Supervisory explicitness and consistency also had moderate effects on reducing role ambiguity and role conflict. Supervisory consistency contributed to some extent to subordinate performance and job knowledge although these appeared to be enhanced by subordinate involvement in determining standards. Thus, the leader's behaviors in the contingent-reward path–goal process seem to contribute in varying degrees to subordinate effort and performance by clarifying subordinates' expectations that payoff will accrue to them as a consequence of their efforts. To a lesser extent, some of the contingent-reward behaviors also contribute indirectly to improved performance and satisfaction with supervision by reducing role ambiguities and role conflicts.

Effects on Participation

Further qualification is needed about the effect on subordinate role ambiguity, effort, and performance. Dossett et al. (1983) found in a laboratory study with 40 undergraduates that although productivity on a clerical task was highest as expected when a supervisor set high, clear, standards for them and also gave them friendly support, participation by itself of the subordinates in setting the goals did not contribute to their productivity. This failure of participation in setting goals to make a difference may be explained by the character of the participation. Neider (1980) demonstrated in a study of performance in retail stores that only when the participation process clarifies the linkage of effort and performance and only when the rewards given for high performance are valued are we likely to see positive effects from such participation.

This clarification also depends on the competence of the leader. Podsakoff et al. (1983) found that an expert leader who worked at setting and clarifying goals did decrease his subordinate's sense of role ambiguity. But the reverse was true for the leader who was inexpert. His efforts resulted in increasing a subordinate's sense of role ambiguity!

Other Moderating Effects on Contingent-Rewarding

Some other conditions which will make it useful for a leader to structure reward contingencies and to set and clarify goals have been listed by Yukl (1981):

> When the leader has substantial authority and discretion to administer tangible rewards to subordinates.
>
> When subordinates . . . are dependent on the leader for [the valued rewards].
>
> When performance outcomes are primarily determined by subordinate effort and skill rather than by events beyond the subordinate's control.
>
> When it is possible to measure subordinate performance accurately.
>
> When the work is repetitive, boring, and tedious, rather than varied, interesting, and meaningful. [p. 194]

> Goal setting is most useful:

> When objective performance indicators are available for use in setting specific goals.
>
> When performance outcomes are highly dependent on subordinate effort and are not strongly affected by fluctuating conditions beyond the control of subordinates.
>
> When subordinates have at least a moderate amount of achievement motivation to be aroused by challenging goals and deadlines. [p. 195]

Why Is Contingent Reward Underutilized?

As we have noted earlier, the contingent rewards for compliance with agreed-upon performance may be in the form of praise and recognition but also in the form of recommendations for increases in pay and promotion. Both forms seem to be underutilized in practice despite the evidence that contingent reward is efficacious leader behavior which can provide subordinates with role clarity and role acceptance, satisfaction, and performance. Linking pay increases with effort and performance remains greatly underutilized in industry according to an interview study of 845 U.S. workers by Yankelovich and Immerwahr (1983). Only 22 percent said that there is a direct relationship between how hard they work and how much they get paid. The interviewers reported that 73 percent of employees said their job effort declined because people often get the same pay increases regardless of how hard they work. They felt they would benefit little from working harder; the benefits would all go mainly to their employers. At the same time, as noted earlier, 61 percent said they want a closer link between performance and pay. Since only 20 percent of all U.S. workers are now unionized, the blame for this cannot be placed on the usual union emphasis on seniority and cost-of-living increases rather than increases based on merit.

Underutilized Feedback

The cost-free but equally efficacious use by supervisors of authentic praise and commendation for work well done is equally underutilized. A small sample of industrial psychologists suggested that time pressures, poor appraisal methods, doubts about the efficacy of positive reinforcement, discomfort to leader and subordinate, and lack of skill were partly responsible (Komaki, 1981).

Commonly observed also is that supervisors actually say and believe they are giving feedback to subordinates, yet their subordinates do not feel they are receiving it. This is exacerbated by the difference in importance subordinates and supervisors attach to various kinds of feedback. In a metropolitan transit organization, Greller (1980) found that subordinates attached more importance than do supervisors to feedback from the task itself (i.e., self-reinforcement), their own comparisons to the work of others, and to co-worker's comments about their work. On the other hand, supervisors attached more importance than their subordinates to their own comments to their subordinates, and to recommendations for rewards such as raises, promotions, and more interesting assignments.

On occasion, feedback about one's job performance may be counterproductive. Kiggundu (1983) reported that with 138 head-office employees, it yielded negative rather than the expected positive results.

Problems with Incentive Payment Schemes

Payments for the amount of work completed rather than for the hours worked, or a straight salary, directly link rewards earned to the amount produced. Yet, such contingent reward plans often are avoided in favor of noncontingent reward plans such as straight salaries. Proponents of piece-rate payments point to the greater overall output generated when workers are paid for the quantity and/or quality of their output than when workers are paid for the hours they work, or by salary. When rewards are made fully contingent on performance, such as when employees are placed on a straight piece-rate or straight commission basis, productivity is likely to be raised (as much as 30 percent according to some studies).

But critics argue that piece-rate payments are exploitative and fail to take into account the factors outside the workers' control that affect their productivity. Also, payment for quantity may result in reduced quality. Group norms, rather than management standards, may underlie how much is produced. Piece rates may be the cause of much worker dissatisfaction and conflict among themselves and with management. Self-interests are promoted which may be in conflict with co-worker and organizational interests. For instance, shoe store salespeople on straight commission for pairs of shoes sold may rush to "tie up" customers instead of allowing co-workers to deal with them, may refuse to handle customer complaints and returns, and may avoid helping as needed with the store's housekeeping.

Salaried employees whose pay is not closely linked to their performance can engage in self-planning, self-direction, and self-control, if committed, loyal, and involved in the organization's purposes. Developing subordinates into self-reinforcers is a leadership goal which can obviate much of the need for contingent reinforcement. While contingent rewards can work and may be necessary where subordinate self-reinforcement is unlikely, the side effects of contingent rewards need to be considered.

Payments to workers contingent on quantity and/or quality of performance can improve such performance if workers are clear how their performance results in the desired output, if they understand how the incentive pay is calculated, if they trust management to keep payment rates from being reduced, if there is no fear of overproduction followed by layoff, and if workers feel the payment schedules are equitable (Bass & Barrett, 1981). Surprisingly, less important seems to be worker expectations that their increased effort will result in greater productivity and how important making money is to them (Schwab & Dyer, 1973).

If pay is to be associated with performance, favored are pay increases associated with experience, worth of the work done, promotions, and ratings of meritorious performance. Group bonus plans, profit sharing, and sharing in bonuses for successful group efforts to reduce costs of production are seen to better reflect the extent that the individual's output depends on colleagues, supervision, and organizational practices and policies.

Supervisors' Lack of Control of Rewards

Another reason managers may fail to utilize contingent reward is that they themselves may lack the necessary reputation required so that they can deliver the necessary rewards. Managers who fulfill the self-interested expectations of their subordinates gain and maintain the reputation for being able to deliver pay, promotions and recognition. Those who fail to deliver lose reputation in the eyes of their subordinates and therefore no longer can be seriously seen as effective transactional leaders (Tsui, 1982).

Noncontingent Reward May Work

A final reason why contingent reward may be underutilized is that noncontingent reward sometimes works reasonably well to bolster performance. Thus, Podsakoff et al. (1982) reported that among 72 supervisors of 101 subordinates of a large, nonprofit organization, contingent rewards by supervisors did correlate with subordinate performance as expected (.26) but noncontingent rewards (I feel well treated by my supervisor no matter what I do) correlated almost the same with subordinate performance (.20). Nevertheless, as shown below, subordinate satisfactions were much higher, especially with their supervisor, when supervisor praise and recommendations for promotion and pay were contingent on subordinate effort and performance.

	Subordinate Satisfaction with				
Supervisory Behavior	**Work**	**Super-visor**	**Peers**	**Pay**	**Adminis-tration**
Contingent reward	.43	.68	.27	.21	.39
Noncontingent reward	.11	.27	.00	− .01	.14

Noncontingent reward may provide a secure situation in which subordinates' self-reinforcement takes care of the contingent elements of consequence to performance. Overall subordinate sense of obligation to the organization for providing the noncontingent rewards may also generate the subordinate effort to realize adequate performance. The Japanese experience is exemplary. In the top third of Japanese firms like Toyota, Sony, and Mitsubishi, employees and company feel a sense of lifetime mutual obligation. Being a good member of the family does not bring immediate pay raises and promotions but overall family success will bring year-end bonuses. Ultimately, opportunities to advance to high levels and salary will depend on overall meritorious performance. Similarly, many of our best managed firms such as IBM tend to emphasize straight salaries based on the position held, seniority, and merit for all employees, blue collar as well as white collar, professional and managerial, rather than making employee earnings contingent on hours they work or pieces of work they produce.

Chapter 8

Management-by-Exception, Negative Feedback, and Contingent Aversive Reinforcement

WHAT IN COMMON HAVE management-by-exception, negative feedback, and contingent aversive reinforcement? It is this. Leaders who primarily or exclusively practice management-by-exception, negative feedback, or contingent aversive reinforcement intervene only when something goes wrong. As long as subordinates are meeting performance standards, the servocontrol mechanism remains quiet. But if a subordinate's performance falls below some threshold, the mechanism is triggered. At the emotionally mildest level, the leader feeds back information to the subordinate that the threshold has been crossed. The negative feedback may be accompanied by clarification and encouragement if the leader is someone who also values use of contingent reward. At the other extreme, it may be accompanied by disapproval, reprimand, or worse.

Negative feedback, particularly if impersonal and buttressed with positive support, can provide the novice subordinate with needed advice on what *not* to do. But when supervisors manage by exception and negative feedback forms the exclusive contribution of the supervisors to their leadership relations with their subordinates, it is likely to be relatively ineffective in contrast to contingent reward. When the intervention is that of reproof or penalization, it can be counterproductive.

Delegation, which may be used to motivate and develop subordinates as well as free the leader for other duties, may be confused with management-by-exception but it can be much more than management-by-exception. A leader can delegate responsibilities to a subordinate and subsequently practice management-by-exception. But the leader can also delegate responsibilities and follow up the delegation with needed reclarification, with inquiries about whether additional help will be required, with encouragement, and with periodic requests for progress reports as well as praise and reward for successful subordinate efforts.

The most cited reason for leaders avoiding contingent positive reinforcement is that they too often practice management-by-exception, that is, they intervene with negative feedback or disciplinary action when employee performance falls too far below standards. They apply contingent aversive reinforcement (Komaki, 1981). But even here manager's discomfort at giving negative feedback is even more self-defeating. When supervisors are faced with poor subordinate performance which they attribute to lack of subordinate ability, the supervisors often tend to "pull their punches." They distort their feedback and make it more positive than it should be (Ilgen & Knowlton, 1980). But clearly, strong leaders do not shy away from applying strong sanctions against subordinates who fail to live up to the leader's expectations about them.

Contingent aversive reinforcement by leaders in response to followers who fail to meet standards can take many forms ranging from mildest to most severe. They can provide information on what went wrong; they can reprimand, censure, or blame; they can bring about penalties, fines, or loss of job; loss of security, freedom, or life. A manager who only intervenes with such reinforcement when subordinates fail to meet standards is practicing management-by-exception. Although she was open to suggestions from her subordinates, Helena Rubenstein was devastating to her employees when things did not go her way. She was not reluctant to discharge those whom she felt were failing to carry out orders.

It is in this regard we may see a big difference between the more transformational leader who is free of inner id–superego struggles and the more transactional manager who cannot face up to his organizational responsibilities to reprimand a subordinate, particularly one with whom the manager is closely associated. Such transactional managers may not find it difficult to sign a form or press a button which results in laying off a hundred distant employees, but will go to extreme lengths to avoid discharging an incompetent immediate assistant. A transformational leader with a strong developmental orientation would also avoid discharging the incompetent employee but rather attempt remedial steps of one type or another until convinced the case was hopeless. The charismatic leader might also avoid taking disciplinary action against the assistant, perhaps mistaking blind loyalty and ingratiation for competence.

Mintzberg (1975) argued that although management-by-exception was popularly seen as the norm such managerial practice was more myth than fact. It is popular mythology that

> the good manager, like the good conductor, carefully orchestrates everything in advance, then sits back to enjoy the fruits of his labor, responding occasionally to an unforeseeable exception. [p. 51]

The good manager must do a lot more than just ''sit back'' to handle exceptions to his planned outcomes. Nevertheless, some managers are predisposed to use this approach. Other managers, due to work overloads, for example, are forced to do it. According to our quantitative studies in Chapter 12, management-by-exception contributes less to subordinate productivity and effort than do transformational leader behavior or contingent reward.

Management-by-exception follows directly from the emphasis on management as controller. When the ship is on course, nothing needs to be done. The manager needs only to watch to see if it veers off course. Only then is it necessary for the manager to signal that an error has occurred and that corrective action is needed. Management-by-exception is consistent with the cybernetics of negative feedback—feedback that signals the system to move back toward its steady-state base. The manager is alert for deviations and provides the negative feedback as needed. Standards are set. Only if the standards are not met by subordinates (or not likely to be met) does the manager intervene between the subordinate and the work being done by the subordinate (Drucker, 1954).

Management-by-Exception Behaviors

Among the Reserve Officer Training Corps (ROTC) cadets queried by Yukl and Van Fleet (1982) many critical incidents were seen to reflect leader standard setting, discipline, and criticism. Fairly common incidents which stress performance to meet requirements included:

> Checks to see that tasks are accomplished satisfactorily.
> Emphasizes scholastic as well as military achievement.

Shows concern about the appearance of cadets.
Expresses disappointment that the unit did not perform better.

Fairly common incidents of criticism and discipline included:

Calmly points out a person's deficiencies.
Uses specific examples of errors rather than general criticism.
Explains to a person why he is being disciplined.

Air Force officers during the Korean War were seen in critical incidents to set high standards of performance which subordinates were expected to meet. Incompetent persons were removed from positions of responsibility.

Sims (1977) found a factor in a supervisor's behavior which dealt with contingent punishment. Items heavily loaded in the factor included:

> Your supervisor would get on you if your work was not as good as the work of others in your department.
> Your supervisor would give you a reprimand (written or verbally) if your work was consistently below acceptable standards. [p. 126]

Criticism–discipline was one among 19 categories of leadership behavior observed in six studies by Yukl (1981). This contingent aversively-reinforcing leader behavior was defined by Yukl as "the extent to which a leader criticizes or disciplines a subordinate who shows consistently poor performance, violates a rule, or disobeys an order; disciplinary actions include an official warning, reprimand, suspension, or dismissal" (p. 125).

Examples were:

> The supervisor was annoyed that a subordinate kept making the same kind of errors and warned him to make a more concerted effort.
> The supervisor called me in to tell me that I had neglected to include two items of information in an important report. [p. 125]

Illustrative of management-by-exception in the quantitative analyses of Chapter 11 are such items as "As long as the old ways work, he/she is satisfied with my performance" and "As long as things are going all right, he/she does not try to change anything." Note that this behavior is not the same as laissez-faire supervision. In the latter, there is discouragement in taking initiatives and minimum pressure to produce. Communication is severely curtailed. The laissez-faire leader is likely to absent himself or withdraw when faced with deviations from expectations while the manager-by-exception remains alert to such deviations and will take suitable corrective actions when they occur.

Effectiveness of Contingent Aversive Reinforcement

Less-supportive results were reported by Podsakoff et al. (1982) for contingent punishment than for contingent reward. According to 101 subordinates of 72 supervisors in a large not-for-profit organization, as expected, contingent rewards by supervisors enhanced subordinate performance and satisfaction. Contingent reprimand, disapproval, or penalization had no effect on performance and satisfaction. And noncontingent punishment was highly counterproductive. Similarly, Fulk and Wendler (1982) obtained little supportive results for contingent negative reinforcement. Contingent approval or disapproval by achievement-oriented leaders was conducive to subordinate role clarity but failed to have much effect on subordinate motivation or performance. Naturally, subordinates found contingent approval more acceptable than contingent disapproval.

According to our results in Chapter 12, military officers see contingent reward as contributing about 25 percent of the variance in unit effectiveness and management-by-exception only 5 percent. However, when 400 fourth-year West Point cadets were asked to describe critical incidents of good and bad leadership they had encountered, incidents involving contingent sanctions were the most frequently mentioned (44 percent) as indicative of bad leadership although they also were mentioned as appearing in 28 percent of the incidents describing good leadership (Adams et al., 1981). Again, with various civilian samples mentioned in Chapter 12, management-by-exception proved to be counterproductive leadership.

Why Attention to the Negative Rather Than to the Positive?

Obviously, there is no reason why in practicing management-by-exception, a manager could not also take cognizance of positive deviations from standards and engage in contingent reward as well. But ordinarily, it is the negative deviations from standards that are monitored in management-by-exception. Yet if contingent reward is more efficacious, why use contingent punishment?

Reasons for this may be organizational. The organization may be a flat structure with many subordinates reporting to a designated supervisor. The latter's time is fully occupied just monitoring the negative deviations. Failure to pay attention to the negative deviations may invite disaster. Full preoccupation with the possible negative deviations inhibits attention to the positive, particularly in the absence of clear goals, clear policies, long-term objectives, and stable outside environments.

Managers may lack or may lose their power to provide or recommend rewards. Faced with continuing demands for productivity, managers have been found to increase their tendencies to use punishment if they lose their ability to provide rewards contingent on subordinate performance (Greene & Podsakoff, 1981).

Larson (1980) suggested that subordinate performance that is below standards is more salient for a supervisor than subordinate performance that exceeds standards. Thus, in a laboratory study, "supervisors" needed a smaller sample of work to evaluate a subordinate who was performing below average than to evaluate one who was performing above average (Fisher, 1979). In the same way, managers in business organizations report less difficulty identifying poor performance than good performance (Scontrino, 1979).

> This asymmetry may exist because the criteria for minimally acceptable (and hence also for poor) perform..nce are frequently more clearly defined than are the criteria for superior performance, and because poor performance often has a more significant impact upon the work group's functioning than does superior performance. This latter factor may serve to sensitize supervisors to the early signs of poor performance. [Larson, 1980, p. 199]

Nevertheless, Fisher (1979) also observed that like people in general, the students acting as supervisors were reluctant to give negative feedback. The saliency of the poor performance must outweigh this reluctance. It must also outweigh how much the supervisors like rather than dislike their subordinate. They may avoid giving negative feedback for poor subordinate performance in order to avoid risking deterioration of their interpersonal relations with the subordinate. They also may be less likely to attribute the poor performance as the subordinate's fault if relations are good with the subordinate.

Supervisors are likely to be more sensitive to subordinate failure if how well the supervisors do their job depends on how well the subordinates have completed assignments. Such sensitivity, in turn, is likely to result in rather quick resort to disapproval. The same will be true if the supervisors' pay, recognition, or promotion depend on the subordinates' performance (Larson, 1980).

Supervisors attribute different degrees of responsibility to subordinates for their performance. One supervisor may praise a subordinate for what could be accomplished despite the uncontrollable obstacles to reaching desired standards. Another supervisor might see the same subordinate responsible for the failure despite the obstacles.

Larson also suggests that supervisors may vary in the implicit theories they have about feedback in general as well as about the consequences of feedback to specific subordinates. Reprimands may be seen as risking retaliation; praise may be seen as lacking in credibility.

Again, the use of contingent disapproval rather than contingent approval may be a matter of the leader's values. Disapproval is more likely if rationality, objectivity, and certainty are regarded as more important than adaptability, and if security is valued as more important than affiliation. A leader oriented toward contingent disapproval will be searching for homogeneity, regularity, standardization, safety, and consolidation (Quinn & Hall, 1983).

Emphasis on disapproval, reprimand, and penalties will be greater if the leader interprets the poor performance of subordinates as the result of their lack of motivation rather than their lack of ability. Experience appears to make some difference. Experienced supervisors are more likely to focus attention on the environment rather than the subordinate as the reason for the subordinate's poor performance (Mitchell & Kalb, 1982). Again, if good performance is seen as due to greater effort, supervisory approval will be greater than if it is seen by the leader to be due to the ability of the subordinate (Knowlton & Mitchell, 1980).

Improving the Utility of Contingent Aversive Reinforcement

According to Blanchard and Johnson (1982), reprimand as well as praise should be timely. It should be specific to the behavior involved, not to the person. Particularly important will be to note what was done wrong and how the supervisor feels about it. But again the reprimand should conclude on a positive note of expectation that subordinate performance is going to improve. One failure at a time should be considered by itself. Subordinates can readily accept feedback from their supervisors about undesirable behavior actually observed by the supervisors. But the subordinates as persons, should never be attacked. That is, a sales manager should reprimand a salesperson for observed failure to call back a customer, but not attack the salesperson for being someone who is lazy and incompetent.

Importance of Diagnosis

The particular actions leaders should take after they have identified subordinate failure to meet responsibilities and to adequately complete assignments depends on the leaders' diagnosis of the reasons. If the supervisors sees consistently poor performance by a subordinate while coworkers continue to perform well, then supervisors can correctly attribute the subordinate failure to lack of effort or ability. If lack of effort is the diagnosed cause, punitive action may be taken; if lack of ability is seen as the cause of subordinate failures, then training or replacing the subordinate may be most appropriate (Mitchell & Wood, 1980).

If the supervisor believes the subordinate's poor performance was due to the environment or the difficulty of the assignment, then the leader's "negative signaling" should be to recommend a change in the working conditions or the task rather than criticizing the subordinate.

Negative deviations in subordinate performance from what is expected by the supervisor can be caused by numerous other factors along with the environment outside the control of the subordinate so that although corrective action and negative feedback is needed, it must be given with minimal penalization of the subordinate. For example, subordinates' poor performance can result from the following:

1. The supervisor and employee have failed to reach an understanding of what is expected—that is, what precisely constitutes satisfactory performance.
2. The employee lacks some necessary knowledge or skill and does not know where or how to acquire it.
3. The employee is not challenged by the job.
4. The employee is not committed to producing the needed results.
5. The employee feels that he/she has too many goals to achieve or an impossible mixture of goals.
6. The employee lacks adequate feedback from the supervisor about his/her progress.
7. The employee's work is hampered by an existing process, method, or system.
8. The employee's work is adversely affected by the failure of others to meet their commitments and his/her failure to influence them. [Anonymous, 1981, p. 13]

Failure to appreciate what is expected calls for further clarification of role requirements, not punitive actions. Failure due to lack of knowledge calls for training or transfer if training is unlikely to be profitable. Lack of challenge calls for enlarging the task, transfer, increased extrinsic incentives, or acceptance of reality by the subordinate who must find his satisfaction elsewhere. Lack of committment may be aided by increasing employee involvement in the planning or control process. Goal overload and conflict calls for goal clarifications and the establishing of priorities. Lack of adequate feedback will require more timely and specific feedback. Process, method, and system problems call for redesign, transfer, or greater tolerance. Subordinate failure due to the failure of co-workers shifts the application of all of the above possible remedial actions to the others surrounding the subordinate.

To sum up, it is important that the messages managers communicate to subordinates when they are performing inadequately do not threaten the self-esteem of the subordinate. Moreover, the negative feedback should concern itself with behavior within the control of the subordinate rather than due, for example, to organizational or equipment failures outside the subordinate's control. The disapproval should be coupled with clarification of what changes in behavior will put it back on the path to the desired goals.

Revson and Kitchener

World class leaders who made frequent use of management by exception included E. I. Dupont, the industrialist, President Gerald Ford, and Argentina's Evita Peron (Bass, 1984).

Many world class leaders, no matter how transformational in outlook, did not hesitate to reprove, reprimand, and discipline. In fact, their own self-confidence, egos, and freedom from the ordinary id–superego conflict made it easier for them to do so in comparison to the typical supervisor. Among industrial executives, Charles Revson was noteworthy in this respect. Revson never praised anyone. Fear was the ruling motivation for those who worked for him.

> Charles Revson . . . mistreated executives and abused them personally to such extent that men of proven capacity who held high positions in nationally known corporations before their employment by Revlon suffered humiliation and impaired efficiency during [their] employment and left Revlon to escape mistreatment; these practices of . . . Charles Revson reduced working conditions for executives at Revlon to a state of wide-

spread ill-repute and ridicule until by 1957 the recruitment and replacement of executives at Revlon had become extraordinarily difficult; the rate of turnover of Revlon executives became a subject of ribald humor. [Tobias, 1976, p. 173]

Among the military, Kitchener was extreme in this respect, even if the failure was not the fault of the erring officer. When commander-in-chief of the Egyptian Army,

Kitchener inevitably appeared ungrateful to his English officers, and sometimes positively savage to their Egyptian and Sudanese comrades who were all terrified of him. His standards were exalted, and he would not tolerate any form of failure, weakness or even sickness. Any officer, who, after doing his utmost, failed nevertheless to execute an order to Kitchener's satisfaction as a result of some act of God, such as a sudden storm or a mechanical breakdown, for which he (the officer) had no responsibility, had to reconcile his mind to the fact that his misfortune had set him apart, like a leper. In Kitchener's eyes he had become the victim of a fatal accident, and was finished. That was hard and, in a normal sense, unjust. It was, however, "Kitchener's way," and the position had to be understood and accepted. [Magnus, 1968, p. 114]

Unintended Consequences of Contingent Reinforcement

The damaging effects on morale and performance of Revson-like leadership require little further comment, but what often is not as apparent are the unintended consequences of contingent reinforcement, even when the reinforcement is a reward.

Reaction to Manipulation

Transactional leadership depends on the power of reinforcement. On the one hand, no one questions that *generally* subordinate behavior can be influenced by such reinforcement. Nevertheless, many caveats need to be considered. First, if promises of reward or threats of punishment for subordinate performance are seen as coercive or manipulative, as we have noted earlier, a variety of unintended consequences may appear. Additionally, more subtle consequences may also surface.

Expounding on the principles of leadership, Vice-Admiral J. B. Stockdale (1981) argued that people do not like to be programmed.

You cannot persuade [people] to act in their own self interest all of the time. A good leader appreciates contrariness. . . . some men all of the time and all men some of the time knowingly will do what is clearly to their disadvantage if only because they do not like to be suffocated by carrot-and-stick coercion. I will not be a piano key; I will not bow to the tyranny of reason. [p. 15]

One is likely to see counterdependent followers particularly working in opposition to what was intended by the leader's contingent rein-forcements. But much of this reverse twist may be seen in independent and even dependent followers. Among five styles of leadership—direc-tive, manipulative, consultative, participative and delegative—Bass et al. (1975) found manipulative leadership least satisfying and effective to subordinates. And their reactions to it may be counterproductive.

Subordinates may take shortcuts to complete the exchange of reward for compliance. For instance, quality may suffer if not as closely monitored by the leader as quantity of output. Second, leaders and subordinates need to be clear about the exchange. Complicated piece-rate systems which are a form of contingent reward are likened to the ambiguous experimental situations which generate neuroses in rats. They are likely to induce "game playing" and fear of "rate busting." The subordinate may react defensively rather than adequately. Reac-tion formation, withdrawal, or hostility may ensue. Third, the schedule of reinforcements, their timeliness, variability, and consistency have considerable effect on their influence.

Contingent negative feedback is a two-edged sword. Reprimands may not only generate inhibition of the subordinates' undesirable behavior, and increased clarity about what is desirable behavior (Reitz, 1971. They also generate anxiety which in turn can result in a variety of dysfunctional behaviors to cope with the anxiety, such as reaction for-mation, guilt, and hostility. This is particularly true of highly motivated subordinates who are already overloaded or under stress. They will be predisposed to interpret well-intentioned negative feedback as a per-sonal attack.

The generally negative consequences of aversive reinforcement by leaders appear to hold across a variety of conditions. Podsakoff et al. (1984) concluded from surveys of 1,946 government employees and hos-pital pharmacists in six samples that while contingent reward by super-visors, as expected, did enhance subordinate satisfaction and perfor-mance, contingent punishment did not, and noncontingent punishment was counterproductive. Situational factors such as the availability of substitutes for leadership and characteristics of the subordinates' jobs did not alter the conclusions reached.

Despite the heavy reliance of the Soviet system on piece-rate and quota systems, overall productivity of employees remains low in both quality and quantity partly at least due to the very incentive plans under which managers and employees must work. Russian payment schemes also include fines and penalties for failure to meet monthly quotas as well as bonus payments for success. An unintended consequence of the contingent positive and aversive reinforcement associated with meeting monthly quotas is the monthly cycle of slowdown and speed-up in effort and performance. To meet the 30-day quota, "storming" occurs during the last ten days. Storming involves long overtime and weekend efforts following which rest and recuperation are needed during the first ten days of the next month. In particular, quality suffers severely in the process (Smith, 1975).

Individual Differences in Reaction to Contingent Reinforcement

People differ considerably in their preference for external compared to self-reinforcement. Task-oriented subordinates and experienced subordinates generally are more likely to be self-reinforcing. Interaction-oriented and self-oriented subordinates are more likely to be sensitive to both positive and aversive reinforcement from others (Bass, 1967). Parsons et al. (1981) isolated three dimensions of consequence along which 339 utility company managers differed from each other. The managers varied in their preference for external feedback, that is, for being told, "Even though I may think I have done a good job, I feel a lot more confident of it after someone else tells me so." They also differed in their ability and tendency to reinforce themselves, that is in agreeing that, "If I have done something well, I know it without other people telling me so," and, "As long as I think that I have done something well, I am not too concerned about how other people think I have done."

Individuals with strong drives to succeed who meet devastating disapproval and defeat react differently to their feelings of disappointment. When Secretary of Defense James Forrestal was removed from office by President Truman with whom he was competing, he was without the emotional resources to cope with the sudden loss of his powerful position. Overly sensitive to others, highly insecure about himself, he lacked the self-confidence to maintain self-reinforcement. He lacked the self-guiding alternatives of the task-oriented rather than the self-oriented personality for channeling his high degree of motivation. Psychosis and suicide were the way out for him. On the other hand, Winston Churchill suffered several major setbacks in his career. He was forced out of the Cabinet in 1915 for the Gallipoli disaster in World War I for which he was responsible. In the 1930s, he had to remain out of power because of his stand on the need to rearm against the growing Nazi threat. Again, he was turned out of office in the first election after victory in World War II, because he was disapproved of by the public for his social and economic views. Nevertheless, the effects of each of these disappointments were to stimulate rather than to inhibit him. He could cope with such disappointments because of his many talents, his strong relation with his wife, and his inner, self-reinforcing strength. He could withdraw from power, make a realistic appraisal of his situation, and emerge with new insights on how to rise again (Zaleznik, 1967). Richard Nixon was a phoenix rising again and again from the ashes of a lost Presidential election in 1960, a lost gubernatorial election in 1962, and the forced resignation from the Presidency in 1974. Ten years later he was back in public as an American elder statesman.

A Model for Contingent Reinforcement

Figure 8 attempts to represent some of the most important linkages among contingent positive and aversive reinforcement by leaders and the resultant effort of their followers and subordinates.

Leaders may reward followers to encourage the followers' acceptance of their work roles. Followers comply with the leaders' directions in order to gain the rewards promised by the leaders for such compliance. If the followers succeed, they earn material rewards in addition to satisfaction and enhanced self-esteem. In turn, these all contribute to self-reinforcing of the followers' role behavior and a continuation and renewal of their efforts to maintain it and comply with what is expected of them. This process also depends on the extent the leaders clarify such expectations. Such clarification promotes followers' understanding of their roles and builds followers' confidence, further contributing to their compliance.

If the followers fail to comply and the failure is attributed by the leaders to lack of follower clarity and understanding, then the leaders will renew their clarification of what they expect. If positively reinforcing leaders attribute the failure of their followers to lack of motivation,

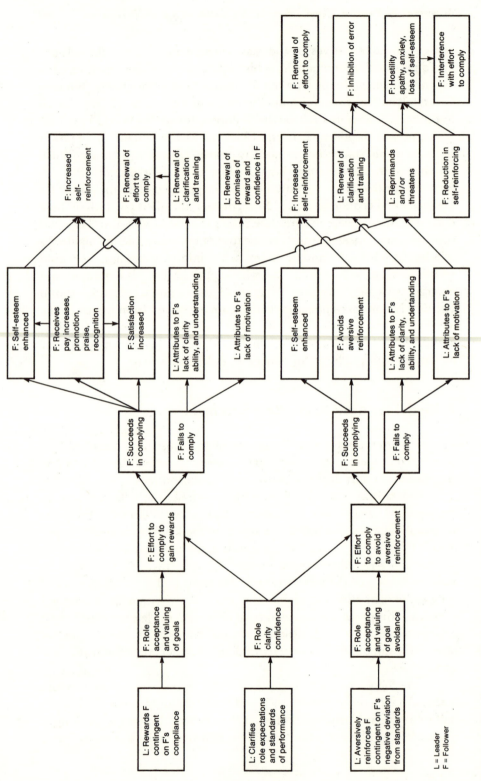

Figure 8 Contingent Reinforcement and Follower Effort

L = Leader
F = Follower

the leaders will renew their promises of reward and confidence in the followers. Of course, they may shift to aversive reinforcement such as reprimand with the unintended consequences of followers' withdrawal, anxiety, and so forth.

Leaders practicing contingent aversive reinforcement such as management-by-exception will foster followers' efforts to comply with clarified standards to avoid negative consequences for failure. If followers succeed in complying, they avoid being aversively reinforced and may increase in self-esteem and self-reinforcement. If they fail and leaders attribute the failure to lack of clarity, ability, and understanding, the leaders will renew clarification and attempt to improve followers' ability through training, thus increasing the likelihood of ultimate successful performance by followers. On the other hand, if aversively reinforcing leaders attribute followers' failure to comply to lack of follower motivation, they are likely to reprimand or threaten, possibly generating the unintended effects on followers of hostility, apathy, anxiety, and loss of self-esteem. In turn, there will be a reduction in self-reinforced effort and interference with the efforts of followers to comply.

Part V

Antecedents of Transformational Leadership

AT THE BEGINNING OF Cameron Hawley's novel *Executive Suite,* Avery Bullard, President of the Tredway Corporation, could not decide whom to choose as his successor from among his five vice-presidents.

> An idea flashed. He would get them together tonight for one last look. . . . He'd put some kind of proposition before them . . . anything . . . the possibility of building a new factory in North Carolina. It would hit them cold. . . He would toss out the idea and then sit back. . . . watching, listening, judging. Then he would pick the man who showed up best. (p. 5)

This initially leaderless group discussion contained the situational elements of stress, ambiguity, and social uncertainty. No one was appointed leader. Differences in competence and leadership potential among the participants would be accentuated and readily observable to Avery Bullard (Bass, 1954). The unstructured situation here might permit one of the participants to emerge who could transform it to a team situation with set goals and ways to achieve them.

Chapter 9

The Organizational Environment

IN THE PRECEDING CHAPTERS, we made some mention of historical forces, current states of affairs, and individual differences in needs and abilities which promote the emergence of transformational or transactional leadership and moderate their effectiveness. We now will expand this discussion and systematically examine the impact on transformational leadership of the external environment, the organizational environment, and the individual leader's personality. In identifying conditions which will bring on transformational rather than transactional leadership, we will try to discern the antecedents for the emergence of charisma, individualized consideration, and intellectual stimulation, on the one hand, and the emergence of leadership by contingent reward and management-by-exception, on the other. What we shall see is that whether or not transformational or transactional leadership emerges in a given situation will depend upon (1) the historical, social, economic, and cultural milieu in which the leadership occurs—the external environment; (2) the immediate organization, task, superiors, peers, and subordinates of the leader—the organizational environment; and (3) the personality and values of the leader. (the subject of the next chapter).

The External Environment

Whether transformational or transactional leadership will occur within an organization will depend to some extent on what is happening or has happened outside of it. Transformational leadership is more likely to reflect social values and to emerge in times of distress and rapid change; transactional leadership, in a well-ordered society. Transformational leadership is likely to be more common in societies where parents are seen as saviors and controllers of their children; transactional leadership, where parents are seen as helpers.

Leadership and Traditional Values

Leadership patterns in Chinese society still are influenced by Confucian precepts that leaders are expected to set moral examples for their followers. There is also the Taoist tradition of developing followers. The best leader works himself out of his job and makes the people feel that their accomplishments can be the results of their own efforts. But such stimulus for transformational leadership in Singapore, Taiwan, or mainland China is offset by the equally strong transactional Mandarin tradition of the importance to the leader of being able to manipulate rewards and punishments of followers. Values from all three traditions continue to affect Chinese leadership (Waley, 1939).

Times of Trouble

The structure of the external environment will determine whether the leadership that develops within it is more transactional or more transformational. In a well-structured environment with clear and strong norms, sanctions and institutions in which the social and economic status quo is reasonably satisfying, more of the leadership which occurs is likely to be transactional. On the other hand, in distressed societies, whose institutions are unable to cope with violations of expectations and need dissatisfactions, more of the leadership which emerges is likely to be transformational.

As we have noted earlier, crisis conditions are the time when charismatic leaders emerge. Churchill is called back to power only when Britain faces alone an overwhelming German onslaught; de Gaulle returns to settle the Algerian crisis; Hitler wins a plurality (38 percent) of the German vote in reaction to political and economic crisis; Khomeini emerges as undisputed leader out of the Iranian revolutionary upheaval. Charismatics even invent the crises (i.e., Hitler's burning of the Reichstag in 1933). Our most charismatic President, Kennedy, rides into office on the wave of national concern for a nonexistent "missile gap" favoring the U.S.S.R. over the United States (the facts were opposite).

Lenin's revolutionary transformation of one autocracy led by the czar into another led by a "dictatorship of the proletariat" was seen by him to depend on his correct appraisal of the crisis conditions. The moment to strike is when power can be seized and broad support obtained for the seizure. This then can be followed by a broad reeducation of the masses —that is, their transformation (Meyer, 1962). A parliamentary democracy in Russia survives only a few months in 1917 as a replacement for a thousand-year-old system of monarchy and aristocracy based on culture, organization, and traditions of coerciveness stretching back to Norse and Mongol invaders and to Byzantium. For Lenin, the new democracy only adds to the distress of military defeat and dislocation. The old regime is more readily replaced by what will be another long-lived autocracy based again on coerciveness. The Marxist economy incorporates many of the coercive old traditions in the transformation from the old regime to the modern Communist state.

American politicians find it easier to serve as transactional leaders operating a well-structured system governed by rules of law, rather than the capriciousness of individuals and power blocs. American political leaders, particularly congressmen faced with election every two years, must tend toward transactional rather than transformational leadership. They must think of exchanging votes from their electoral constituencies for promises to assist the voters. They must think of exchanging promises of legislative action for support from special interest groups. Only those in "safe seats" can better afford to think about long-term transformations. In addition, since both the Democratic and the Republican parties represent wide political spectrums, ideological transformations promoted by the Democratic Party's radical left or the Republican Party's radical right are seldom as popular as remaining nearer to the moderate centers which more often support practical compromises and negotiated exchanges. Political leaders build up credits (chits) and therefore influence with other politicans by supporting the other politicians when possible to do so. In exchange, they expect to "call in the chits" when needed in the future for exchange. Favors are rendered in exchange for earlier favors received.

Times of Change and Discontinuity

But the current social and political scene in the United States contains elements conducive for the emergence of transformational leadership.

Historical dislocation has increased, that is, peoples' sense of continuity with the past has become increasingly fractured by the pace of social and technological change. These shifts in belief and identification occur more readily as a consequence of our mass media's flood of imagery, "interminable exploration and flux" (Lifton, 1974). The institutions of family, school, government, and church have all been weakened. Naisbitt (1982) noted ten "megatrends" in American society: (1) from an industrial economy to one based on information creation and distribution, (2) from human-run to run by automated technology, (3) from a self-sufficient to a global economy, (4) from a short- to a long-term framework of decision-making, (5) from a bottom-up to a top-down approach, (6) from an institutional to a self-help perspective, (7) from a representative democracy to a participatory one due to instantaneously shared information, (8) from hierarchical structures to informational networks, (9) from the movement of the population from snowbelt to sunbelt, and (10) from an either/or to a multiple-option society. It becomes easier for transformational leadership to occur in the absence of strong institutions supporting the status quo, and with the ferment of social, economic, and technological disruptions of Naisbitt's megatrends. In the 1984 Presidential campaign, Gary Hart's "New Ideas" were an unsuccessful transformational attempt to recognize these trends.

Quinn and Hall (1983) see an environment in ferment as one of high intensity and high uncertainty. Leadership which comes to the fore is idealistic and transformational. Once intensity drops and some of the uncertainty disappears, such leadership receives less favor. Winston Churchill's career from 1930 to 1945 is illustrative. Rejected all during the 1930s by a pacifist-minded country, Winston Churchill immediately was given extraordinary powers to take charge as the peerless leader of the British from the moment World War II really heated up for the British in May 1940 until Germany was defeated in 1945. Within a month of the victory, Churchill was turned out of office by the electorate who again wanted no part of Churchill to lead Britain in its postwar recovery.

Marketplace Effects

We expect that transformational leadership is more likely to appear in an organization, particularly at its top, if the organization is located in a turbulent marketplace. The stresses and dislocations outside the firm are reflected inside. Leadership needs to provide new solutions, stimulate rapid response, develop subordinates, and provide reasons for coping. On the other hand, we expect that transactional leadership is more likely to appear in an organization embedded in a stable marketplace. The focus here is likely to be on long-term agreements and contracts. Departures can be monitored and contingent rewards provided.

More transformational leadership within organizations is needed in downturns of the economy and times of budget cutting. Anxiety and uncertainty are high. As much or more must be done with fewer resources. Under such conditions, managers are needed who will be proactive rather than reactive. They need to engage in the intellectual stimulation of

> re-examining priorities; re-assessing benefits of different activities; exploring, exchanging, and sharing of resources with others; searching for alternative sources of support; scanning for innovative, new models of service and production that require less use of resources; restructuring roles and reorganizing operations to mazimize use of human and technical resources. [Lippitt, 1982, p. 398]

They also need to engage in inspirational leadership to mobilize volunteers' time and energy. They need to support individualization in consideration by avoiding the "across-the-board" cutbacks common to many organizations in times of economic recession. Broad and long-term perspectives are required to maintain R & D, employee development and a future growth orientation for when the business cycle turns upward again. The transformational efforts of Eastern Airlines' Frank Borman and Chrysler's Lee Iacocca were much in the news in the early 1980s as they engaged in turning around their firms.

Societal Norms for Parenting

Demause (1982) argued that the foundations of psychohistory lie in the changing norms for childraising. As seen in historical accounts, these systematic changes provide a reason to expect in the last half of this century an increase in individualized consideration, an increase in leadership based on intellectual stimulation and a decrease in charismatic leadership in comparison to earlier years. The change is attributed to changes in parenting practices. Prior to the eighteenth century, Demause could find few accounts of empathy in parents with their children's needs or the motivation in parents to satisfy their children. People expressed tenderness toward children but mostly when the child was asleep or dead. Going further back in history to pagan and classical times, parental regard was even less. Infanticide and abandonment were widely practiced. With the growth of the Church and the Reformation this gave way to parenting which declared that the child could have love when the parent had full control over it or when the child reached the parent's goals. Only in the present century have we seen norms established for parents to see themselves primarily as helping the child to reach its goals.

Parent–child relations are assumed to be mirrored in leader-follower relations when the children develop into adult leaders and followers. In pagan times when infanticide and abandonment were widely practiced by parents, children who survived looked to their parents as their saviors from death or abandonment. By the beginning of the Industrial Revolution, a parent came to be seen as the child's authoritative controller who frees the child only when it has reached goals set by the parents.

Perceptions are displaced from parent to leader. Leaders during the earlier times could more easily be identified as saviors and powerful authorities. They could more readily display transformational leadership. The same was true in the world of parental authoritative controllers. Common leadership patterns which emerged were paternalistic and transactional to the extent that owners and managers directly linked usually very modest material benefits or their denial to hours served or work done. For the child of the Spock generation, with parents whose model is to give love and help the child to reach the child's goals, in a society which fosters children's rights, transformational leadership which emerges must develop more out of individualized consideration, mentoring, and intellectual stimulation rather than the charisma of the savior.

Organizational Environment

Whether organizations are organic or mechanistic (Burns & Stalker, 1961) should make a difference. We speculate that transformational leadership is most likely to appear in organic organizations where goals and structure are unclear, but where warmth and trust are high, members are highly educated and are expected to be creative. On the other hand, transactional leadership is most likely to appear in mechanistic organizations where goals and structure are clear and/or where members work under formal contracts.

Other examples of how organizational characteristics are likely to foster the emergence of transformational or transactional leadership can be cited. For instance, whether a military unit is a combat unit or a support unit will make a difference.

Combat Versus Support Services

To the degree that military combat units, in contrast to military combat support units, can be faced with more turbulent environments, greater stress, more life-and-death emergency situations, with greater demand for individual initiative, risk, and commitment to unit goals, there is greater need for charismatic leadership to promote performance stimulation and transcendence of self-interest. More transformational leadership should emerge in combat than in combat support units. Evidence of this is seen in our quantitative explorations in Chapter 12.

Technology

Woodward's (1965) seminal study and investigations which have followed point to the importance of an organization's technology to what leadership takes place within it. In firms engaged in continuous processing such as occurs in petrochemcial refineries, decisions are more likely to be made by committees of experts. Such decisions set policies and precedents. In the firms engaged in producing a unit, say the architectural plans for a building, a single, authoritative figure, the master architect, is more likely to wield the power to decide. Decisions here do not set precedents. We would guess that transformational leadership is easier to accomplish in unit production than in the continuous processing firm. More individualized attention to subordinates is possible. The spotlight is already shining on the master craftsman. Intellectual stimulation is central to the creative process often involved in the unit production of a new turbine for a damsite or a new clothing fashion or the building of a new prototype machine.

Universities

Modern universities, particularly American public universities, as state agencies represent organizations in which transformational leadership is less likely to be seen. Changes are particularly difficult to effect in the public university, embedded as it is in a state bureaucracy, often further enmeshed with union rules and contracts, as well as departmental and faculty norms and traditions. Changes often occur mainly as a consequence of political trade-offs among powerful coalitions.

Instead of leadership which provides vision, individualized consideration and intellectual stimulation for the university's goals of conservation, dissemination, and creation of information, leadership must focus on the use of the budget process to practice management-by-exception, and where it can, to practice contingent reward. Much leadership is actually substituted for by organizational processes such as mandated committee reviews, collegial decision-making, and tenure regulations. Nevertheless, the goals of universities, to conserve, disseminate, and advance the frontiers of knowledge, are very broad. They allow much latitude on how to make the goals into operational objectives. Highly endowed, independent, private universities may be transformed by a strong leader such as Robert Hutchins at the University of Chicago or Charles Eliot at Harvard.

Business Firms

According to Peters and Waterman (1982), the 60 best-managed U.S. firms are organizations in which we would expect considerable transformational leadership to appear. (Some care is needed in evaluating the Peters and Waterman conclusions. Their popular style and selective interviewing suggests that they appear to have found what they went looking for.)

In their action orientation, the firms seem to use both transformational and transactional processes. They are inspired by visions of big goals but take small steps toward the big objectives rather than waiting until they have all the answers on what is required. Intellectual stimulation is high. The firms are at the forefront of new ideas, new products, and new services. But contingent, incremental thinking is also the norm. The firms take small risks with small experiments instead of deciding in advance what will and what won't work.

The firms are open to transformation. They are organic rather than mechanistic. They are ready, willing, and able to change rapidly to meet the conditions they must face in today's turbulent world. The firms' flexibility makes their transformation easier. They use ad hoc temporary task teams to work on problems as they arise. Teams are expected to emerge with recommendations which can be described and justified in one page rather than 500-page reports. Relations are kept informal. Influence depends on who has the information and expertise rather than what is to be found on an organization chart. Leaders are not bound by traditions, rules, and sanctions. Again, change is easier to effect.

At all levels in these well-run firms, transformational leaders are needed:

> Leaders with charisma, who can give a sense of mission to others.
>
> Leaders who can establish and breakoff intensive relations.
>
> Leaders who are concerned with ideas, ideas they can convert into images to excite colleagues and heighten expectations.
>
> Leaders who are risk-takers whenever opportunities are seen.
>
> Leaders who cannot tolerate the pedestrian situation but push for excellence. [Zaleznik, 1977]

Nevertheless, these well-run firms also are characterized by managers who also can practice transactional leadership as well. In these firms, subordinates know they will be able to get their rewards if they carry out arrangements as agreed upon with their superiors. Management-by-exception is also practiced in that as long as employees carry on as planned, their superiors leave them to do their work. But superiors remain available for guidance and assistance as needed. Both superiors and subordinates understand small-group dynamics, how small groups work well together, and how to be a good group member. They also understand how decisions actually are made in organizations.

Team Effects

Shull et al. (1970) identified four types of teams: routine operations, engineered, craft tasks, and heuristic. The types increase successively in their professionalism and in the nonrepetitiveness of their tasks. We expect to see more transformational leadership as we move from routine operating to heuristic teams.

In the routine group of technical "locals" with repetitive tasks, the decision unit is a staff with an appointed leader. It is most system-oriented. The group concerns itself with specifying quantity and quality objectives along with critical control points and sequencing. Economy and efficiency are sought by the group. Higher authority specifies objectives and clarifies contingencies. Control is by control points and individual responsibility. Here, we expect to see transactional leadership emphasizing contingent reinforcement rather than transformational leadership.

In the engineer group, where tasks are nonrepetitive, but technical specialists are still required along with a designated project leader, the group process is characterized by control points, periodic review, and specific quantity and quality objectives. Yet there is more independent planning and individual responsibility, still with strong emphasis on economy and efficiency. There is more negotiation with higher author-ity about the inputs and outputs of the project unit. Feedback mechan-isms about the adequacy of performance are available. Here we expect transactional leadership to be more prominent, but some transforma-tional leadership is likely to emerge.

In the craft group, the "tailor-made" definition and solution of problems reside with the group of skilled personnel. The task may still be somewhat repetitive. The decision team is more likely to engage in independent action, diagnosis, and consultation with peer review. There will be consultations with higher authority for planning and con-trol. Professionalism is the norm. Here somewhat more transforma-tional leadership may appear, we expect, but transactional leadership, is still likely to be dominant.

In the heuristic team, faced with nonrepetitive, ill-structured tasks, independent analysis and solution with full participation and majority rule (or consensus) is pursued by the team. It is more person-oriented. There is open support or disagreement. There is little time constraint. Creativity is sought. Higher authority seldom is involved in planning and control. Here, we expect the most transformational leadership to be observed along with some degree of transactional leadership.

Policy Substitutes and Supports

To some extent, firms that practice Theory Z (Ouchi, 1981), the Japan-ese model for its elite companies, substitute organizational policy for what a transformational leader might do. For example, each such Jap-anese organization has a specific, stated policy which presents a clear picture to its members of its objectives and values. There is heavy emphasis on transcendence of self-interest for the sake of harmonious relations with others and for the good of the organization.

On the other hand, policy also substitutes for many elements of transactional leadership. Applicants are carefully screened in the attempt to insure that all who are hired will endorse the philosophy and values of the organization. In exchange for commitment to the firm for their whole working career, the employee is provided the security of permanent employment by the firm. Superiors are expected as a matter of policy to attend to the individual needs and concerns of their subordinates.

There are other trade-offs and exchanges involved in Theory Z. Theory Z emphasizes work-group, job-related decisions. In exchange for the added power to make such decisions, workers must live in a system with a high degree of peer pressure and oversight. Submergence of the self is mandatory. Career-long psychological commitment to the firm means that employees must accept a restriction in the range of opportunities available to more mobile employees. They may have to resign themselves to less satisfying working conditions (Robbins, 1983). (But, in the Japanese situation, highly dissatisfied employees reflect shamefully on their management who feel a strong sense of disgrace if they cannot restore harmony and satisfaction among their employees.)

Subordinates and Superiors of the Leader

Leadership is a reciprocal relationship between leaders and followers, but no direct evidence is as yet available on how superiors and/or subordinates of leaders impact on the leaders' tendencies to be transformational or transactional. However, we can make some educated guesses based on what we know about their impact on leadership behavior, in general. The experience and capabilities of the superiors of the leaders and the subordinates of the leaders would be expected to contribute to the tendencies of the leaders to be transformational or transactional.

Superiors and subordinates influence the performance of leaders by serving as reference groups. The leaders' behavior is affected to the degree they identify with their own superiors or their subordinates and perceive they are similar to their superiors or subordinates. The leadership behavior of focal supervisors is also affected by both their superiors' and their subordinates' expectations of them (Pfeffer & Salancik, 1975). More specifically, Crowe et al. (1972) observed that both autocratic and democratic managers behaved democratically with democratic subordinates and autocratically with autocratic subordinates. Thus, subordinates are capable of stimulating behavior from leaders that is even contrary to the leaders' own preferences.

Blanchard and Johnson (1982) suggest that when subordinates are immature, untrained, or inexperienced, they seek and need instructive (transactional) leadership which clarifies objectives and how to reach them, but they also need individualized consideration (transformational) which aims at subordinate development, growth, and change so that subordinates can become self-reinforcing and leadership can become delegative.

We can speculate further about other attributes of subordinates that may cause their leaders' to be transformational or transactional. For instance, as noted earlier, charismatic leadership depends on subordinates' imbuing their leaders with extraordinary value and power. A developing process may be at work. According to Zaleznik (1967), early in their relationship, most subordinates idealize their boss and overestimate his other strengths. Here, charismatic leadership is possible. However, this initial phase is followed by depreciation. Subordinates' own fantasies create and destroy unrealistic images of their boss.

Despite such a process, highly dependent subordinates will continue to seek and comply with their leader's initiatives. On the other hand, subordinates who pride themselves in their own rationality, skepticism, independence, and concern for rules of law and precedent are less likely to succumb to the blandishments of the charismatic leader or the leader who emphasizes emotional inspiration. We guess that subordinates will be resistant to charismatic leadership if they are equalitarian, self-confident, highly educated, and high in status. They will be less responsive to individualized consideration and intellectual stimulation if they are inflexible. On the other hand, subordinates will be more receptive to transactional leadership if they are oriented toward extrinsic motivation, or if they are readily responsive to promised rewards, threats of punishment, and the accomplishment of short-run objectives.

Some subordinates already value higher-level work outcomes that provide personal growth, feelings of personal development and self-fullfillment from using their own capabilities, feelings of worthwhile accomplishment and challenge, and feelings of independent thought and action. Other subordinates do not. Abdel-Halim (1980) found that salespeople differed from each other in this way. It would seem to follow that transactional leaders promising satisfaction of such higher-level needs would have an easier time in contingently rewarding those who already value such outcomes. Increasing subordinates' valuation of such outcomes would be a task for the transformational leader.

Hollander (1978) clearly elucidated the two-way exchange in transactional leadership.

Leadership is an influence relationship between two, or usually more, persons who depend upon one another to achieve certain common goals within a situation. . . . This relationship is built over time. It involves an exchange in which benefits are traded between the leader and the follower. [p. 152]

Both leader and follower "give something and get something." How much each has to offer the other is of paramount importance to the transactional exchange. On the other hand, the impact of the follower on the transformational leader lies in the extent to which the follower is ready or made ready by the leader to consider a broader, higher set of common goals. The direct benefits, particularly immediate ones, recede from view. Such transformation will be more difficult with followers who are more highly resistant to change or more highly self-interested.

Interchangeability and Mutuality

Hollander further sees that the two-way character of transactional leadership suggests that leader-follower positions are interchangeable.

Being a leader or a follower is not a fixed state of affairs. Leaders may seem to "hold" positions of authority, but they still require some following. And followers have the potential to become leaders. [p. 153]

For Burns (1978), transformational leaders have the capabilities to make their followers into leaders. This would be seen most clearly in the transforming effects of mentoring. "Mutual charisma" is a possibility. We attribute special endowments and responsibilities to all in the "chosen" group. We have complete faith in each other. The Jews collectively were the chosen people. All Calvinists, by their faith, were predestined for salvation.

Mutual inspiration and intellectual stimulation are distinct possibilities although intellectual stimulation is more likely to be a one-sided affair. For example, Price and Garland (1981) found in a laboratory experiment that followers were most likely to comply with the influence attempts of their leaders when the leaders were seen to be high in competence and the followers perceived themselves to be low in competence. It follows that, compared to those who see themselves as highly competent, those who see themselves as low in competence will be more ready to be transformed by an inspiring, intellectually superior leader endowed with charisma.

The Task

The task itself, the work to be done, may stimulate transformational leadership efforts. Suppose, for example, the task requires cooperative efforts among subordinates but provides only for individual material incentives. Earlier we cited the example of shoestore clerks who are paid solely for the pairs of shoes they sell. Customers are "rushed" and tied up. No direct incentives are provided for the other functions which need to be done such as dealing with customer complaints and returns, stocking and restocking, and keeping the store tidy. The manager needs to clarify the larger objectives and to develop among the clerks the motivation to achieve store-wide goals of satisfied clients and properly stocked goods, although achieving these goals may have only long-term or indirect effects on the clerk's monetary self-interests. Again, policies (such as group bonus plans) might substitute for such transformational leadership efforts.

Team sports require that the team members submerge their self-interest for the team to be successful. Basketball, soccer, and hockey are illustrative. The team coach is transformational to the extent he emphasizes the importance of victory and the need for individual players to sacrifice their personal interests for the good of the team. The performance of players in team sports also benefits from the emotional arousal possible from pep talks.

A Summary of Situational Effects

No simple figure can fully describe the many environmental, organizational, and task variables we have discussed as antecedents of leadership in this and preceding sections. However, Figure 9 is an effort to sum up some of the important aspects of the situation of consequence to the leader–follower interaction.

The charismatic process is stimulated in an ill-structured crisis environment of organic organizations in a society with norms for parents as saviors. Individualized consideration is favored in organic organizations where environmental norms are for parents as helpers. Intellectual stimulation can thrive best when the environment is ill structured and where children are raised to cope with increasingly difficult problems as they mature. Contingent reward and management-by-exception are favored in well-structured, stable, and orderly environments, and mechanistic organizations with pragmatic norms.

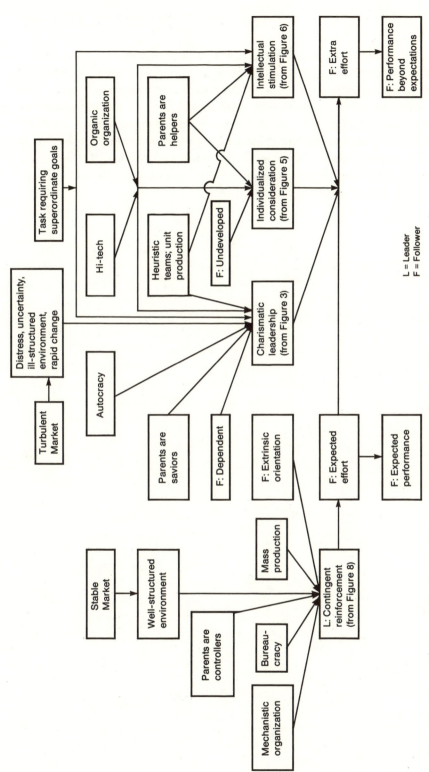

Figure 9 Situational Antecedents of Transactional and Transformational Leadership

We need to learn the extent to which organizational climate, structure, task, and objectives can give rise to the need for more transformational and more transactional leadership. Furthermore, we expect that in more effective organizations, leaders will become more transformational in leadership style as they move up the organizational ladder. At the same time, we also surmise that more transactional leadership is likely to be needed at lower levels in such organizations. If this is true, there are obvious implications for the selection and development of junior and senior executives.

Chapter 10

The Individual Personality

THE IMPORTANCE OF the individual personality of the leader and the led to charismatic leadership was discussed in Chapter 3. In Chapter 4, we saw some of the interplay between the leader's individualized consideration and the subordinate's developmental needs. In Chapter 5, the role of competence and intellect figured strongly in the leader's intellectual stimulation of the led. Now we turn to some broader implications of how transformational leadership, in general, is affected by the personality of the individual leader.

Revolutionary destruction of the old order does not necessarily mean that a transformational man-on-a-white horse will automatically arise to radically alter government and society. Revolutions can produce republican and democratic successor governments (e.g., the United States, the Third French Republic). But if a transformational leader happens to be on the scene, often the form that the new government will take will be strongly influenced by the personality of the leader. Louis Napoleon transformed the liberal Revolution of 1848 into the conservative Second Empire shortly after coming to power. While we are not espousing a Great Man theory of history, we do note how important a role individual differences in personality and values play in whether transformational or transactional leadership emerges in a given situation.

Personality and Values and Leader Behavior

A review of how personality and values shape leader behavior will be found in Bass (1981, pp. 41–145). For instance, personally assertive believers in authoritarianism will be directive with their subordinates. Changes in situation are likely to have little effect on their personal predilections to be directive. On the other hand, leaders who espouse egalitarianism will change their style as a consequence of the situational demands placed on them (Farrow, 1976).

Psychohistorians generally have concentrated their attention on individual charismatic leaders. They have accounted for such leadership mainly as a consequence of individual personality and its development (e.g., Davis, 1975). For example, one line of reasoning suggests that talented individuals turned inward and independent by early family experiences such as the early loss of their fathers, compensate for their lack of a father by the development of a strong sense of self-esteem, self-reliance, and the feeling that they have special missions to perform. (For instance, Franklin D. Roosevelt and Joseph Stalin were made fatherless early in life.) Furthermore, we read about the influence of the strong mothers of Douglas MacArthur, Dwight Eisenhower, Gary Hart, Harry Truman, Winston Churchill, and Napoleon Bonaparte, as well as of Roosevelt. This suggests the likelihood of a shaping of the sons directed by their mothers' strong needs for achievement, power, or recognition which could only be accomplished through their sons' successes.

Modeling

In Chapter 3, we introduced some of the requisite abilities, interests, and traits that characterize the charismatic leader, such as self-confidence and self-determination. The inner conflicts of the charismatic were seen to be resolved in the political or organizational arena. For the transformational leader, in general, additional personal elements can be added, such as modeling.

Many examples can be found of transformational leaders developing models for their own behavior from leaders who came before them.

> aspiring leaders . . . read about the lives of former leaders. They wrote biographies or sketches of them. . . . Napoleon was reputed to carry a copy of Plutarch's *Parallel Lives* . . . Mao Tse-tung recalled from his youth reading not only about Chinese heroes but also about Washington . . .

Napoleon, Catherine of Russia, Peter the Great, Gladstone, Rousseau, Montesquieu and Lincoln . . . Woodrow Wilson wrote a biography of George Washington . . . Stalin wrote a laudatory essay on Lenin, Trotsky wrote a critical evaluation of Stalin, John F. Kennedy sought to discover the sources of political independence in *Profiles in Courage* . . . and Churchill between the wars chronicled the life of his ancestor Marlborough. [Paige, 1977, p. 196]

The Desire for Revolutionary Immortality

What drives leaders toward transformational rather than transactional leadership may be a personal sense and desire for revolutionary immortality. Lifton (1974) defined this as a sense of participating in permanent revolutionary ferment, "of transcending individual death by living on indefinitely within this continuing revolution. Some such vision is present in all revolutionaries." Trotsky spoke about "permanent revolution"; Hitler, a Thousand Year Reich. Contrast this with the indifference of Louis XV about what would happen after his death. He survived a 60-year reign noted for its failure to adapt to new economic, social, and political trends despite many signs of impending disaster for the monarchy. He summed up his feelings with: "Après moi, le déluge!" Transactional leaders have a tendency to be lost by history.

Inner Conflicts and Their Resolution

Consistent with what we noted in Chapter 3 about how charismatic leaders deal with inner conflicts, Wolfenstein (1967) suggests that the revolutionary political leader, one who is aiming to transform government or society, is a person initially faced with unresolved oedipal conflict. But like charismatics in general, he can externalize the conflict to resolve it. He is one "who escapes from the burden of Oedipal guilt and ambivalence by carrying his conflict with authority into the political realm" (p. 307). However, as we have noted before, he does seem to have strong ego ideals as a consequence of having resolved his id–superego conflicts.

Earlier, we noted that would-be transformational leaders, leaders with vision, willingness to encourage others to look at old problems in new ways, and to hold on to inner convictions despite continuing disappointments, are persons who can withdraw and refocus their energies, who can remain master of their own fate, who have a variety of other strengths and talents which can carry them during the times of troubles and adversities. The legends of the great transformational heroes, Moses, Buddha, Jesus, and Mohammed include withdrawal from difficulties and later return with renewed and strengthened faith in self and one's teachings.

Adversity produces a heightened sense of self (Zaleznik, 1967).

> In reaching decisions and charting a course for a corporation, considerable clarity of vision and accuracy in perception are necessary. The heightened sense of self . . . is both a resource and a hazard in corporate management and the fate of the individual. It is a resource in that the investment in self preserves the independence necessary to weigh opinions and advice of others. While it is good common sense to encourage subordinates to offer recommendations, in the final analysis a major policy cannot be advanced apart from the convictions of the chief executive. How does he achieve the conviction necessary to seal a decision? If he is dependent on others as a result of an impoverishment of self-confidence, it will be very difficult indeed for him to foster a position that will guide the destiny of the organization (Zaleznik, 1967, p. 63).

In times of trouble in the marketplace, industrial corporation leaders must mobilize their own inner strengths.

> This requires . . . listening to one's own internal dialogue between positive and negative feelings, supports for risk-taking and supports for caution, and reflecting on different alternatives for action (Lippitt, 1982, p. 398).

The Consummate Transformational Leader

Charles de Gaulle exemplified the transformational political leader. His personality and its development were critical to his success in his transformational efforts. Twice the savior of France, Charles de Gaulle's "will to grandeur" demonstrated the triumph of his own personality over national and international conflict. He was raised in a family that maintained an unpopular set of beliefs in monarchism as against the popularly supported Third Republic. But issues were examined within the family on their own merits. There was moderation, dignity, firmness, and self-respect in family deliberation. The values inculcated transcended self-interest. Of great importance were culture, Christianity, and love of country and its history. Valued as highly was the soldier as defender of the nation and carrier of the Christian faith. But also conveyed was a profound sense of distress with what was happening to France following the Franco-Prussian debacle in 1870. At the same time, de Gaulle's whole education at home and in school stressed the Greek ideals of self-sufficiency, self-control, and the mastery of events through the force of character. De Gaulle emerged as an adult leader with tremendous inner strengths, a person who wanted to be right rather than merely immediately successful. At the same time, service to France and its grandeur was his lifelong mission, not the success of a particular social or economic ideology. This called for him to be a good role player with an astute sense of timing. He had to work for long-range goals in support of high ideals. The "cause" was crucial. Charles de Gaulle made himself the "voice of the nation" (Hoffman & Hoffman, 1970).

> History calls him in emergencies, and he calls the French on behalf of France. He has to serve the present needs of France, to protect her legacy, and to guarantee her future. He must maintain her personality, so that she can keep playing on the world stage; he must, in his own moves, follow only what he deems the national interest, apart from all categories, ideologies, and special interests. He is a unifier, by being above and lifting others above their daily selves. [Hoffman & Hoffman, 1970, p. 266]

He was "destiny's instrument." As he said in his own memoires, his role was to give France's inspiration from the summit, hope of success, and ambition to sustain the nation's "soul." In doing so, de Gaulle's own personal needs were fulfilled by the role he played:

> France provides Charles de Gaulle not only with the transcendence he needs, but also with the limits he craves. To be "France's champion" means depending on no one, yet being oneself completed; but the need to preserve France's personality, the subordination of the self to her service imposes prudence, harmony, moderation, and protects both the nation and the missionary from the excesses of those (like Napoleon or Hitler) who use their nation as tools of personal glory or to work out their ideological or psychological obsessions. [Hoffman & Hoffman, 1970, p. 267]

But de Gaulle was not alone in his search for personal glory. It is common enough in world-class leaders and may distinguish those such as Gerald Ford who remain more transactional from those such as Fidel Castro who become more transformational.

Activity and Involvement

Leaders differ in the extent to which they involve themselves in their subordinates' efforts. Intellectually stimulating and inspiring transformational leadership calls for personalities that are more active, self-starting, and proactive. Transactional leaders can remain more reactive and less involved, particularly if they practice management by exception rather than contingent reward.

Adult Experience

Childhood and adolescent experiences contribute heavily to the formation of the personality of the transformational leader. By early adulthood, we are likely to see a person who already has developed some strength to stand alone despite all the organizational and societal pressures to conform. Such inner direction is not stamped out in the interests of organizational harmony. For the developing transformational leader, there continues to be reinforcement during early adulthood for individual initiative, for gaining of visibility, and for establishing a reputation in the larger organization as a first-rate problem solver. He learns to place organizational loyalties ahead of local departmental interests. This last tendency was illustrated by a current board chairman of a large multinational corporation. As a young middle manager in a small unit of the organization which was engaged in an intergroup competition with other small units of the organization, he joined with one of the opposing units during the heat of the competition, a most unusual and surprising gambit.

While the superego is shaped by family, school, and peer expectations and standards and by cultural norms, we cannot lose sight of the extent personality continues to be shaped during adulthood by various experiences and reinforcements. Young radicals become old conservatives. Middle-aged leaders are "born again." Values and practices are revolutionized by media and technological advances. Military service may provide an education in leadership. Mentors in one's organization may open up whole new ways of viewing issues. To a considerable degree, whatever the personalities of U.S. Presidents before they reach the office, the sudden increase in power and role demands and the many problems which they have never faced before generate experiences of success and failure which have marked effects on the person. The self-assured, astute politician Lyndon Johnson entered the office in 1963 as the culmination of his life planning for the position. By 1968, as a consequence of the Vietnam fiasco, he had made up his mind not to run for another term and he quietly exited into obscurity.

More generally, Lord Acton's well-known adage sums up the impact on personalities of holding unlimited authority and power: "Absolute power corrupts absolutely." The office shapes the leader's personality just as the leader's personality affects how the leader will use the office.

Christenson (1979) argued that we should pay less attention to what U.S. Presidential candidates say in campaigns and more to what we know about their records based on how they have behaved as adult public office holders before becoming candidates. Conservative candidates almost always promise lower taxes, less Federal spending, a balanced budget, a bigger military budget, and a harder line toward the Soviet Union. Liberal candidates almost always promise more concern for the disadvantaged and the environment and less reliance on the military. The campaigns tell us how good the candidates are as campaigners and as campaign leaders but little about their future performance as Presidents.

Christenson mentions the possibility of trying to forecast presidential performance from early childhood and adolescent experience but rejects this in favor of attending to what the candidates' record was as an adult in carrying out his responsibilities as an officeholder prior to becoming a candidate for the Presidency. He was prophetic in 1979 in the case of Ronald Reagan. Much of Ronald Reagan's performance as President could be forecast from what he said and did as governor of the state of California in dealing with taxation, social welfare, the state's educational systems, and so on.

Motivation to Lead

Personality differences also are seen in the extent many people gain charismatic visibility and celebrity status, but not all use such status to take on leadership roles. Astronauts such as John Glenn and Frank Borman built political or business positions out of their early feats as space explorers. Other astronauts did not. The difference depended on personal career interests, energy levels, and commitments. Opportunities were taken by some but rejected by others without the same motivations and commitment.

But what personality differences sort out leaders who tend to be transformational from those who tend to be transactional? What moves some to attempt to reshape the world around them while others are content to maintain it in good working order? Erikson (1969) suggested that the transformational leaders, Martin Luther and Mahatma Ghandi, could not cope satisfactorily with their own particular personal problems so they projected them onto a world stage to adequately deal with them. They repressed their own feelings about themselves. By transforming society rather than themselves, they achieved resolution of their personal problems.

Differences in Individual Traits

We speculate that this willingness to confront the present with the drive to influence its transformation is likely to be stronger among those who are more socially bold, but not necessarily more sociable. That is, they must be assertive, yet they need to be able to withstand the affiliative pressures to do what is more immediately satisfying to their colleagues and themselves. On the other hand, the transactional leader would be more responsive to such affiliative pressures.

Quite obviously, the intellectual stimulator who transforms collegial solutions to problems must be thoughtful and introspective. On the other hand, we guess that transactional leaders are likely to be seen as more cooperative and friendly. We assume it takes more energy to try to influence change than to support the status quo. To sum up, we speculate that those leaders who are more frequently transformational are likely to be higher (than those leaders who are more frequently transactional) in social boldness, introspection, thoughtfulness, and general energy but not sociability, cooperativeness, and friendliness. Needed is an examination of how much transformational and transactional leadership is associated with the personality and values of a sample of executives who have been tested on measures of authoritarianism, assertiveness, introspectiveness, need for achievement, maturity, integrity, field independence, creativity, and originality. These traits would be expected to be more highly related to transformational rather than to transactional leadership. On the other hand, transactional leaders would be expected to relate more strongly to measures of conformity, sense of equity, and preference for social rather than political approaches. The transformational leader is more likely to find satisfaction in power; the transactional leader, in affiliation. A hypothesis needing to be tested is that personality, per se, is more important to transformational, particularly charismatic leadership, in contrast to transactional leadership. That is, more self-determining behavior such as de Gaulle's is expected in transformational leadership. Transactional leaders are expected to be more subject to situational effects.

Differences in Power, Objectives, and Access to Information

Particularly strong in effect is likely to be the impact of the leader's attitude and approach to power, objectives, and access to information. Transformational leadership is likely to appear more often when leaders emphasize long-term objectives, and where leaders and subordinates differ the most in power and access to information. On the other hand, transactional leadership is likely to correlate highest with leader emphasis on short-term objectives, and where leaders and subordinates are more equal in power and access to information.

Successful Leadership and Popularity

If one reads the literature on successful leadership, one is likely to conclude that what is needed is for the would-be leader to be valued, popular, and liked by those on whom he proposes to exert influence. He must have established idiosyncrasy credit with his prospective followers. His initiatives must be assertive, but not aggressive. He needs to be considerate to those with whom he must work and concerned more about the common tasks to be done than his own self-aggrandizement. Nevertheless, when we look at the personality and values of one of the most successful leaders of our times—Lyndon Johnson—we see a pattern of quite different, contradictory personal traits and requirements. Much of what we have accepted about what is needed for success as a leader is inadequate to explain success and leadership without considering the extent to which the leadership was transactional and/or transformational. Despite his unpopularity among his peers in both locations, Lyndon Johnson succeeded in transforming the San Marcos college campus, where he was a student, and the power structure of the U.S. Senate in which he served from 1948 to 1963, as senator and vice-president. His Great Society program and his orchestration and enlargement of the Vietnam confrontation transformed the United States itself and had social, political, and economic effects on the country that are continuing. But he made extensive use of transactional leadership, gaining and using his power to coerce and reward in exchange for compliance and support.

Despite his own lack of ideals and principles, he invented and successfully sold new solutions to old problems, he stimulated his supporters to exhaust themselves in his behalf, he did bring protégés along with him into power, and he gained charisma as he gained power, success, and visibility.

Although he was born poor and died wealthy, what drove him was the need for power and the need to dominate. He manipulated those around him in transactional exchanges to gain such power and then used the power as a lever for more of it.

A despised, intensely disliked young Lyndon Johnson, after a leave of absence, returned as a senior college student to Southwest State Teachers College in San Marcos, Texas, in June 1930. He was unwelcome and unable to join the élite influential group on campus. When he graduated in August 1931, he was the most powerful, most important "big man on campus," still despised and disliked but with his personally selected followers in control of the student newspaper and student employment service. He was extremely authoritarian to his followers. He was extremely submissive toward faculty and administration. He was driven by a continuous urge to dominate his fellow students. He was extremely assertive in his relations with them.

Johnson seems to have had few characteristics in common with the majority of emergent leaders in the experimental social science literature such as popularity, intellectual competence, and integrity. What he did have was an extraordinary need to assert himself, to dominate, and to stand out no matter what the costs to himself or others. He also had the willingness and ability to use surprise, trickery, and deceit, as well as political acumen. In one year's time, he completely transformed the campus life of over 1,000 students as well as the futures of a number of them who were forced to leave before graduation, or who became his supporters and subordinates in later life (Caro, 1982).

> Lyndon Johnson's rise would be spectacularly rapid; yet in relative terms, what achievement was more spectacular than his achievement at San Marcos, where within a little more than a year after returning from Cotulla, not only did he create a political organization on campus, he created *politics* on that campus—created it and, unpopular though he was, reaped power from it? [Caro, 1982, p. 200]

The same pattern was seen again in his successful political career as he rose to become majority leader of the U.S. Senate and ultimately President of the United States. As Johnson's career progressed in Washington, he made conscious efforts to please arch-conservatives and arch-liberals. As regards his values, he was a chameleon. He took maximum advantage of opportunities that Roosevelt's New Deal provided him yet complained bitterly to his conservative friends about the damage it was doing to the nation.

> One facet of Lyndon Johnson's political genius was already obvious in 1940: his ability to look at an organization and see in it political potentialities that no one else saw, to transform that organization into a political force, and to reap from that transformation personal advantage. He . . . [tranformed] a social club [the White Stars], a debating society [the Little Congress] and . . . the Democratic Congressional Campaign Committee . . . into political forces that he used to further his own ends. [Caro, 1982, p. 607]

In this latter effort, he engineered a politically devastating blow to what had been his own very close friend, mentor, and supporter, Sam Rayburn, long-term Speaker of the House of Representatives.

Also seen here in Lyndon Johnson were skills which are seldom brought up as important in the behavioral science literature except to suggest that such Machiavellian talents for bluffing, bluster, and baloney are likely to get the would-be leader in trouble. Tact is good, but not insincerity; trust is good, but not dependency. Authenticity and openness are encouraged. Clearly, transformational leadership can take place in the absence of tact, trust, authenticity, and openness. The transformational leader can be loved, idolized, and revered, or he can, like Joseph Stalin, transform a country in which he was hated, feared, and reviled. As we have noted earlier, numerous transformational leaders such as Field Marshal Kitchener and Charles Revson were unpopular and disliked by most of their associates.

With reference to the charismatic factor in transformational leadership, Tucker (1970) noted: "To be a charismatic leader is not necessarily to be an admirable individual." For Weber (1958), "the manic seizure and rage of the Nordic beserker or the demagogic talents of a Cleon are just as much 'charisma' as the qualities of a Napoleon, Jesus, or Pericles" (p. 73).

Values figured strongly in Machiavelli's (1513/1962) admonitions to the Prince. The Prince had to be prepared to be "not good" when this was advantageous to his position. He must appear to be religious, sincere, humane, and faithful. He had to make himself feared but not hated and had to appear as always successful.

Personal Defects

By now, it should be obvious that personal strengths figure strongly in the development and performance of transformational leaders. Such leaders emerge to the extent they can display charisma, individualized consideration, and intellectual stimulation. Nevertheless, personal weaknesses may result in leaders who attempt but fail to be transformational despite their charisma, consideration, or intellect.

William Bligh of *Bounty* fame was one of history's best examples of a leader who had the makings of a great naval commander but who was fatally flawed by his inability to tolerate incompetence and to deal with a false image that was created about him.

William Bligh seems to have been maligned by intense publicity campaigns by Fletcher Christian's brother, Edward, and James Morrison, boatswain's mate of the *Bounty,* who both manufactured and published tales about Bligh, the tyrant, to excuse Fletcher Christian's mutiny. Only several years after the mutiny did the focus on Bligh as tyrant emerge. The facts appear otherwise. Bligh was more benevolent and humanitarian than most naval captains of his day. In fact this may have been one of his problems. James Cook, with whom he had sailed, was his model. Bligh laid down a variety of antiscurvy procedures to which traditional seamen objected. Bligh followed Cook's scheme of three eight-hour shifts instead of four hours on, four hours off, which provided a great deal more normal rest. The results were unusually excellent records for health and safety on the longer voyages he commanded.

Until the mutiny, Bligh had shown a considerable amount of individualized consideration to Christian. The petty altercation between Bligh and Christian that supposedly led to the mutiny was far outweighed by what seems to be the major reason—the sexual frustration of Christian and the other mutineers on having to leave Tahiti and their Tahitian wives. Conditions for the mutiny were aided greatly by the shortage of skilled personnel and supervision. Bligh was the only regular Navy officer aboard the *Bounty*. He had continual problems with his own carpenter whom he could not control through disciplinary action for fear of losing his services. When Bligh made mistakes, they usually were errors on the side of leniency based on his judgments about the effects of his actions on the ship's effectiveness. For above all, Bligh was a highly competent, duty and task-oriented, sailor, seaman, and navigator. This was demonstrated by his direction, after the mutiny, of the overloaded small boat: he sailed 3,400 miles in 36 days from the mid-Pacific through the hazardous Torres Strait to Timor. Again, his main problem here seems to have been the failure of subordinates when responsibilities had to be delegated. His technical competence was repeatedly shown in his career following the mutiny when, despite the unwarranted reputation he had earned from the later false publicity about the mutiny, he was successful in command positions on ships of increasing importance, starting with taking another ship back to Tahiti for the breadfruit trees and including meritorious command of ships of the line during the Battle of Copenhagen and the Battle of Camperdown. He often was on the best of terms with many of his more capable subordinates, with his patron, Joseph Banks; and with his immediate superiors including Horatio Nelson and the higherups of the Admiralty. But his interpersonal behavior was flawed. He generated serious interpersonal problems with temperamental outbursts due to his frustration and intolerance of technical incompetence. Bligh verbally abused his immediate lieutenants, calling them "rascals and scoundrels" in front of the ship's company. In Bligh's court-martial case dealing with his command of HMS *Warrior* (74 guns) this verbal abuse was seen "to lessen their dignity as officers and was degrading in the extreme" (Kennedy, 1978, p. 337).

Bligh's manner of directing activities when he was in command of the *Warrior* was not likely to endear him to anyone. If he wanted something done quickly, he acted energetically, frequently swearing at the quartermasters or men who were standing around, shaking his fist and waving his hands. Bligh was "a rather articulate verbal abuser." This was not directed personally at any individual. He became furious when there was neglect of some action because of inattentive officers. Bligh himself acknowledged his anxiety when responsible for the direction of the complex orders requiring the ready responsiveness of his subordinates and their crews. He attributed his "warmth of temper" to his "zeal for the service." But he claimed that mutual support of superior and subordinate rather than discipline, as such, was the way that obedience could be assured in ships of war.

At the same time, Bligh repeatedly displayed a great deal of individualized consideration. He voluntarily taught navigation to his midshipmen and warrant officers, and dined regularly with his officers, even those who had testified against him at a court-martial. In modern day terms, he was a technically competent, benevolent autocrat who took pride in his work and tried to ensure that everyone else around him were equally as task-oriented as he was. "His kindness was always apparent when the people he dealt with treated him politely and deferentially. When they were insolent or disobedient, they brought out the worst in him 'sending him into paroxysms of rage.' " Bligh "was not harsh like Cook who had a foul temper and a violent streak when it came to flogging." Nor was he like (the naval hero, Horatio) Nelson, a man adored by his men, "who treated mutineers with extreme violence" (Kennedy, 1978, p. 398).

Personal Values and Transformational Leadership

Clearly, the leaders' personal values must be understood to understand their transformational efforts. Whether or not top-level managers will endorse and engage in consideration reflected in the encouragement of employee participation in the decision-making process depends on how much and why the managers value such participation. Dickson (1982) found that if managers more strongly held humanistic values, they appreciated and encouraged participation as a means of communication. Those who most focused on the value of the organization, by contrast, saw participation as the means to gain employee acceptance of the decisions. Those who were concerned about avoiding employee alienation saw participation as a moral right and as a way of increasing employee morale. The same participative leadership behavior could result with different intentions and from quite different values. At the same time, those who gave the strongest endorsement to the work ethic saw less use in participation.

Leaders with specific values, principles, and ideals that are not mirrored in the current state of affairs are likely to be stimulated into transformational efforts. Whether the values served are good or bad, whether the transformational leaders are wearing white hats or black hats, depends on the authenticity of interests ultimately served by the transformation.

Morality and Leadership

For Burns (1978), transformational leadership is moral if it deals with the true needs of the followers as defined by the followers based on informed choice. The leader is guided by near-universal ethical principles such as respect for human dignity and equality of human rights. The leadership mobilizes and directs support for "more general and comprehensive values that express followers' more fundamental and enduring needs" (p. 42). Moral leadership helps followers to see the real conflict between competing values, the inconsistencies between espoused values and behavior and the need for realignments in values, changes in behavior, or transformations of institutions.

Burns argued that if followers' need levels were elevated by leaders, such leadership was immoral if the followers' needs were not authentic. Hitler was immoral in seeing the art of leadership as consolidating the attention of people against a single adversary, of making it appear that different opponents belong in the same category, and in encouraging brutality to achieve goals. Conspiratorial fantasies created fictional needs which could only be satisfied by destroying the imagined conspirators. Hitler transformed German society at the expense of the tens of millions who were enslaved and who died as a consequence.

Leadership that provides pseudosolutions to pseudoproblems to satisfy pseudoneeds exploiting group fantasies and group delusions is immoral leadership. Inventing and encouraging group delusions—a favorite of demagogues—is transformational leadership at its worst. According to Demause (1982), group delusions are group fantasies which

> ward off feelings of paranoid collapse and provide relief from what feels like an intolerable state of emotional dissonance between the relatively calm external world and the turmoil of [one's] internal world. The intolerable ambivalence of the collapse stage is now avoided by splitting: the repressed narcissistic rage gets directed toward the enemy, while the unfulfilled love and grandiosity are projected onto the group itself. The country is now seen as infinitely precious and superior, but endangered from the *outside,* not from one's own hostility. [p. 186]

A kind of nonauthentic need fulfillment can follow to deal with the group delusion. Holsi and North (1965) found that the paranoia content in German communications kept increasing until World War I was declared. The declaration of war fulfilled the need created by the paranoid delusion. As a consequence of the declaration of war, anxiety declined sharply. Now the external enemy and the actions to be taken could be clearly identified. Declarations of war bring a deluded sense of relief after all the uncertainties leading up to them. Victory is then equated with moral value and the rightness of the cause (Demause, 1982).

Moral Leadership and Organizational Well-Being

The well-being of organizational life is better served in the long run by moral leadership. That is, transformations that result in the fulfillment of real needs will prove more beneficial to the organization than transformations that deal with manufactured needs and group delusions. A strong argument can be made for encouraging organizational leaders to wear white hats, not black hats, to subscribe to a code of ethics of what is right and what is wrong, ethics that are accepted as such in their society and by their profession. Nevertheless even here we may be faced with contradiction. As Jesus, a great transformer said, "It is written that . . . but I say to you. . . . '' The transformational leader may be a breaker and changer of what society has regarded heretofore as right and wrong.

In the organizational context, transformational leadership that is moral implies influencing change consistent with ethical principles of one's society and profession, of articulating and raising consciousness about authentic needs and inconsistencies and providing subordinates with the opportunity to understand and make choices.

Morality among leaders contributes to an organization's well-being and goes hand-in-hand with the integrity of leaders. For example, in the military,

> saying what one means and meaning what one says . . . being upright, honest, and sincere is . . . vital. Soldiers . . . depend upon others to support them as they risk their lives in combat. They have always had to depend upon the word of their subordinates and superiors. . . . Lives, careers, battles, and the fate of nations have hung upon the ability of military leaders to state all the true facts to the best of their knowledge, regardless of what effect these facts might have on themselves or others. Subordinates must be able to trust their leaders implicitly. Nothing can disrupt the morale and effectiveness of an organization more quickly than an untrustworthy, quibbling, or temporizing leader. Cheating, violating a trust, sacrificing others for selfish interest, gaining unfair advantage; these are the cancers in a military society that must be rooted out wherever found, if that society is to retain its vitality and life. [Hays & Thomas, 1967, p. 52]

Integrity, in turn, is central to the reputation of the successful military leader. Reputation determines the leader's influence and effectiveness with his superiors, peers, and subordinates. Credibility is lost, sometimes irretrievably, as a consequence of revealed duplicity. Nevertheless, duplicity in the sense of surprising the enemy is what wins battles.

Personal Values and Performance

England and Lee (1974) listed six ways in which leaders' personal values influence their performance. What leaders see as important, as right, and as good influence their perception of situations, other individuals, groups, and problems as well as the leaders' decisions and solutions to problems. Success and achievement, what is ethical, and what organizational constraints to accept or resist are also delineated by the leaders' personal values.

Personal values of leaders are of such importance that clarifications of their own values and those of their group, institution, and community are essential.

> The clarification, creation, and testing of value guides to action and evaluation should become as familiar [to a leader] as the creation and testing of empirical propositions in scientific research. Skills in recognizing and changing discrepancies between values and other forms of reality should be taught. [Paige, 1977, p. 199]

Idealistic Versus Pragmatic Values

Transformational leaders vary from the highly idealistic to those without ideals. Transformational leaders like Charles de Gaulle and Woodrow Wilson prided themselves on their high ideals. Other transformational leaders such as Franklin D. Roosevelt valued their own pragmatism as well. Roosevelt commented to his confidant, Harold Ickes, "Of course, it is not well to go into a fight unless we know that we can win" (Caro, 1982, p. 588). Illustrating his complete absence of social economic and political ideals, Lyndon Johnson expressed New Deal liberalism when meeting with liberals and old-fashioned conservatism when meeting with conservatives. Nevertheless, like everyone else, whatever their ideals and values, transformational leaders are responsible for their own actions and are to be judged accordingly, sometimes soon after they take action (Stockdale, 1981). In other cases, the judgments can only be made, if ever, long afterward.

Managers, especially lower-level managers, tend to value pragmatism. What works in practice is seen as more important than what is theoretically true. Maintaining productivity, profitability, and current standards are seen as important, right, and good (Bass et al., 1979). It would seem to follow that more transactional rather than transformational leadership is to be expected from the typical lower-level manager or bureaucrat for whom cooperativeness and conformity are more valued than individual initiative and creativity.

Leadership and the Purpose of Enterprise

Managers' values depend on their beliefs about the purposes of their enterprises. Whether they will be transformational or transactional will depend to some extent on their belief that they are part of a system whose purpose is to maximize profits, satisfy various constituencies, or contribute to the quality of life. Hay and Gray (1974) see the history of management in the past century as having undergone three evolutionary phases: profit maximizing, trusteeship, and quality of life management. Profit maximizing of the late nineteenth and early twentieth century stressed the single objective of profitability as overriding all other considerations. This was replaced by trustee management which saw itself engaged in balancing the system involving the interests of the owner, managers, employees, suppliers, customers, clients, and community. More recently a management has emerged which places a premium on the quality of life created by the system managed. Hay and Gray, as well as a sampling of executives by the author, suggest that trusteeship is most popular among organizations and their managers today although a minority remain as nineteenth-century profit maximizers and another minority are late twentieth-century advocates of quality of life management.

We expect that profit-maximizers will be transactional leaders and quality of life managers will be transformational. In between, trustee managers will tend to be both transactional and transformational.

Profit-Maximizers

Profit maximizing managers would appear more suitable for transactional leadership with its emphasis on self-interest and labor as a commodity to be exchanged for money. There is little room for the transformational factor of charismatic leadership among managers whose sole focus is on the values of profit maximization. There would be no room in relationships for subjective feelings or emotions. Relations should remain strictly "businesslike," unsentimental, and a matter of management obtaining the best possible earnings at the lowest possible costs for services rendered or goods provided. Transactional contingent reward and punishment fit profit maximization values.

One should see little concern in profit maximizing managers about the developmental needs of individual employees, as such. At most, employee development would be seen as a benefit provided employees in exchange for services rendered. Or, developmental activities would be justified if seen to contribute to long-term profitability. If possible, no more than subsistence or minimum wages would be paid. Belief in Social Darwinism leads to acceptance of the idea that employees and managers have achieved their highly differentiated roles, rights, and rewards as a consequence of their different inborn ambitions and capabilities.

Intellectual stimulation of employees, we suggest, would be regarded as not worth the effort or as possibly dangerous by profit maximizers. For them, most meaningful would be the epitome of transactional relations between employees and management—straight commission payments or piece-rate incentive payments directly proportional to goods sold or pieces of work completed by employees. "Everyone has a price; it is just a matter of establishing it."

Trustee-Oriented Managers

Pragmatic incremental changes rather than giant leaps are likely to be encouraged in trusteeships. Here also transactional leadership will be seen in the negotiations and bargaining in organizations driven by fluctuating coalitions of constituencies and interests.

Transactional contingent reward processes should be most favored by profit maximizers, and least acceptable to managers who subscribe to the importance of the quality of working life. For the latter, employees will become self-reinforcing as a consequence of their involvement in planning and control of their own work. Employee commitment to the organization and loyalty to it will increase as a consequence. In between profit-maximizers and quality of life managers in the transactional use of contingent reward, we suggest, would be trustee-oriented managers. They would be expected to reject straight piece-rate payment because of its potential unintended effects on the system such as employee slowdowns in fear of rate-busting, or misguided emphasis by employees on quantity instead of quality of output. Contingent reward would be introduced by trustee managers through merit pay and performance appraisal systems.

Similar speculations can be offered about the use of the transactional process of management-by-exception. In the value-world of profit maximization, the price is set between management and employees for employees' time, effort, and work done. Management must intervene if and when employees fail to live up to the contract. Intervention may take the form of reprimand, fines, or discharge. The objective function in the Soviet Union has not been profit but output. Nevertheless, in this culture of output maximization no matter the cost, as practiced in the Soviet Union, fines are levied (as much as 30 percent) for failure to reach monthly production quotas. Many other kinds of penalties may be faced for failure to meet production quotas as established by central planning in Moscow.

The monitoring aspects of management-by-exception may be particularly important for the trustee manager. Keeping alert to system imbalances will be critical but when a fault is found the corrective action may be directed to another part of the system as well as to the location where the fault surfaces. The transactional leadership of management-by-exception is least likely to be seen, we guess, in quality of life managers who expect that employees themselves will take responsibility to monitor what they are doing. The employees will take corrective steps as necessary, assuming they have the training and experience to do so.

Quality of Life Managers

Transformational leadership may shift what management sees as its purpose from profit maximizing to trusteeship management or from trusteeship to quality of life management. In addition, possibilities can be entertained of finding some transformational leadership in trusteeship organizational cultures. Here, the various constituencies can be influenced by transformational leadership to compromise or resolve their conflicting interests by transcending them for the sake of larger organizational needs. Transformational leaders can be the basis of mobilizing coalitions of interests to achieve cooperative effort toward larger organizational interests.

Almost by definition, quality of life management calls for the transformational focus on even broader long-term societal needs and objectives transcending the firm's own immediate interests. A sense of contributing to the greater good is fostered. A consciousness of mission is seen in the value that what is good for society is good for our company.

At the same time, quality of life management accepts the transformational leader's focus on the individualized development of employees as a major objective of value in its own right. Trustee management is likely to accept the need for such development, but only as a means to several ends, namely, satisfying employees' needs for growth and building a more effective system.

The transformation of subordinates by intellectual stimulation is most likely to be seen among managers believing in quality of life management. Employee participation is seen to provide valued growth opportunities, and to foster the achievement of solutions to problems of the social costs of business to the environment and to society. Managers valuing trusteeship also may foster intellectual stimulation but their transformational efforts will be constrained by the overall objective of maintaining a system in balance.

Values Determine Intervention

Which values are held by managers will determine how they interpret a problem situation and how and whether they will intervene. For example, workers are observed standing idle. The profit maximizer is likely to see a violation of "contract." Employees are paid to work, not to stand idle. Equipment is being underutilized. The employees are shirking their obligations. Corrective action will be taken by reprimanding the employees. The manager with trustee values will intervene only after determining whether the idleness is due to shirking or to failure of directions or deliveries of supplies. The quality of life manager is only likely to intervene to ask if some help is wanted. Or the quality of life manager may not intervene at all, expecting that the talking among workers occurring during the observed idleness is needed or appropriate.

Situation Specificity

In the preceding sections of this chapter, we have looked at the impact on transformational leadership of the external and internal organizational environments as well as the impact of personality and its development. Nevertheless, it may be that a combination of both effects is required to understand the emergence of transformational leadership in many instances. The need for charismatic and inspirational leadership, for example, is situation-specific. Practicing leaders need to be made aware of the potential and legitimacy for such transformational leadership when circumstances call for it.

Georgette (April 9, 1918), Ludendorff's major effort to drive the British back to the English Channel, provoked Field Marshall Sir Douglas Haig to issue a most unusual Order of the Day to all ranks. The language was very uncharacteristic of him:

> There is no other course open to us but to fight it out! Every position must be held to the last man: there must be no retirement. With our backs to the wall, and believing in the justice of our cause, each one of us must fight on to the end. The safety of our homes and the freedom of mankind alike de-

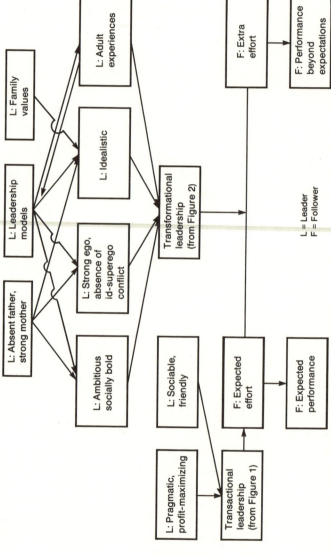

Figure 10 Personal Antecedents of Transactional and Transformational Leadership

pend on the conduct of each one of us at this critical moment. [Toland, 1982, p. 156]

Such emotional words, coming from the ordinarily cool and stolid Haig, inspired many of the reserve troops who were moving to the front lines to plug the gaps. An Australian subaltern issued orders to his section that its position would be held until relieved. "If the section cannot remain here alive, it will remain here dead, but in any case it will remain here" (Toland, p. 159).

Ordinarily, Haig was not a charismatic leader. But his "back to the wall" message in 1918 did transform war-weary troops in Flanders.

Figure 10 is a model describing the effects of the personal antecedents discussed in this chapter.

Part VI

Quantitative Explorations

KELVIN DECLARED THAT "if you can't measure it, you don't know what you are talking about." At the very least, if you can't measure it, you might not know what you are talking about. Leaders vary. To know here what we are talking about, we need to measure how much and in what ways and transformational and transactional leaders vary from each other.

Chapter 11

Behavioral Description of Transactional and Transformational Leadership

WITH THE DEFINITIONS OF transactional and transformational leadership in mind, and encouraged by the results of the pilot study about the value of the conceptualization in Chapter 2, we set out to analyze quantitatively (1) the transactional leader's emphasis on exchange with followers of benefits for compliance and (2) the transformational leader's emphasis on mobilization and direction of followers toward expanded, higher, or transcendental objectives.

Intensity of Leadership

We first attempted to demonstrate that leaders defined as transformational would display more intensive leader behavior than leaders defined as transactional. Results failed to support the hypothesis, which was based on an arousal and opponent process of motivation described in Chapter 1.

Sheridan et al. (1982) constructed behaviorally anchored rating scales of the intensity, extremity, and direction of leadership activities on seven dimensions: task direction, participation, consideration, performance feedback, integrity, performance rewards, and representation. For example, on the performance feedback scale, the highest, most positive item, the item which emerged empirically, judged at 90 points on a 100-point scale, was, "The supervisor lets employees know what performance areas they are good in and what areas need improvement if they are to advance their career plans." Almost as high in point value was, "The supervisor frequently tells subordinates his/her impression of their work performance."

A neutral item worth about 55 points was, "The supervisor criticizes employees for unsatisfactory work, but seldom comments on good work." At the bottom of the performance feedback scale at ten points was, "The supervisor complains about the performance of a subordinate to everyone except the individual being criticized." Slightly higher in point value was, "The supervisor gives all subordinates the same performance evaluation regardless of how well they do their job."

Fifty-two MBA students were tested using the seven leadership activity scales. The characteristics of transactional leaders were defined for them as: (1) recognized what it was you wanted to get from your work and tried to see that you got what you wanted if your performance warranted it; (2) exchanged rewards and promises of reward for your effort and good performance; and/or (3) was responsive to your immediate self-interests if they could be met by your getting the work done.

The students were asked to indicate on the seven leadership activity scales the highest, usual, and lowest level of activity of a transactional leader for whom they had worked or they knew well enough to rate.

Similarly, an additional 50 MBA students were given the following definition of transformational leader and asked to rate the activity levels of one for whom they had worked or knew well enough to rate: (1) motivated you to do more than you originally expected to do, (2) raised your level of awareness about important matters, (3) increased your level of needs from need for security or recognition to need for achievement or self-actualization, and/or (4) led you to transcend your own self-interests for the good of the team or the organization.

The working hypothesis was that transformational leaders would be described as displaying a more intensive pattern of leadership activity levels. No significant differences were found in intensity on five of the seven dimensions. However, contrary to expectations, as seen in Table 1, transactional leaders were described as being significantly higher in intensity of consideration for the personal needs and feelings of subordinates. They were also described as significantly higher in intensity of performance feedback—the extent the supervisor evaluates employees' work and keeps them informed about how well they are doing on the job.

In retrospect, the greater intensity of immediate feedback was logi-

Table 1 Mean Ratings of the Most Intense, Usual, and Least Intense Incidents Displayed by Transactional and Transformational Leaders

	50 Transactional Leaders	52 Transformational Leaders
Task direction		
Most intense	88.2	85.1
Usual	61.2	65.4
Least intense	40.5	34.2
Participation		
Most intense	79.7	78.8
Usual	63.7	60.2
Least intense	39.9	37.9
*Consideration**		
Most intense	90.3	87.4
Usual	74.5	68.8
Least intense	52.1	43.6
*Performance feedback**		
Most intense	84.9	81.4
Usual	73.0	65.0
Least intense	52.9	47.8
Integrity		
Most intense	85.5	81.4
Usual	69.9	65.0
Least intense	55.1	47.8
Performance rewards		
Most intense	81.4	80.6
Usual	67.0	65.1
Least intense	45.4	45.4
Representation		
Most intense	85.4	83.5
Usual	68.0	65.6
Least intense	44.1	44.9

* $p < 01$ for the overall differences between transactional and transformational leaders.

cally coherent with the exchange relationship emphasized in transactional leadership. The results for the intense consideration of personal needs did not mirror what was found for the frequency of such behavior. The sample of 50 and 52 MBA's were also asked to complete Stogdill's (1963) version of the Leader Behavior Description Questionnaire (LBDQ) describing the person whom they were rating. Here results were identical for the frequency (not intensity) of behavior by the transactional and transformational leaders. The mean was 21.7 for transactional and 21.8 for transformational leaders on their responses to the scale of consideration for their subordinates. The figures were 17.6 and 17.3, respectively, for their responses to the scale of initiation of structure.

These results suggested that again, as in the pilot study, subordinates, in retrospect, can point out and describe at least one transformational leader they have known. Transformational leaders are not a rarity. Second, except for when they dealt with the immediate personal needs of the subordinates or with providing feedback, the intensity, extremity, and direction of most leader behaviors were not what distinguished transactional and transformational leaders. Third, the widely used measures of initiation and consideration did not differentiate between transformational and transactional leaders. We concluded that we should move on to examining the frequency with which various specific kinds of behavior were observed in transactional and transformational leaders. Furthermore, we felt that merely asking respondents to identify a transformational or transactional leader did not engender confidence that we were adequately discriminating between the two types of leaders. Therefore, we set out to develop a reliable and valid instrument to discriminate between transformational and transactional leadership behavior.

Response Allocation Analysis

Our next step was to compile specific transformational and transactional items and then to make a reliable distinction between them. Several sources were used.

The open-ended responses of the 70 executives in our pilot study detailed in Chapter 2 were one source of items describing transformational leaders. A survey of the literature (Bass, 1981) with particular attention to influence processes, charisma, and the dynamics of exchange furnished numerous additional items describing transformational and transactional leaders. A total of 142 items were drafted. These were then submitted to 11 graduate MBA and social science students enrolled in a seminar on leadership. Each student was given a detailed definition of transformational and transactional leadership and also asked to read pertinent sections on the distinctions in Bass's review (1981, pp. 20, 455, 609–611). They also were asked to clarify the meanings for themselves of such terms as charisma, idiosyncrasy credit, esteem, and power. Following this, each student alone sorted the 142 items into three categories: transformational, transactional, or "can't say."

Seventy-three of the 142 items were selected for inclusion in a revised questionnaire. An item was selected as transformational if 8 or more of the 11 judges identified it as transformational and none or 1 identified the item as transactional. An item was selected as transactional if 9 or more judges of the 11 identified an item as transactional and none or 1 identified the item as transformational.

A clearly transformational item, one on which all 11 judges agreed was transformational was: "He/she makes me go beyond my self-interests for the good of the group."

A clearly transactional item on which all 11 judges agreed was transactional was: "He/she makes me concentrate on my self-interests rather than what is good for the group."

An example of a confusing item, seen by five judges as transformational; by four as transactional; and by two as "can't say" was: "I put all my effort into accomplishing each task as a consequence of his/her leadership."

Another example of an ambiguous item which ten judges marked "can't say," was: "He/she carries out the promises he/she makes."

Subordinates' Scaled Descriptions of Their Superiors

We next set out to see if the items that were identified as either clearly transformational or clearly transactional by the judges could be scaled for psychometric studies using the same two dimensions.

The 73 items were randomly scrambled in a questionnaire displayed at the end of this chapter, which was given to a total of 104 U.S. Army colonels, foreign officers, and civilians of equivalent rank. All were attending Army War College. The U.S. Army officers made up over 95 percent of the sample. Less than 2 percent were female. Of the superiors chosen to be described by our respondents, 91.3 percent were full colonels or general officers, 1.9 percent were lieutenant colonels, and the remaining 6.7 percent were civilians of equivalent rank. They were distributed as follows: Infantry, 26.9 percent; Artillery, 11.5 percent; Armor, 11.5 percent; Support, 22.1 percent; Other, 25.0 percent. Respondents had known their superiors as follows: over two years, 12.5 percent; over one but less than two years, 47.1 percent; over six months but less than a year, 37.5 percent; under six months, 2.9 percent.

MEANS AND VARIANCES OF THE ITEMS OF THE LEADERSHIP QUESTIONNAIRE (FORM 1)

Item	Mean	Var.	Item	Mean	Var.	Item	Mean	Var.
1	2.58	1.35	26	2.24	1.44	51	2.13	1.37
2	2.66	1.25	27	2.55	1.39	52	2.54	1.30
3	3.41	0.85	28	2.45	1.19	53	1.97	1.46
4	2.76	1.15	29	2.17	1.31	54	1.62	1.26
5	2.87	1.22	30	2.09	1.10	55	2.29	1.25
6	3.31	1.01	31	2.17	1.30	56	1.73	1.39
7	2.14	1.22	32	2.12	1.06	57	1.68	1.20
8	2.76	1.14	33	3.00	1.15	58	1.60	1.28
9	2.27	1.18	34	2.60	1.10	59	2.53	1.24
10	2.14	1.30	35	2.27	1.29	60	2.39	1.33
11	2.73	1.25	36	2.00	1.15	61	2.38	1.20
12	2.75	1.22	37	2.56	1.45	62	2.48	1.35
13	2.27	1.36	38	2.24	1.41	63	1.47	1.21
14	2.25	1.31	39	2.25	1.35	64	1.08	1.09
15	1.98	1.13	40	2.62	1.30	65	1.54	1.19
16	2.06	1.30	41	2.61	1.35	66	2.90	1.18
17	2.25	1.45	42	2.18	1.32	67	2.16	1.25
18	2.43	1.40	43	2.75	1.11	68	2.17	1.32
19	2.03	1.15	44	2.68	1.04	69	1.91	1.11
20	2.62	1.42	45	2.40	1.10	70	1.50	1.35
21	1.75	1.25	46	2.87	1.15	71	1.80	1.27
22	2.59	1.30	47	0.91	1.15	72	1.68	1.19
23	0.79	1.14	48	1.47	1.14	73	1.38	1.19
24	1.77	1.29	49	1.97	1.18			
25	2.12	1.27	50	2.78	1.36			

Respondents were asked to describe their current immediate superior (or another in their recent past whom they knew better). The respondents were asked to judge how often their superior displayed each of the 73 behaviors or attitudes using the following scale: A, frequently, if not always; B, fairly often; C, sometimes; D, once in a while; E, not at all. The anchors bore a magnitude–estimation-based ratio to each other of 4:3:2:1:0 according to Bass et al. (1974). Scoring was therefore A = 4, B = 3, C = 2, D = 1, E = 0. That is, for instance "fairly often" implies a frequency three times as much as "once in a while" and is so scored as three points; "once in a while" is scored as one point.

The means and variances are shown below for each of the 73 items. The most frequently observed leader behavior was the transactional item that indicated that more than fairly often, respondents, on the average, felt that their leader was satisfied if they met agreed-upon standards for good work. This was item 3 which had a mean of 3.41 for the 104 leaders. In comparison to all the other items, the variance of .85 in response to this item was smallest. The greatest variance of 1.46 occurred in item 53: "Whenever I feel it necessary, I can negotiate with him/her about what I can get for what I accomplish." This item averaged 1.97, which meant it occurred "sometimes." At the same time, it was rare ($\overline{X}$ = .79) for any of these 104 leaders to be described as "makes me concentrate on my self-interests rather than what is good for the group" (item 23).

Scales of Transactional and Transformational Leadership

Internal consistency analyses were used to set up two scales. Items first identified from the response allocation analysis as transactional or transformational were pooled as one or the other to generate transactional and transformational item summation scores. Split-half reliabilities were .86 and .80, respectively. But the transformational scores correlated .72 with the transactional scores. Those who scored high in transactional leadership did likewise in transformational leadership. Those who were seen to exhibit little transactional leadership were also seen to show infrequent transformational leadership.

A factor analysis was called for.

LEADERSHIP QUESTIONNAIRE

Directions: Listed below are descriptive statements about superiors. For each statement we would like you to judge *how frequently* your current immediate superior (or another superior in your recent past whom you know better) has displayed the behavior described.

Use the following for the five possible responses.

Key:	A	B	C	D	E
	Frequently, If Not Always	Fairly Often	Sometimes	Once in a While	Not At All

When the item is irrelevant or does not apply, or where you are uncertain or don't know, leave the answer blank.

1. _____ Makes me feel good to be around him/her.

2. _____ Makes me feel and act like a leader.

3. _____ Is satisfied when I meet the agreed-upon standards for good work.

4. _____ Makes me feel ready to sacrifice my own self-interests for the good of the group.

5. _____ Makes me feel we can reach our goals without him/her if we have to.

6. _____ I earn credit with him/her by doing my job well.

7. _____ Assures me I can get what I personally want in exchange for my efforts.

8. _____ Makes me go beyond my own self-interests for the good of the group.

9. _____ Puts suggestions by the group into operation.

10. _____ Finds out what I want and tries to help me get it.

11. _____ You can count on him/her to express his/her appreciation when you do a good job.

12. _____ Commands respect from everyone.

13. _____ I put all my effort into accomplishing each task as a consequence of his/her leadership.

14. _____ Because of him/her, I am less concerned about my own immediate needs and am concerned about our group reaching its objectives.

15. _____ Gives personal attention to members who seem neglected.

16. _____ Earns my esteem by helping me to get what I want.

17. _____ Is a model for me to follow.

18. _____ In my mind, he/she is a symbol of success and accomplishment.

19. _____ Has provided me with new ways of looking at things which used to be a puzzle for me.

20. _____ Is a good team player.

21. _____ Talks a lot about special commendations and promotions for good work.

22. _____ I am ready to trust his capacity and judgment to overcome any obstacle.

23. _____ Makes me concentrate on my self-interests rather than what is good for the group.

24. _____ Makes me do more than I expected I could do.

25. _____ Is content to let me continue doing my job in the same way as always.

26. _____ Is an inspiration to us.

27. _____ Makes me proud to be associated with him/her.

28. _____ Lets me know how I am doing.

29. _____ Has a special gift of seeing what it is that really is important for me to consider.

30. _____ His/her ideas have forced me to rethink some of my own ideas which I had never questioned before.

31. _____ Makes clear what I can expect if my performance meets designated standards.

32. _____ Enables me to think about old problems in new ways.

33. _____ Is a dominant figure in our group.

34. _____ Makes me feel that as long as I do my job satisfactorily I can expect to move ahead.

35. _____ Makes sure that payoffs for good subordinate performance are made as quickly as possible.

36. _____ Inspires loyalty to him/her.

38. _____ Increases my optimism for the future.

39. _____ Is inner-directed.

40. _____ Inspires loyalty to the organization.

41. _____ I have complete faith in him/her.

42. _____ Excites us with his/her visions of what we may be able to accomplish if we work together.

43. _____ Treats each subordinate individually.

44. _____ Spends time talking about the purposes of our organization.

45. _____ Arouses my awareness about what is really important.

46. _____ Accepts me for what I am as long as I do my job.

47. _____ Is a father-figure to me.

48. _____ I decide what I want; he/she shows me how to get it.

49. _____ Sets standards for me which can be easily maintained.

50. _____ Encourages me to express my ideas and opinions.

51. _____ Motivates me to do more than I originally expected I would do.

52. _____ Heightens my motivation to succeed.

53. _____ Whenever I feel it necessary, I can negotiate with him/her about what I can get for what I accomplish.

54. _____ Asks no more of me than what is absolutely essential to get the work done.

55. _____ Provides means for me to communicate with others.

56. _____ Encourages me to put my free time to good use.

57. _____ Tends to spend his/her time "putting out fires" rather than focusing on long-term considerations.

58. _____ Only tells me what I have to know to do my job.

59. _____ Gives us a vision of what needs to be done and depends on us to fill in the details.

60. _____ Encourages understanding of points of view of other members.

61. _____ As long as things are going all right he/she does not try to change anything.

62. _____ Gives me a sense of overall purpose.

63. _____ Tells me what I should do if I want to be rewarded for my efforts.

64. _____ I cannot succeed in reaching our goals without him/her.

65. _____ Gives me what I want in exchange for showing my support for him/her.

66. _____ Has a sense of mission which he/she transmits to me.

67. _____ Sees to it that my needs are met.

68. _____ Makes everyone around him/her enthusiastic about assignments.

69. _____ As long as the old ways work, he/she is satisfied with my performance.

70. _____ I model my own behavior after his/hers.

71. _____ It is all right if I take initiatives but he/she does not encourage me to do so.

72. _____ There is a close agreement between what I am expected to put into the group effort and what I can get out of it.

73. _____ Without his/her vision of what lies ahead of us, we would find it difficult, if not impossible, to get very far.

74. _____ The person I am describing is
    A. Male
    B. Female

75. _____ If military, the person I am describing is a
    A. Colonel or above
    B. Lt. colonel
    C. Major
    D. Captain
    E. Lieutenant

76. _____ If civilian, the level of the position of the person I am describing is:
    A. First-line supervisor
    B. Second-line supervisor
    C. Third-line supervisor
    D. Fourth-line supervisor
    E. Fifth-line supervisor or higher

77. _____ How long have you worked with the person you are describing?
    A. Three months or less
    B. Over three but less than six months
    C. Over six months but less than one year
    D. Over one but less than two years
    E. Over two years

78. _____ The branch of service of the person I am describing is:
    A. Infantry
    B. Artillery
    C. Armor
    D. Support
    E. Other

For items 79–82: A = extremely effective; B = very effective; C = effective; D = only slightly effective; E = not effective

79. _____ The overall work effectiveness of your unit can be classified as:

80. _____ Compared to all other units you have ever known, how do you rate the unit's effectiveness?

81. _____ How effective is your superior in meeting the job-related needs of the subordinates?

82. _____ How effective is your superior in meeting the requirements of the organization?

For items 83–84: A = very satisfied; B = fairly satisfied; C = neither
satisfied nor dissatisfied; D = somewhat dissatisfied;
E = very dissatisfied

83. _____ In all, how satisfied are or were you with your superior?

84. _____ In all, how satisfied are you that the methods of leadership used by
your superior are or were the right ones for getting your group's job
done?

Chapter 12

Factors of Transactional and Transformational Leadership

THE RESULTS REPORTED in this chapter were the basis for structuring this book. The quantitative analyses that produced the basic factor structure will be detailed here. This will be followed by a brief review of investigations of the correlations of the leadership factors with measures of subordinate satisfaction, extra effort, and performance. Results of tests of the model of the relation between transformational and transactional leadership will also be presented.

Factor Analysis

A principal components factor analysis was run with varimax rotation, for the data from 104 military officers, described in Chapter 11, who completed the Leadership Questionnaire describing their immediate supervisors. Seven factors emerged with eigenvalues above 1.0 and accounted for 89.5 percent of the common variance among the 73 items.

Table 2 shows the final rotated factor matrix of seven factors and 73 items. Unfortunately, for such an analysis of 73 items, approximately six times as many or 450 respondents were needed to obtain highly stable outcomes. However, the factor results reported here for the 104 cases did not change substantially in structure when we added an additional 72 senior military officers to the sample. Subsequently, when the

Table 2   Varimax Rotated Factor Matrix

	Factor							
Item	*I*	*II*	*III*	*IV*	*V*	*VI*	*VII*	h^2
1	.83	.06	.26	.16	.13	.03	− .14	.96
•2	.69	.11	.31	.28	.00	.12	− .17	.91
3	.55	.24	.50	.08	.09	.00	.00	.86
4	.61	.07	.33	.10	.31	.03	− .22	.93
5	.27	.03	.40	.20	− .09	− .04	.08	.78
6	.46	.33	.42	.06	.11	− .08	− .13	.78
7	.31	.42	.40	.18	.20	.20	− .13	.92
8	.56	.09	.43	.07	.20	.16	.05	.93
9	.74	.10	.29	.04	.12	.09	.11	.86
10	.61	.14	.50	.11	.03	.15	− .18	.89
11	.55	.28	.50	− .03	.05	− .05	− .09	.89
12	.83	.08	.00	− .03	.02	− .04	− .03	.95
13	.73	.28	.06	− .05	.06	.17	.07	.90
14	.67	.07	.28	.02	.11	.18	.04	.93
15	.53	.09	.56	.09	.10	.03	− .06	.89
16	.65	.13	.30	.17	.27	.22	− .01	.94
17	.86	.13	.20	.17	.10	.11	− .06	.96
18	.79	.13	.09	.13	.16	.07	.04	.96
19	.57	.01	.08	.01	.46	.29	− .03	.91
20	.81	.04	.16	.08	− .12	.09	− .02	.93
21	.20	.44	.29	.04	.07	.19	− .14	.87
22	.80	.15	.02	.17	.33	.00	− .02	.96
23	− .20	.14	− .01	.02	.02	.48	.04	.77
24	.32	.14	.13	− .09	.19	.63	.08	.80
25	.20	− .03	− .02	.67	− .05	− .02	.03	.80
26	.85	.16	.10	.11	.19	.07	− .03	.96
27	.83	.17	.18	.17	.17	.10	− .14	.97
28	.56	.13	.44	− .16	.12	.14	− .09	.92
29	.79	.17	.26	− .04	.26	.13	.06	.93
30	.27	.07	.06	− .15	.69	.18	− .03	.85
31	.46	.41	.16	− .02	.18	.06	.18	.87
32	.48	.09	.12	− .16	.59	.17	− .02	.90
33	.23	.10	− .01	− .13	.11	.03	− .10	.86
34	.39	.36	.36	.22	.32	− .05	.13	.85
35	.62	.27	.38	.01	.20	.05	− .06	.91
36	.50	.29	.15	− .08	.19	.08	− .04	.84
37	.85	.19	.18	.07	.02	.11	.00	.96
38	.73	.27	.11	.24	.13	.15	− .05	.90
39	− .02	.08	.01	.01	− .04	.07	.03	.59
40	.86	.05	.12	.09	.00	.02	− .06	.92
41	.88	.18	.00	.17	.13	.00	− .10	.96
42	.75	.28	− .03	.15	.01	.12	− .16	.92
43	.73	.10	.42	.00	− .12	.00	.09	.89
44	.32	.08	.28	− .05	.14	.08	− .14	.83
45	.68	.21	.07	.05	.29	.09	− .08	.91
46	.64	.12	.06	.39	.27	− .09	.02	.89
47	.45	.32	.00	.06	.27	.12	.08	.68
48	.38	.41	.31	.08	.27	.18	.10	.86

Table 2 (Continued)

Item	I	II	III	IV	V	VI	VII	h^2
				Factor				
49	.29	.33	.18	.23	−.08	.02	.04	.76
50	.83	.17	.16	.19	.07	.04	−.12	.96
51	.65	.23	.06	−.13	.21	.37	.07	.91
52	.64	.19	.15	−.16	.14	.22	.15	.87
53	.35	.58	.01	−.03	.24	−.06	−.08	.83
54	.05	.32	−.09	.33	+.02	.02	.40	.75
55	.68	.10	.20	.02	.22	−.10	−.03	.90
56	.33	.22	.19	.02	.14	.19	−.11	.82
57	−.48	.01	.00	−.04	−.14	.22	.22	.83
58	−.13	.05	−.07	.08	−.04	.06	.64	.76
59	.56	.06	.19	.27	.09	.02	−.10	.86
60	.81	.13	.28	.16	.08	−.02	−.03	.94
61	.15	.01	.03	.66	−.01	.08	.15	.84
62	.75	.20	.14	.07	.21	.02	−.02	.91
63	.06	.67	.11	−.14	−.06	.10	.07	.86
64	.16	.15	.02	.18	.20	.63	.10	.83
65	.16	.61	.12	.09	−.01	.21	.04	.81
66	.77	.15	.08	−.09	.10	.05	−.03	.92
67	.71	.14	.29	.07	.08	−.01	−.14	.93
68	.90	.15	.14	.06	.08	.02	−.03	.96
69	.15	.10	.15	.72	−.08	.05	.06	.92
70	.66	.30	.07	.16	.09	.14	−.02	.90
71	−.16	.00	.03	.21	.06	.14	.49	.73
72	.31	.62	.02	.20	.08	.12	.06	.80
73	.37	.26	−.13	.24	.00	.46	.03	.81

analysis was repeated to include the additional 72 cases, the first five factors emerged in the same way, but the last two had to be abandoned as independent factors as will be explained. What follows now are the details about the five surviving factors.

Factor I—Charismatic Leadership

In the original analysis with 104 cases, charismatic leadership behavior accounted for 64.9 percent (66 percent in the enlarged sample) of the 89.5 percent of variance of consequence. It clearly was transformational. It concerned the faith and respect in the leader and the inspiration and encouragement provided by his (or her) presence. Items most heavily loaded on this factor (.70 or above on the analysis and reanalysis) are shown below, along with their mean frequency of occurrence for the 104 cases shown in parentheses. Also, the factor loadings are shown in italics for the same items when the sample was expanded to 176 cases.

Loading on Factor I	Item No.	Item
.90 (.80)	68	Makes everyone around him/her enthusiastic about assignments (2.17)
.88 (.87)	41	I have complete faith in him/her. (2.61)
.86 (.86)	17	Is a model for me to follow (2.25)
.86 (.82)	40	Inspires loyalty to the organization (2.62)
.85 (.84)	26	Is an inspiration to us (2.24)
.85 (.84)	37	Inspires loyalty to him/her (2.56)
.83 (.80)	1	Makes me feel good to be around him/her (2.58)
.83 (.79)	12	Commands respect from everyone (2.75)
.83 (.85)	27	Makes me proud to be associated with him/her (2.55)
.80 (.79)	22	I am ready to trust his/her capacity to overcome any obstacles. (2.59)
.79 (.83)	50	Encourages me to express my ideas and opinions (2.78)
.79 (.71)	29	Has a special gift of seeing what it is that is really important for me to consider (2.17)
.79 (.74)	18	In my mind, he/she is a symbol of success and accomplishment. (2.43)
.77 (.71)	66	Has a sense of mission which he/she transmits to me (2.90)
.75 (.72)	42	Excites us with his/her visions of what we may accomplish if we work together (2.18)
.74 (.81)	60	Encourages understanding of points of view of other members (2.39)
.73 (.73)	38	Increases my optimism for the future (2.24)
.71 (.75)	62	Gives me a sense of overall purpose (2.48)

Factor II—Contingent Reward

This cluster of transactional leadership behavior items was recognized in the analysis for the 104 cases as much of what is currently prescribed in the *One Minute Manager* (Blanchard & Johnson, 1982). It is the contingent supervisory behavior implied in path–goal theory. It accounted for 6.3 percent of the variance among the 73 items. (The figure was 7.2 percent for the 176 cases.) Most highly loaded items (above .40 on the analysis and reanalysis) were:

Loading on Factor II	Item No.	Item
.67 (.70)	63	Tells me what to do if I want to be rewarded for my efforts (1.47)
.62 (.55)	72	There is close agreement between what I am expected to put into the group effort and what I can get out of it. (1.68)

Loading on Factor II		Item No.	Item
.61	(.53)	65	Gives me what I want in exchange for showing my support for him/her (1.54)
.58	(.56)	53	Whenever I feel like it, I can negotiate with him/her about what I can get from what I accomplish. (1.97)
.44	(.40)	21	Talks a lot about special commendations and promotions for good work (1.75)
.42	(.44)	7	Assures me I can get what I personally want in exchange for my efforts (2.14)
.42	(.48)	48	I decide what I want; he/she shows me how to get it. (1.47)

Factor III—Individualized Consideration

Considerate and supportive leadership behavior directed toward the individual subordinate accounted for 6.0 percent of the common variance for the 104 cases and 6.3 percent for the 176 cases. Loadings above .35 on the analysis and reanalysis were as follows for the 104 and 176 cases (in italics):

Loading on Factor III		Item No.	Item
.56	(.34)	15	Gives personal attention to members who seem neglected (1.98)
.50	(.37)	10	Finds out what I want and tries to help me get it (2.14)
.50	(.50)	11	You can count on him/her to express his/her appreciation when you do a good job. (2.73)
.50	(.56)	3	Is satisfied when I meet agreed-upon standards for good work (3.41)
.42	(.54)	6	I earn credit with him/her by doing my job well. (3.31)
.42	(.34)	43	Treats each subordinate individually. (2.75)
.40	(.47)	5	Makes me feel we can reach our goals without him/her if we have to (2.87)

Factor IV—Management-by-Exception (or Contingent Aversive Reinforcement)

This leadership behavior, aroused only when discrepant subordinate performance occurred, accounted for 4.3 percent of the variance for the 104 cases and 3.1 percent of the variance for the expanded sample of 176 cases. High scores on this factor implied a leader who concentrated on maintaining a steady state of affairs, and only intervened when subordinates deviated from expectations. It implied a contingent authorization. The items it contained were originally identified in our response allocation analysis as transactional. Absence of positive feedback was implied, along with the giving of negative feedback as made necessary by failure to maintain standards.

Factor loadings on analysis and reanalysis were as follows:

Loading on Factor IV	Item No.	Item
.72 (.70)	69	As long as the old ways work, he/she is satisfied with my performance. (1.91)
.67 (.63)	25	He/she is content to let me continue doing my job in the same way as always. (2.12)
.66 (.65)	62	As long as things are going all right, he/she does not try to change anything. (2.38)

Other items, which had been in a separate factor for the 104 cases, clustered into this factor of management-by-exception when the sample was enlarged to 176 cases as shown below.

Loading on Factor IV	Item No.	Item
.50	54	Asks no more of me than what is absolutely essential to get the work done (1.62)
.45	71	It is all right if I take initiatives but he/she does not encourage me to do so. (1.8ↄ)
.39	58	Only tells me what I have to know to do my job (1.60)

Factor V—Intellectual Stimulation

Originally seen to be an important aspect of transformational leadership, this factor accounted for 2.9 percent and 6.3 percent of the common variance for the 104 and 176 cases, respectively. Intellectual leadership was clearly involved in the items that were highly loaded on the factor. Items loading on this factor were also correlated substantially with factor I which involves charisma.

Loadings above .45 on analysis and reanalysis were as follows:

Loading on Factor V	Item No.	Item
.69 (.67)	30	His/her ideas have forced me to rethink some of my own ideas which I had never questioned before. (2.09)
.49 (.63)	32	Enables me to think about old problems in new ways (2.12)
.46 (.47)	19	Has provided me with new ways of looking at things which used to be a puzzle for me (2.03)

There were sixth and seventh factors with eigenvalues above 1.0 in the analysis for 104 cases. However, when the sample was expanded to 176 cases, the eigenvalues for these two factors fell below 1.0. -- the threshold value below which factors are abandoned. Thus, when the additional 72 Army officers were added (mainly colonels describing their superiors) to the original 104 to make a total sample of 176 respondents, a somewhat simpler factor structure emerged in that the seventh factor dropped to an eigenvalue of .97 and its items tended to migrate to the fourth factor of management-by-exception or contingent aversive reinforcement. Likewise, the sixth factor faded as a separate entity. As the sample was enlarged, loadings on the three items clustered on the sixth factor dealing with performance stimulation dropped respectively from .63 to .38, from .63 to .14, and from .46 to .31. This led us to abandon it as a separate factor and to include it within charismatic leadership on which its items now had higher loadings.

The items originally loaded above .70 in correlation with the first factor of charisma, ranged in the reanalysis from .71 to .87 in correlation with charisma. The items of the second factor of contingent reward, on reanalysis, increased or decreased slightly in correlation with the factor. Similar results occurred with the items loaded on the factors of individualized consideration, management-by-exception, and intellectual stimulation.

A Scale of Extra Effort

A dependent variable of consequence to us is the exertion of extra effort by subordinates beyond ordinary expectations. A number of the questionnaire items fell into this conceptual domain and can be used to form a scale showing how highly a leader motivates subordinates beyond original expectations.

Transformational Factor			Transactional Factor			
I	III	V	II	IV	Item	Item
.33	.13	.53	.18	− .08	24	Makes me do more than I expected I could do
.61	.18	.46	.24	− .09	51	Motivates me to do more than I originally expected I would do
.58	.04	.37	.31	− .05	52	Heightens my motivation to succeed

As shown to the above left, heightened effort of subordinates beyond expectations was seen to be most strongly associated with charismatic leadership (factor I) and intellectual stimulation (factor V), more modestly with contingent reward (factor II), even less so with individualized consideration (factor III), and not at all with management-by-exception (factor IV).

For the 176 cases, the three items had an average intercorrelation of .64. When responses to the items were added together, they formed an index with an estimated Spearman–Brown reliability of .84.

A Scale of Inspirational Leadership

Yukl (1981) had identified inspirational leadership as one cluster of leader behaviors among 19 categories. We noted such a three-item cluster within our set of charismatic items. Further inferences about the meaning of inspirational leadership could be obtained by a closer examination of the three items used by our sample of 176 Army officers to describe their superiors which were highly loaded on the charismatic factor and which were directly concerned with inspiration. The items formed a close-knit cluster. Their mean intercorrelation was .77. When combined into a three-item scale, they had an estimated Spearman–Brown reliability of .91.

Their correlations with the five transformational and transactional factors are shown below.

Transformational Factor			Transactional Factor			
I	III	V	II	IV	Item	Item
.84	.00	.23	.18	.05	26	Is an inspiration to us
.84	.17	.14	.18	.07	37	Inspires loyalty to him/her
.82	.17	.14	.06	.03	40	Inspires loyalty to the organization

While it can be seen that subordinates were inspired primarily by the factor of charismatic leadership, some slight degree of loyalty to the leader was also inspired by the leader's individualized consideration and contingent rewarding. The leader's intellectual stimulation appeared also to have a slight but generally inspiring effect. Loyalty to the organization was enhanced by the three transformational factors—charisma, consideration, and intellectual stimulation.

Thus, while inspiration may result to some modest degree from intellectual stimulation or individualized consideration, its main association is with the emotional, nonintellectual arousal of charismatic leadership.

Active–Proactive Versus Passive–Reactive Leadership

The factor scores for each of 176 cases were intercorrelated to generate a matrix which was then subjected to a higher-order factor analysis. Two factors emerged: (1) active–proactive leadership and (2) passive–reactive leadership with loadings as shown below:

First Order Factors	Higher-Order Factors	
	Factor I'	Factor II'
	(Active–Proactive Leadership)	*(Passive–Reactive Leadership)*
I. Charisma	.90	.00
II. Contingent reward	.78	.20
III. Individualized consideration	.84	−.01
IV. Management-by-exception	.16	.44
V. Intellectual stimulation	.72	.00

As can be seen, transformational leadership involved three active dimensions: charisma, individualized consideration, and intellectual stimulation. Transactional leadership involved one active dimension, contingent reward, and one passive dimension, management-by-exception. The active dimension appeared to be the kind of leadership required for high-performing systems (Vaill, 1978). On the other hand, the passive dimension (factor II') correlated .88 with a cluster of laissez-faire items: "Only tells me what I have to know to do my job," "It is all right if I take initiatives but he/she does not encourage me to do so," and "Asks no more of me than what is absolutely essential to get the work done." The cluster correlated −.11 with active–proactive leadership (factor I'). This laissez-faire cluster correlated .45 with the *first-order* management-by-exception (factor IV) for the 176 cases.

Reputation for charisma, individualized consideration, intellectual stimulation, and contingent reward involve proactive foresight, planning ahead, and taking steps when necessary in anticipation of perceived opportunities and threats. On the other hand, maintaining discipline or managing-by-objectives involves more of a "wait-and-see" policy which at its extreme becomes laissez-faire avoidance of being drawn into the situation or taking initiatives or responsibility for it.

Figure 11 displays the relations between the first-order and higher-order factors.

One would think that active–proactive leadership is opposite to passive–reactive leadership in occurrence. The analyses suggest otherwise. Some leaders are seen to display a lot of both. Others are seen to display neither, while still others are high on one dimension and low on the other. One may speculate that those leaders who are both frequently proactive and also frequently reactive create a lot more uncertainty in their subordinates than those who are high on one dimension and low on

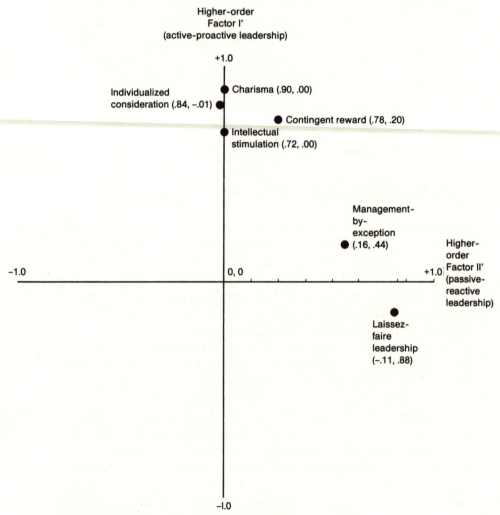

Figure 11   Relation of First-order and Higher-order Factors

the other. The charismatic leaders who suddenly withdraw from the scene leave a lot of people guessing and wondering about their return.

We cannot, at this time, rule out the possibility that these results are due partly or fully to the military sample and the particular measurement we employed. That is, we have only used scales of frequency. It may be that the two higher-order factors of activity and passivity are reflections of the total emphasis on discrimination among cases according to the frequency with which they were judged to display various leadership behaviors. For instance, if judgments had been about quality, duration, or intensity, different higher-order factors would probably have emerged.

Activity and passivity have proved useful dimensions for characterizing the political styles of U.S. Presidents. Barber (1968) contrasted Calvin Coolidge and his successor, Herbert Hoover, according to their different political styles—their different ways of meeting the demands of the Presidential role. A tired, bored Calvin Coolidge slept 11 hours a day. In contrast, hardworking Herbert Hoover immersed himself in detail, in commissioning policy studies, and in endless rounds of conferences, always searching for factual solutions.

Length of Acquaintanceship

Multivariate analyses were completed for the 104 cases comparing mean ratings on each factor according to the length of acquaintanceship of subordinates and superiors. Forty subordinates who had described superiors they had known for less than one year were compared with 62 who had described superiors they had known for one year or more. The multivariate analysis did not find either the univariate differences for individual factor scores, or the multivariate differences in assigned ratings as a function of length of acquaintanceship of 1.98 versus 2.03 to be of statistical or practical consequence.

Combat Versus Combat-Support

Systematic differences in factor scores for charismatic leadership and individualized consideration were observed when 40 officers in combat organizations were compared with 35 officers in combat support service. Table 3 displays the results. It can be seen that combat officers were found by their subordinates to display more transformational leader-

Table 3 Multivariate Analysis of Variance of Factor Scores of Combat and Combat Support Officers (N = 75)

	Type of Service		
Factor	Combat	Combat Support	P
Transformational			
I. Charisma	2.65	2.12	< .05
III. Individualized consideration	2.83	2.17	< .01
V. Intellectual stimulation	2.05	1.63	< .05
Transactional			
II. Contingent reward	2.63	1.55	< .05
IV. Management-by-exception	2.04	2.08	> .05

ship. They also were seen to be significantly higher on the transactional factor of contingent reward, but were the same as combat support officers in management-by-exception. Thus, combat officers were seen to be higher than combat service officers in active–proactive but not in passive–reactive leadership.

Satisfaction and Effectiveness

In another section of the Leadership Questionnaire (see Chapter 11), items 83 and 84 were included which dealt with how satisfied respondents were with their superiors' leadership behavior: "In all, how satisfied were you with your superior?" and "In all, how satisfied are you that the methods of leadership used by your superior are or were the right ones for getting your group's job done?" Five-point scales were used as follows: 4 = very satisfied, 3 = fairly satisfied, 2 = neither satisfied nor dissatisfied, 1 = somewhat dissatisfied, 0 = very dissatisfied.

In the same way, four questions, items 79, 80, 81 and 82, dealt with effectiveness: "How would you rate the overall work effectiveness of your unit?"; "Compared to all other units you have ever known, how do you rate the unit's effectiveness?"; "How effective is your superior in meeting the job-related needs of the subordinates?"; and "How effective is your superior in meeting the requirements of the organization?" Five-point scales used were as follows: 4 = extremely effective, 3 = very effective, 2 = effective, 1 = only slightly effective, 0 = not effective.

Indexes of perceived effectiveness and satisfaction were obtained by simple summing of ratings from a respondent. Reported coefficient alphas for these two indexes were .81 and .91, respectively (Bass et al., 1975).

Table 4 shows the correlations obtained between the five leadership factor scores and the indexes of perceived satisfaction and effectiveness. These two indexes actually formed a single criterion since they correlated .85 with each other. Perceived effectiveness and satisfaction with the leader went hand-in-hand. It is clear that while both the transformational and transactional leadership factors were seen to be positively associated with satisfaction and effectiveness, transformational leadership factors, particularly charisma and individualized consideration, were more highly related than transactional leadership factors to satisfaction and effectiveness. Charisma, by itself, was practically synonymous with satisfaction and rated effectiveness, correlating .91 and .85 with the two criteria. Individualized consideration was next highest in correlation (.76 and .70) followed by intellectual stimulation (.55 and .47).

The transactional factor of contingent reward correlated .45 and .41 with effectiveness and satisfaction while the transactional factor of management-by-exception correlated only .29 and .23 with the two criteria.

Additional Studies

A number of additional small and large sample studies have been completed. These include examinations based on the five factors enumerated earlier of the self-perceived discrepancy between actual leadership behavior of technical directors and what the directors think it ought to be; the extent to which world-class leaders' transformational leadership can be identified in terms of the factors by student judges from biographical accounts of the leaders; and the relation of leadership to specific aspects of extra effort and effectiveness of professionals, educational administrators and industrial managers.

Table 4 Correlations Between Factor Scores and Perceived Satisfaction with the Leader and the Leader's Effectiveness (N = 104)

Factor	Satisfaction	Effectiveness
Transformational		
I. Charisma	.91	.85
III. Individualized consideration	.76	.70
V. Intellectual stimulation	.55	.47
Transactional		
II. Contingent reward	.45	.41
IV. Management-by-exception	.29	.23

Self-Perceived Discrepancies

A small sample of 11 technical superiors of a large medical equipment manufacturer completed a shorter Form 2 containing 31 of the 73 items of Form 1 from which factor scores could be obtained. They rated their own actual leadership behavior and what they thought it ought to be. Mean factor scores were calculated for what they saw was their actual behavior and what they thought it ought to be. Results were as follows:

| | Mean Scores | | |
Factor	Actual	Ought	Deficiency
Transformational			
I. Charismatic leadership	2.25	3.02	− .77
III. Individualized consideration	1.86	2.23	− .37
V. Intellectual stimulation	2.17	2.27	− .10
Transactional			
II. Contingent reward	1.86	2.23	− .37
IV. Management-by-exception	1.28	1.29	− .01

These managers felt particularly lacking in charismatic leadership and their ability to inspire subordinate performance. They also saw they should be doing more to individualize consideration and provide contingent rewards. On the other hand, they were satisfied with their more modest tendencies to provide intellectual stimulation and management-by-exception.

A Study of World-class Leaders through Survey Questionnaires Applied to Their Biographical Accounts

A total of 198 undergraduates each elected to study one from a total of 67 leaders, 58 men and 9 women. After reading one or more biographies and periodical accounts about them, they each completed Form 4 of the Multifactor Leadership Questionnaire about the leader they had studied as if they were an "average subordinate or follower" of the leader. On this form, ten items, many newly written, were included for each of our five factors: charismatic leadership, individualized consideration, intellectual stimulation, contingent reward, and management-by-exception. Individual scores for each rater on each factor were obtained by adding the results for the 10 items each with possible responses of 0 to 4, then dividing the sum by 10 to yield an average response to the 10 items of each scale. Even though the judgments of the raters depended on which particular biographical accounts they had read, a picture emerged of the leaders which generally is consistent with their different reputations.

As a whole, the 67 leaders scored higher on the transformational than the transactional factors. As before, A or 4.0 meant "frequently if not always displays the behavior" and E or 0.0 meant "never does so." The mean results were as follows for the transformational factors: charisma (3.2), intellectual stimulation (2.9), and individualized consideration (2.7). For the transactional factors, they were: contingent reward (2.4), and management-by-exception (2.1). The transformational factors were considerably higher than those found for real-life but ordinary administrators and professionals as shown later in Tables 5 and 6. Similar patterns emerged for the world class leaders whether they were military, political, or industrial. There were no significant differences between the 58 men and 9 women who were studied. Nor did it matter if the student rater was male or female.

Reliabilities of the scales, as assessed by coefficient alphas, were as follows: charisma, .82; individualized consideration, .84; intellectual stimulation, .78; contingent reward, .74; and management-by-exception, .60.

Since we had two to six subordinates describing each of the 67 leaders, we completed a multivariate analysis. We examined the extent to which there was more variance when the "subordinates" who were contrasted on the five scales were describing different leaders than when the "subordinates" were describing the same leader. The multivariate F-ratio was highly significant. Then we converted the resulting F-ratios for the three transformational and two transactional scales to eta coefficients to determine the construct validity of the scales; that is the extent each scale value was a meaningful discrimination of leader behavior. The etas were correlations, which could vary from 0 to 1.0. They were as follows: charisma, .79; individualized consideration, .77; intellectual stimulation, .77; contingent reward, .66; and management-by-exception, .69.

Consistent with other survey results, the three transformational factors correlated .63 on the average with each other and only .34 on the average with the two transactional factors. Also, they correlated more highly with rated satisfaction with the leader and his or her effectiveness than did the two transactional factors as shown on the next page.

Factor	Satisfaction with Superior	Effectiveness of Leadership
Transformational leadership		
I. Charismatic leadership	.64	.58
III. Individualized consideration	.50	.40
V. Intellectual stimulation	.52	.34
Transactional leadership		
II. Contingent reward	.28	.21
IV. Management-by-exception	− .10	− .17

There appeared to be reasonable consistency between the differential patterns of scores obtained for the leaders and their general reputation. For example, among the nine U.S. Presidents in the sample (John Adams, Gerald Ford, John F. Kennedy, Abraham Lincoln, Richard Nixon, Franklin D. Roosevelt, Theodore Roosevelt, Lyndon B. Johnson, and Harry Truman), John F. Kennedy and Franklin D. Roosevelt earned the highest scores in charismatic leadership (3.7). Consistent with the results, a recent *Newsweek* (Anonymous, 1983 B) poll found that of all our Presidents, 30 percent of the national survey would most like to see Kennedy as President today. The next highest favorite was Franklin D. Roosevelt with 10 percent of the nominations.

Among the top 10 of our 67 leaders in charisma were 3 black leaders —Andrew Young (4.0), Martin Luther King (4.0), and Malcolm X (3.7).

Two women leaders were near the top of the list of 67 in individualized consideration (Eleanor Roosevelt at 3.8 and Margaret Thatcher at 3.5).

Most important for our continuing argument here was that some of the industrial leaders studied such as George F. Johnson (Endicott–Johnson Shoes), Thomas J. Watson, Sr. of IBM, and Alfred P. Sloan of General Motors were seen to be as high in charismatic leader behavior as their military and political counterparts (Bass et al., 1984).

A Study of 45 Professionals and Managers

Forty-five New Zealand professionals and managers completed the Multifactor Leadership Questionnaire, Form 4, to describe their immediate superior. Sixty-four percent were male; 36 percent, female. Coefficient alphas, means, and standard deviations as shown in Table 5 were found with this sample. As can be seen in Table 5, on the average,

Table 5 Relations of Transformational and Transactional Factor Scale Scores on the Multifactor Leadership Questionnaire (Form 4) to Selected Variables for 45 New Zealand Professionals and Managers

| | | | | Variable | | | | | | | | |
| | | | | Effectiveness | | | | Satisfaction | | | | |
Factor	Male Sex	Organ. Level	Extra Effort	Unit[a]	Unit[b]	Job[c]	Org.[d]	Sup.[e]	Meth.[f]	Spec. Incid.	Coeff. α	Mean	S.D.
Transformational													
I. Charisma	−.11	.23	**.50**	**.29**	**.41**	**.58**	**.56**	**.54**	**.59**	.23	.93	2.35	.69
III. Individualized Consideration	−.11	−.22	.25	.21	**.36**	**.65**	**.62**	**.51**	**.59**	**.39**	.88	2.58	.59
V. Intellectual Stimulation	−.09	.15	**.49**	**.32**	**.51**	**.48**	**.52**	**.51**	**.52**	**.48**	.87	2.50	.63
Transactional													
II. Contingent Reward	−.06	.14	**.38**	.25	**.29**	**.40**	**.43**	**.34**	.27	**.53**	.80	2.27	.55
IV. Management-by-exception	**.28**	−.21	**−.28**	−.09	.08	−.15	−.03	−.09	−.13	.00	.66	2.51	.52

Statistically significant correlations shown in bold type where

p < .01 when r = .37

p < .05 when r = .28

[a] Overall work effectiveness of your unit?
[b] Effectiveness compared to other units?
[c] Superior meets job-related needs?
[d] Superior meets requirements of the organization?
[e] Satisfied with superior?
[f] Satisfied with superior's methods?

leaders were seen to display the behavior for any factor somewhere between sometimes (2.0) and fairly often (3.0). Individualized consideration (2.58) was slightly more frequently observed and contingent reward slightly less frequently observed (2.27) than the other factors.

The standard deviations in the transformational leadership factors (.69, .59, .63) were slightly more than the standard deviations in the transactional leadership factors (.55 and .52). One effect was associated with sex. Male superiors were more likely to display management-by-exception than their female counterparts.

Respondents described themselves at organizational levels as follows: first, 20 percent; second, 11 percent; third, 18 percent; fourth, 18 percent; and fifth, 20 percent. We had expected to see more transformational and less transactional leadership at higher organizational levels. Results were more complex. Slightly more charismatic leadership may have been seen at higher levels according to Table 5. Slightly more individualized consideration and management-by-exception were seen at lower levels.

Extra effort was most strongly associated with charisma and intellectual stimulation, as expected. But contingent reward appeared to make more of a contribution to extra effort than did individualized consideration. Management-by-exception was counterproductive.

Generally, as expected, the transformational factors were more strongly associated than the transactional factors with effectiveness, particularly to the extent the superior was seen to contribute to meeting the requirements of the organization and to meeting job-related needs. Transformational leadership was also more satisfying. Contingent reward made a more modest contribution to effectiveness and satisfaction, while management-by-exception was generally of no consequence.

Respondents were asked to think of a specific incident in which their supervisor affected the effort or performance of themselves or others. They then were asked to rate how much the effort or performance was affected and in what way: *A*, increased a great deal; *B*, increased to some extent; *C*, decreased to some extent; or *D*, decreased a great deal. These alternatives were then scored as $+2$, $+1$, -1, -2.

Results in Table 5 suggest that, in the short run when dealing with a specific incident, those superiors who most frequently display contingent reward and intellectual stimulation make more of a contribution to improvement than do supervisors who more frequently are charismatic or display individualized consideration. Least likely to contribute to improving a specific situation are supervisors who engage more frequently in management-by-exception.

In all, we determined that highly reliable measures of the five factors could be obtained; that hierarchical level had a complex association with the transformational and transactional factors; and that while, in the short run, managers who practiced contingent reward were most likely to contribute to subordinate performance, in the long run the greater payoff came from transformational factors, particularly if we were concerned about leadership effects on the organization and work to be done.

A Study of 23 Educational Administrators

These were mainly high level members of New Zealand's South Island central administration; 71 percent saw themselves at the fourth and fifth organizational levels; only 29 percent below this. Again, 65 percent were male; 35 percent female. They completed a somewhat modified questionnaire. Absent were the question about a specific critical incident and two management-by-exception items which had been found in the 45 professional–managerial sample to be unrelated to most of the 10 items in the cluster. As shown in Table 6, the sex of supervisors had more of an effect among these administrators than among the previous sample of 45 professionals and managers. Females were significantly more likely to engage in contingent reward.

Again, management-by-exception was more likely to be seen at lower levels. This may be a consequence of greater spans of control at lower levels.

The distribution of means was similar to the 45 professional–managerial samples, but there was a noticeably larger standard deviation. Coefficient α reliabilities were higher than before, partly due to modifications in the questionnaire (Form 4).

In the aggregate, extra effort and effectiveness, particularly when job and organizationally relevant, were more highly associated with transformational than transactional factors. Management-by-exception was counterproductive. Contingent reward was reasonably satisfying, but charismatic leadership even more so. For these educational professionals, intellectual stimulation was also quite satisfying as a leadership method.

In all, results here combined with those obtained for the 45 professionals and managers added further confidence to the utility of our efforts.

A Study of 256 Supervisors and Managers

These were 256 U.S. supervisors and managers from a Fortune 500 firm who completed a shorter version of 37 items of the five scales embedded

Table 6 Relations of Transformational and Transactional Factor Scale Scores on the Multifactor Leadership Questionnaire (Form 4) to Selected Variables for 23 New Zealand Educational Administrators

| | | | | Variable | | | | | | | | |
| | | | | Effectiveness | | | | Satisfaction | | | | |
Factor	Male Sex	Organ. Level	Extra Effort	Unit [a]	Unit [b]	Job [c]	Org. [d]	Sup. [e]	Meth. [f]	Coeff. α	Mean	S.D.
Transformational												
I. Charisma	−.13	−.18	**.72**	.36	**.61**	**.88**	**.76**	**.73**	**.83**	.95	2.44	.81
III. Individualized Consideration	−.10	−.16	**.60**	**.40**	**.52**	**.77**	**.63**	**.54**	**.68**	.91	2.30	.76
V. Intellectual Stimulation	−.23	−.04	**.76**	.20	.37	**.70**	**.66**	**.47**	**.66**	.89	2.21	.67
Transactional												
II. Contingent Reward	−.31	−.04	.44	.27	.34	**.58**	.39	**.51**	**.55**	.80	2.25	.87
IV. Management-by-exception	−.03	−.26	−.42	−.16	−.36	−.37	−.48	−.08	−.34	.84	2.65	.66

Statistically significant correlations shown in bold type where

p < .01 when r = .50

p < .05 when r = .40

[a] Overall work effectiveness of your unit?

[b] Effectiveness compared to other units?

[c] Superior meets job-related needs?

[d] Superior meets requirements of the organization?

[e] Satisfied with superior?

[f] Satisfied with superior's methods?

in a larger questionnaire. The coefficient α reliabilities per scale were as follows: charisma, .94; individual consideration, .87; intellectual stimulation, .89; contingent reward, .83; and management-by-exception, .70.

As Table 7 shows, contingent reward as well as the transformational factors correlated highly with an index of satisfaction with the supervisor. Management-by-exception was negatively related with satisfaction with the supervisor. Independent performance appraisals of these same subordinates were found to correlate positively with the charismatic and individualized consideration scores of their superiors. But here, intellectual stimulation, contingent reward, and management-by-exception were found to be of no consequence (Waldman et al., 1984).

Tests of the Model

The data from the previous studies were fitted against the model of transformational leadership shown in Figure 2. The model proposed that transformational leadership augments extra effort and performance above and beyond that due to transactional leadership.

First, the differences in extra effort among subordinates were determined which could be attributed to an optimum combination of the leaders' transactional factor scores for contingent reward and management-by-exception. Then, the leaders' transformational factor scores were added to their transactional scores in an expanded optimum combination.

Table 7 Relations of Transformational and Transactional Factor Scale Scores to Selected Variables for 256 Supervisors and Managers in a Single U.S. Firm

Factor	Extra Effort	Satisfaction with Supervisor	Appraised Performance of Subordinate
Transformational			
I. Charisma	**.88**	**.67**	**.19**
III. Individualized Consideration	**.79**	**.68**	**.24**
V. Intellectual Stimulation	**.80**	**.64**	.08
Transactional			
II. Contingent Reward	**.76**	**.67**	.05
IV. Management-by-exception	**− .24**	**− .27**	− .04

Statistically significant correlations shown in bold type where
p < .05 when r = .12
p < .01 when r = .16

In the same way, the leaders' transformational scores were combined with their transactional scores to calculate the expected augmentation in the extent to which perceived effectiveness or appraised performance of the subordinates could be attributed to the leadership profile.

The tests of the model were completed for 189 U.S. Army colonels, 72 Army officers ranging from lieutenant to lieutenant colonel, and the 256 business managers. These managers were scattered in levels throughout the hierarchy of a Fortune 500 firm. As shown below, in all three samples, the transactional scores alone accounted for 26 to 59 percent of subordinate extra effort. More important, when we added the transformational factor scores to a leader's transactional factor scores, we obtained increments of 25 to 37 percent in accounting for the subordinates' extra effort. In the same way, for the military samples, the transactional scores alone accounted for 18 and 22 percent of the variance in subordinates' perceptions of effectiveness. Gains of 48 and 27 percent accrued from adding the leaders' transformational scores to the equations.

Sample	Only Transactional Factors	Incremental Effect of Transformational Factors	Combined Effects
		Extra Effort	
189 colonels	26%	37%	63%
72 officers	37%	36%	73%
256 managers	59%	25%	84%
		Perceived Effectiveness	
189 colonels	18%	48%	66%
72 officers	22%	27%	49%
		Appraised Subordinate Performance	
256 managers	0%	9%	9%

While transactional scores failed to account for any of the appraised performance of subordinates in the sample of business managers, adding the managers' transformational scores to the equation did result in accounting for 9 percent of the variance in subordinates' performance. None of these results could be attributed to chance effects. The additive relations posited between transactional and transformational leadership in the model shown in Figure 2 of Chapter 2 were supported by the results obtained in all three samples.

Summing Up

To conclude, we have shown in these quantitative studies that

1. five factors are required to understand transactional and transformational leadership;
2. it is possible to measure each of these factors with high reliability so that widely differing profiles can be obtained from questionnaire descriptions of individual leaders;
3. respondents describing the same leaders will produce similar profiles; and
4. as proposed in the model, transformational leadership will contribute in an incremental way to extra effort, effectiveness, and satisfaction with the leader as well as to appraised subordinate performance beyond expectations that are attributable to transactional leadership.

Relation to Clinical Evidence

The quantitative explanations revealed five dimensions of consequence to transformational and transactional leadership. The dimensional structure remains to be verified empirically with samples of larger size and using different methods than we had the opportunity to employ. Our confidence in the factorial structure has been strengthened, however, by the discovery of a report of Zaleznik (1977) since completing these analyses.

Parallel Structures

Based on clinical observations, the psychoanalytically trained Zaleznik distinguished between "managers" and "leaders." His managers displayed transactional leadership; his leaders, transformational leadership. Paralleling our first factor of charisma, he wrote that leaders, but not managers, attract strong feelings of identity and intense feelings of love and hate. Leaders send clear messages of purpose and missions, not ambiguous signals. Zaleznik noted that leaders, but not managers, generate excitement at work and heighten expectations through the images and meanings they provide. Paralleling our third factor of individualized consideration, he wrote that leaders, but not managers cultivate, establish, and break off intensive one-to-one relationships. They reveal empathy for individuals, as such, and what different events mean to different individuals. On the other hand, managers see themselves as role players engaged in an activity whose meaning lies in itself as a process. Paralleling our fifth factor of intellectual stimulation, he wrote that leaders, but not managers, were more concerned with ideas rather than process, ideas which the leaders can articulate and project into images.

On the other hand, consistent with our analyses, Zaleznik's managers engaged more often in transactional activities than did his leaders. As with our second factor of contingent reward, Zaleznik's managers, but not his leaders, made flexible use of rewards and punishments. Similar to our fourth factor of management-by-exception, Zaleznik observed that managers, but not leaders, tried to maintain (not change) a controlled, rational, equitable system. Zaleznik indicated that his leaders were likely to be more active; his managers were likely to be more passive. While managers tolerate the mundane, leaders react to it "as to an affliction."

Although we may be risking premature closure about the fundamental structure of transformational and transactional leadership, our quantitative analyses and Zaleznik's clinical support provides us with some confidence about the validity of the five factors, the transformational factors of charismatic leadership, individualized consideration, and intellectual stimulation, and the transactional factors of contingent reward and management-by-exception.

References

ABDEL-HALIM, A. A. Effects of higher order need strength on the job performance—job satisfaction relationship. *Personnel Psychology*, 1980, *33*, 335–347.

ADAMS, J., INSTONE, D., RICE, R. W., and PRINCE, H. T. II. Critical incidents of good and bad leadership. Paper presented at the American Psychological Association, Los Angeles, 1981.

ADLER, S. Subordinate imitation of supervisor behavior: The role of supervisor power and subordinate self-esteem. Paper presented at International Congress of Applied Psychology, Edinburgh, 1982.

ALDEFER, C. P. An empirical test of new theory of human needs. *Organizational Behavior and Human Performance*, 1969, *4*, 142–175.

ALIAS, A. G. On the psychopathology of schizophrenia. *Biological Psychiatry*, 1974, *9*, 61–72.

ANONYMOUS. The chief executive officer: Personal management styles. *Business Week*, May 4, 1974, *2*, 43–51.

ANONYMOUS. Going down the long lonesome road. *Macleans*, May 25, 1981A, 10–11.

ANONYMOUS. What to do about the marginal employee. *Supervisory Sense*, 1981B, *1*, 7.

ANONYMOUS. The talk of the town. *The New Yorker*, September 12, 1983A, 37.

ANONYMOUS. Kennedy has become America's favorite President. *Newsweek*, November 28, 1983B, 64.

ATKINSON, J. W. *An Introduction to Motivation.* Princeton, NJ: Van Nostrand, 1964.

AYER, F., JR. *Before the Colors Fade: Portrait of a Soldier, George S. Patton, Jr.* Boston: Houghton-Mifflin, 1971.

AYRES, B. D. *The Counseling Function of the Leadership Role.* United States Army Administration Center Leadership Monograph Series, Monograph 11, November, 1978.

BACHARACH, S. B., and LAWLER, E. J. *Power and Politics in Organizations.* San Francisco: Jossey-Bass, 1980.

BANDURA, A. *Social Learning Theory.* Morristown, NJ: General Learning Press, 1971.

BANDURA, A. Self-efficacy mechanism in human agency. *American Psychologist,* 1982, *37,* 122–147.

BARBER, J. D. Classifying and predicting presidential styles: "Two weak" presidents. *Journal of Social Issues,* 1968, *24,* 51–80.

BARLOW, J. A. Mass line leadership and thought reform in China. *American Psychologist,* 1981, *36,* 300–309.

BARTOLEME, S. Executives as human beings. *Harvard Business Review,* 1972, *50,* 62–69.

BASS, B. M. The leadership group discussion as a leadership evaluation instrument. *Psychological Bulletin,* 1954, *51,* 465–492.

BASS, B. M. *Leadership, Psychology and Organizational Behavior.* New York: Harper, 1960.

BASS, B. M. *Organizational Psychology.* Boston: Allyn & Bacon, 1965.

BASS, B. M. Social behavior and the orientation inventory. *Psychological Bulletin,* 1967, *68,* 260–292.

BASS, B. M. *Stogdill's Handbook of Leadership: A Survey of Theory and Research.* Revised and Expanded Edition. New York: Free Press, 1981.

BASS, B. M. A new paradigm for leadership training and research. *International Review of Applied Psychology* (in press).

BASS, B. M., AVOLIO, B., and GOODHEIM, L. A retrospective survey analysis of world-class leadership. School of Management, Binghamton, Working Paper 84–76, 1984.

BASS, B. M., and BARRETT, G. V. *People, Work and Organizations.* Boston: Allyn & Bacon, 1981.

BASS, B. M., BURGER, P. A., BARRETT, G. V., and DOKTOR, R. *Assessment of Managers: An International Comparison.* New York: Free Press, 1979.

BASS, B. M., CASCIO, W. F., and O'CONNOR, E. Magnitude estimations of frequency and amount. *Journal of Applied Psychology,* 1974, *59,* 313–320.

BASS, B. M., and FARROW, D. L. Quantitative analyses of biographies of political figures. *Journal of Psychology,* 1977, *97,* 281–296.

Bass, B. M., Valenzi, E. R., Farrow, D. L., and Solomon, R. J. Management styles associated with organizational, task, personal and interpersonal contingencies. *Journal of Applied Psychology,* 1975, *60,* 720–729.

Bass, B. M., Wurster, C. R., and Alcock, W. A test of the proposition: We want to be esteemed most by those we esteem most highly. *Journal of Abnormal and Social Psychology,* 1961, *63,* 650–653.

Beale, H. K. *Theodore Roosevelt and the Rise of America to World Power.* Baltimore: Johns Hopkins University Press, 1956.

Bennis, W. Leadership transforms vision into action. *Industry Week,* May 31, 1982, 54–56.

Bennis, W. Transformative leadership. *Harvard University Newsletter,* April 7, 1983.

Berger, P. L. Charisma and religious innovation: The social location of Israelite prophecy. *American Sociological Review,* 1963, *28,* 940–949.

Berlew, D. E. Leadership and organizational excitement. In D. A. Kalb, I. M. Rubin, and J. M. McIntyre (Eds.), *Organizational Psychology: A Book of Readings.* Englewood Cliffs, NJ: Prentice-Hall, 1974.

Berlyne, D. E. Arousal and reinforcement. In D. Levine (Ed.), *Nebraska Symposium on Motivation* (Vol. 15). Lincoln: University of Nebraska Press, 1967.

Blanchard, K., and Johnson, S. *The One Minute Manager.* New York: William Morrow, 1982.

Blau, P. M., and Scott, W. R. *Formal Organizations.* San Francisco: Chandler Publishing Company, 1962.

Bradley, D. N. *A Soldier's Story.* New York: Holt, 1951.

Broder, D. Forgetting cause and effect. *Washington Post,* February 12, 1984, F3.

Bromley, D. G., and Schupe, A. D. *Moonies in America: Cult, Church, and Crusade.* Beverly Hills: Sage Publications, 1979.

Burns, J. M. *Leadership.* New York: Harper and Row, 1978.

Burns, T., and Stalker, G. M. *The Management of Innovation.* Chicago: Quadrangle Books, 1961.

Caro, R. A. *The Power Broker: Robert Moses and the Fall of New York.* New York: Knopf, 1974.

Caro, R. A. *The Years of Lyndon Johnson: The Path to Power.* New York: Knopf, 1982.

Christenson, R. M. The record is all. *New York Times,* November 6, 1979, A19.

Clark, B. R. The organizational saga in higher education. *Administrative Science Quarterly,* 1972, *17,* 178–184.

CONSIDINE, B. *The Remarkable Life of Dr. Armand Hammer.* New York: Harper and Row, 1975.

COX, C. M. *Genetic Studies of Genius* (Vol. 2). *The Early Mental Traits of Three Hundred Geniuses.* Stanford, CA: Stanford University Press, 1926.

CROWE, B. J., BOCHNER, S., and CLARK, A. W. The effects of subordinates' behavior on managerial style. *Human Relations,* 1972, *25,* 215–237.

DECI, E. L. *Intrinsic Motivation.* New York: Plenum Press, 1975.

DeFRANK, T. M., CLIFT, E., and BEACH, Y. L. Ronald Reagan's magic. *Newsweek,* February 6, 1984, 22–4.

DEMAUSE, L. *Foundations of Psychohistory.* New York: Creative Roots, 1982.

DICKSON, J. W. Top managers' beliefs and rationales for participation. *Human Relations,* 1982, *35,* 203–217.

DOSSETT, D. L., CELLA, A., GREENBERG, C. I., and ADRIAN, N. Goal setting, participation and leader supportiveness effects on performance. Paper presented at the American Psychological Association, Anaheim, CA, 1983.

DOW, T. The theory of charisma. *Sociological Quarterly,* 1969, *10,* 306–318.

DRACHKOVITCH, M. M. Succession and the charismatic leader in Yugoslavia. *Journal of International Affairs,* 1964, *18(1),* 54–66.

DRENTH, P. J. D., and KOOPMAN, P. L. A contingency approach to participative leadership. In J. G. Hunt, D. Hosking, C. A. Schriesheim, and R. Stewart (Eds.), *Leaders and Managers: International Perspectives on Managerial Behavior and Leadership.* New York: Pergamon, 1984.

DRIVER, M. J., and ROWE, A. J. Decision-making styles: A new approach to management decision making. In C. Cooper (Ed.), *Behavioral Problems in Organizations.* Englewood Cliffs, N.J.: Prentice–Hall, 1979.

DRUCKER, P. *The Practice of Management.* New York: Harper, 1954.

EDEN, D., and SHANI, A. B. Pygmalion goes to boot camp: Expectancy, leadership and trainee performance. *Journal of Applied Psychology,* 1982, *67,* 194–199.

ENGLAND, G. W., and LEE, R. The relationship between managerial values and managerial success in the United States, Japan, India, and Australia. *Journal of Applied Psychology,* 1974, *59,* 411–419.

EOYANG, C. K. Symbolic transformation of belief systems. In L. Pondy, P. Frost, E. Morgan, and T. Dandridge (Eds.), *Organizational Symbolism.* New York: Jai Press, 1983.

ERIKSON, E. *Gandhi's Truth.* New York: Norton, 1969.

ETZIONI, A. *A Comparative Analysis of Complex Organizations.* Glencoe, IL: The Free Press, 1961.

EVANS, M. G. Extensions of a path–goal theory of motivation. *Journal of Applied Psychology,* 1974, *59,* 172–178.

FARROW, D. L. A path–analytic approach to the study of contingent leader behavior. Doctoral dissertation, University of Rochester, 1976.

FERMI, L. *Mussolini.* Chicago: University of Chicago Press, 1966.

FIEDLER, A. F., and LEISTER, A. F. Leader intelligence and task performance: A test of a multiple screen model. *Organizational Behavior and Human Performance,* 1977, *20,* 11–14.

FISCH, G. G. Line–staff is obsolete. *Harvard Business Review,* 1961, *39* (5), 67–79.

FISCHER, L. *The Life of Lenin.* New York: Harper, 1965.

FISHER, C. D. Transmission of positive and negative feedback to subordinates: A laboratory investigation. *Journal of Applied Psychology,* 1979, *64,* 533–540.

FREUD, S. *Moses and Monotheism.* New York: Vintage, 1922/1939.

FULK, J., and WENDLER, E. R. Dimensionality of leader–subordinate interactions: A path–goal investigation. *Organizational Behavior and Human Performance,* 1982, *30,* 244–264.

GALANTER, M. Charismatic religious sects and psychiatry: An overview. *American Journal of Psychiatry,* 1982, *139,* 1539–1548.

GARDNER, J. W. *Excellence: Can We Be Equal and Excellent Too?* New York: Harper, 1961.

GEERTZ, C. Centers, kings and charisma: Reflections on the symbolics of power. In J. Ben-David and T. N. Clark (Eds.), *Culture and Its Creators: Essays in Honor of Edward Shils.* Chicago: University of Chicago Press, 1977, pp. 150–171.

GEORGOPOULOS, B. S., MAHONEY, G. M., and JONES, N. W. A path–goal approach to productivity. *Journal of Applied Psychology,* 1957, *41,* 345–353.

GERTH, H., and MILLS, C. W. *From Max Weber.* New York: Oxford University Press, 1946.

GHISELLI, E. E. Intelligence and managerial success. *Psychological Reports,* 1963, *12,* 898.

GILL, R. W. T. A trainability concept for management potential and an empirical study of its relationship with intelligence for two managerial skills. *Journal of Occupational Psychology,* 1982, *55,* 139–147.

GLASS, A. Pursuing discredited policy. *Washington Post,* February 12, 1984, F3.

GORDON, L. V. The image of political candidates: Values and voter preference. *Journal of Applied Psychology,* 1972, *56,* 382–387.

GRAEN, G. Role-making processes within complex organizations. In M. D. Dunnette (Ed.), *Handbook of Industrial and Organizational Psychology.* Chicago: Rand McNally, 1975, pp. 1201–1245.

GRAEN G., and CASHMAN, J. F. A role-making model of leadership in formal organizations: A developmental approach. In J. G. Hunt and L. L. Larson (Eds.), *Leadership Frontiers.* Kent, OH: Kent State University Press, 1975, pp. 143–165.

GRAEN, G., NOVAK, M. A., and SOMMERKAMP, P. The effects of leader-member exchange and job design on productivity and satisfaction: Testing a dual attachment model. *Organizational Behavior and Human Performance,* 1982, *30,* 109–131.

GREENE, C. N. A longitudinal investigation of performance–reinforcing behaviors and subordinate satisfaction and performance. *Midwest Academy of Management Proceedings,* 1976, 157–185.

GREENE, C. N., and PODSAKOFF, P. M. Effects of withdrawal of a performance-contingent reward on supervisory influences and power. *Academy of Management Journal,* 1981, *24,* 527–542.

GRELLER, M. M. Evaluation of feedback sources as a function of role and organizational development. *Journal of Applied Psychology,* 1980, *65,* 24–27.

GROVE, A. S. My turn: Breaking the chains of command. *Newsweek,* October 3, 1983, 23.

HAMBRICK, D. C., and MASON, P. A. The organization as a reflection of its top managers. Paper presented at the Academy of Management, Dallas, 1983.

HANDY, C. D. *Understanding Organization.* Blatimore: Penguin Books, 1976.

HAWLEY, C. *Executive Suite.* Cambridge, MA: Riverside Press, 1952. (Quoted in Bass, B. M. The leaderless group discussion as a leadership evaluation instrument. *Personnel Psychology,* 1954, *7,* 470–477).

HAY, R., and GRAY, E. Social responsibilities of business managers. *Academy of Management Journal,* 1974, *17* (1), 135–143.

HAYES, S., and THOMAS, W. N. *Taking Command.* Harrisburg, PA: Stackpole, 1967.

HENRY, W. E. Conflict, age and the executive. *Business Topics,* 1961, *9,* 15–25.

HERSEY, P., and BLANCHARD, K. H. *Mangement of Organizational Behavior: Utilizing Human Resources.* Englewood Cliffs, NJ: Prentice-Hall, 1977.

HEWINS, R. *J. Paul Getty: The Richest American.* London: Sedgwick and Jackson, 1961.

HILL, N. Self-esteem: The key to effective leadership. *Administrative Management,* 1976, *31* (8), 24.

HOFFMAN, S., and HOFFMAN, I. The will to grandeur: de Gaulle as political artist. In D. A. Rustow (Ed.), *Philosophers and Kings: Studies in Leadership.* New York: George Braziller, 1970.

HOLLANDER, E. P. *Leadership Dynamics.* New York: Free Press, 1978.

HOLSI, O. R., and NORTH, R. C. The history of human conflict. In E. B. McNeil (Ed.), *The Nature of Human Conflict.* Englewood Cliffs, NJ: Prentice-Hall, 1965.

HOLUSHA, J. Cuts, U.S. aids, and Iacocca were factors in Chrysler turn around. *New York Times,* July 15, 1983, D1, D6.

HOUSE, R. J. A path–goal theory of leadership effectiveness. *Administrative Science Quarterly,* 1971, *16,* 321–338.

House, R. J. A 1976 theory of charismatic leadership. In J. G. Hunt and L. L. Larson (Eds.), *Leadership: The Cutting Edge.* Carbondale: Southern Illinois University Press, 1977, pp. 189-207.

House, R. J., and Mitchell, T. R. Path-goal theory of leadership. *Journal of Contemporary Business,* 1974, *5,* 81-97.

Hummel, R. P. Charisma in politics: Psycho-social causes of revolution as preconditions of charismatic outbreaks within the framework of Weber's epistemology. Thesis, New York University, 1973.

Hunt, D. M., and Michael, C. Mentorship: A career training and development tool. *Academy of Management Review,* 1983, *8,* 475-485.

Hunt, J. G., and Schuler, R. S. *Leader Reward and Sanctions: Behavior Relations Criteria in a Large Public Utility.* Department of Administrative Science. Carbondale: Southern Illinois University Press, 1976.

Ilgen, D. R., and Knowlton, W. A. Performance attributional effects on feedback from supervisors. *Organizational Behavior and Human Performance,* 1980, *25,* 441-456.

Janis, I. L., and Mann, L. *Decision Making.* New York: Free Press, 1977.

Jennings, E. E. *An Anatomy of Leadership.* New York: Harper, 1960.

Jennings, E. E. The mobile manager: A study of the new generation of top executives. Ph.D dissertation, University of Michigan, 1967.

Jessup, J. K. *The Ideas of Henry Luce.* New York: Atheneum, 1969.

Johnson, M. C. Speaking from experience: Mentors—the key to development and growth. *Training and Development Journal,* 1980, *34* (7), 55-57.

Johnston, A. *The Great Goldwyn.* New York: Random House, 1937.

Jung, C. G. *Psychological Types* (R. F. C. Hall, trans.). Princeton, NJ: Princeton University Press, 1971.

Kanter, R. M. *Men and Women of the Corporation.* New York: Basic Books, 1977.

Kaplan, E., and Cowen, E. L. Interpersonal helping behavior of industrial foremen. *Journal of Applied Psychology,* 1981, *66,* 633-638.

Katz, D., and Kahn, R. L. *The Social Psychology of Organizations.* New York: Wiley, 1966.

Keller, R. T., and Szilagyi, A. D. Employee reactions to leader reward behavior. *Academy of Management Journal,* 1976, *19,* 619-627.

Kennedy, G. *Bligh.* London: Duckworth, 1978.

Kerr, S., and Jerimer, J. M. Substitutes for leadership: Their meaning and measurement. *Organizational Behavior and Human Performance,* 1978, *22,* 375-403.

Kiechel, W., III. Wanted: Corporate leaders. *Fortune,* May 30, 1983, 135-140.

Kiggundu, M. N. Task interdependence and job design: Test of a theory. *Organizational and Human Performance,* 1983, *31,* 145-172.

KILMANN, R. Problem management: A behavioral science approach. In M. G. Zaltman (Ed.), *Management Principles for Non-profit Agencies and Organizations.* New York: American Management Association, 1979.

KLAUSS, R., and BASS, B. M. *Interpersonal Communications in Organizations.* New York: Academic Press, 1982.

KLIMOSKI, R. J., and HAYES, N. J. Leader behavior and subordinate motivation. *Personnel Psychology,* 1980, *33,* 543-555.

KNOWLTON, W. A., and MITCHELL, T. R. Effects of causal attributions on a supervisor's evaluation of subordinate performance. *Journal of Applied Psychology,* 1980, *65,* 459-466.

KOLB, D. A. Problem solving and the executive mind. Symposium: Functioning of the Executive Mind. Case Western Reserve University, April 14-17, 1982.

KOMAKI, J. Applied behavior analysis. *Industrial Psychologist,* February 1981, 7-9.

KORMAN, A. K. A hypothesis of work behavior revisited and an extension. *Academy of Management Review,* 1976, *1,* 50-63.

KORMAN, A. K., WITTIG-BERMAN, U., and LANG, D. Career success and personal failure: Alienation in professionals and managers. *Academy of Management Journal,* 1981, *24,* 342-360.

KRAM, K. E. Mentoring process at work: Developmental relationships in managerial careers. Unpublished Ph.D. dissertation, Yale University, 1980.

KRAMER, J. (Ed.), *Lombardi: Winning Is the Only Thing.* New York: Maddick Manuscripts, 1970.

KRAUT, A. Intellectual ability and promotional success. *Personnel Psychology,* 1969, *22,* 281-290.

LANDY, F. J. An opponent process theory of job satisfaction. *Journal of Applied Psychology,* 1978, *63,* 533-547.

LARSON, A. *The President Nobody Knew.* New York: Popular Library, 1968.

LARSON, J. R. Some hypotheses about the causes of supervisory performance feedback behavior. Paper presented at the meeting of the Academy of Management, Detroit, 1980.

LAWLER, E. E., III. Leadership in participative organizations. NATO Conference, Oxford, 1982.

LEVINSON, D. J., DARROW, C. M., KLEIN, E. G., LEVINSON, M. H., and McKEE, B. *The Seasons of a Man's Life.* New York: Knopf, 1978.

LIFTON, R. J. *Revolutionary Immortality: Mao Tse-tung and the Chinese Cultural Revolution.* New York: Random House, 1968.

LIFTON, R. J. *Explorations in Psychohistory: The Wellfleet Papers.* New York: Simon and Schuster, 1974.

LIPPITT, R. The changing leader–follower relationships of the 1980's. *Journal of Applied Behavioral Science*, 1982, *18*, 395–403.

LOCKE, E. A. Toward a theory of task motivation and incentives. *Organizational Behavior and Human Performance*, 1968, *3*, 157–190.

LODAHL, A. Crisis in values and the success of the Unification Church. Bachelor of Arts Thesis in Sociology, Cornell University, Ithaca, NY, 1982 (quoted in Trice and Beyer, 1984).

LUNDBERG, C. The unreported research of Dr. G. Hypothetical: Six variables in need of recognition. In M. W. McCall and M. M. Lombardo (Eds.), *Leadership: Where Else Can We Go?* Durham, NC: Duke University Press, 1978.

LUTHANS, F., and KREITNER, R. *Organizational Behavior Modification*. Glenview, Ill.: Scott, Foresman, 1975.

MACCOBY, M. *The Gamesman*. New York: Simon and Schuster, 1976.

MACHIAVELLI, N. *The Prince*. New York: Mentor Press, 1513/1962.

MAGNUS, P. *Kitchener: Portrait of an Imperialist*. New York: Dutton, 1968.

MAO, T. *Selected Works of Mao Tse-tung*. Peking: Foreign Language Press, 1967.

MARGERISON, C. J. *How Chief Executives Succeed*. Bradford, England: MCB Publications, 1980.

MARTIN, J., SITKIN, S., and BOEHM, M. Founders and the elusiveness of a cultural legacy. Research Report no. 726. Graduate School of Business, Stanford University, 1984.

MASLOW, A. A theory of human motivation. *Psychological Review*, 1943, *50*, 370–396.

MASLOW, A. *Motivation and Personality*. New York: Harper, 1954.

McCALL, M. W., JR. *Leaders and Leadership: Of Substance and Shadow*. Technical Report no. 2. Greensboro, NC: Center for Creative Leadership, 1977.

McCALL, M. W., JR., and LOMBARDO, M. M. Where else can we go? In M. W. McCall, Jr. and M. M. Lombardo (Eds)., *Leadership: Where Else Can We Go?* Durham, NC: Duke University Press, 1978, pp. 151–165.

McCALL, M. W., JR., and LOMBARDO, M. M. *Off the Track: Why and How Successful Executives Get Derailed*. Technical Report no. 21. Greensboro, NC: Center for Creative Leadership, 1983.

MEYER, A. G. *Leninism*. New York: Praeger, 1962.

MEYER, E. C. Leadership: A return to basics. *Military Review*, 1980, *60* (7), 4–9.

MINTZBERG, H. *The Nature of Managerial Work*. New York: Harper and Row, 1973.

MINTZBERG, H. The manager's job: Folklore and fact. *Harvard Business Review*, 1975, *4*, 49–61.

MISSIRIAN, A. K. The process of mentoring in career development of female managers. Unpublished Ph.D. dissertation, University of Massachusetts, 1980.

MITCHELL, T. R., and KALB, L. S. Effects of job experience on supervisor's attributions for a subordinate's poor performance. *Journal of Applied Psychology*, 1982, *67,* 181–188.

MITCHELL, T. R., and WOOD, R. E. Supervisors' responses to poor performance: A test of an attributions model. *Journal of Applied Psychology,* 1980, *25,* 123–138.

MITROFF, I. I. Systematic problem solving. In M. W. McCall and M. M. Lombardo (Eds.), *Leadership: Where Else Can We Go?* Durham, NC: Duke University Press, 1978.

MITROFF, I. I., and MASON, R. O. Business policy and metaphysics: Some philosophical considerations. *Academy of Management Review,* 1982. *7,* 361–370.

MITROFF, I. I., KILMANN, H., and SAXTON, M. J. Organizational culture: Corrective order-making out of an ambiguous world (unpublished manuscript).

MORSE, J. J., and WAGNER, F. R. Measuring the process of managerial effectiveness. *Academy of Management Journal,* 1978, *21,* 23–35.

MUELLER, R. K. Leading-edge leadership. *Human Systems Management,* 1980, *1,* 17–27.

NAISBETT, J. *Megatrends: Ten New Directions Transforming Our Lives.* New York: Warner Books, 1982.

NANCE, J. J. *The Nance Lectures.* Cleveland, OH: Bureau of Business Research, Cleveland State University, 1979.

NEIDER, L. L. An experimental field investigation utilizing expectancy theory view of participation. *Organizational Behavior and Human Performance,* 1980, *26,* 425–442.

NICOL, J. The tight ship and her merry hearts. *Sea History,* 1983, *27* (Spring), 45–46.

NICHOLSON, N., URSELL, G., and BLYTON, P. *The Dynamics of White Collar Unions.* London: Academic Press, 1981.

NIETZCHE, F. *Thus Spoke Zarathustra* (1883). In O. Levy (Ed.), *The Complete Works of Friederich Nietzche.* New York: Gordon Press, 1974.

OBERG, W. Charisma, commitment, and contemporary organization theory. *Business Topics,* 1972, *20,* 18–32.

O'BOYLE, T. F. Rise and fall: Turnabout in fortunes of Mesta Machine is history with a moral. *Wall Street Journal,* January 3, 1984, 1, 31.

O'HIGGINS, P. *Madame: An Intimate Biography of Helena Rubinstein.* New York: Viking, 1971.

OLDHAM, G. R. The motivational strategies used by supervisors. *Organizational Behavior and Human Performance,* 1976, *15,* 66–86.

OLSHAKER, M. *The Instant Image: Edwin Land and the Polaroid Experience.* New York: Stein & Day, 1978.

OUCHI, W. G. *Theory Z: How American Business Can Meet the Japanese Challenge.* Boston: Addison-Wesley, 1981.

PAIGE, G. D. *The Scientific Study of Political Leadership.* New York: Free Press, 1977.

PARSONS, C. K., HEROLD, D. M., and TURLINGTON, B. Individual differences in performance feedback preferences. Paper presented at the Academy of Management, San Diego, 1981.

PATTON, G. S., JR. *War As I Knew It.* Boston: Houghton-Mifflin, 1947.

PAYNE, P. *The Marshall Story.* New York: Prentice-Hall, 1951.

PETERS, T. J. A style for all seasons. *The Executive,* Summer, 1980.

PETERS, T. J., and WATERMAN, R. H. *In Search of Excellence.* New York: Harper and Row, 1982.

PETTIGREW, A. M. On studying organizational cultures. *Administrative Science Quarterly,* 1979, *24,* 570–581.

PFEFFER, J., and SALANCIK, G. R. Determinants of supervisory behavior: A role set analysis. *Human Relations,* 1975, *28,* 139–154.

PODSAKOFF, P. M., TODOR, W. D., GROVER, R. A., and HUBER, V. L. Situational moderators of leader reward and punishment behaviors: Fact or fiction? *Organizational Behavior and Human Performance,* 1984, *34,* 21–63.

PODSAKOFF, P. M., TODOR, W. D., GROVER, R. A., and HUBER, V. L. Relationships between leader reward and punishment behavior and group processes and productivity. *Journal of Management* (in press).

PODSAKOFF, P. M., TODOR, W. D., and SCHULER, R. S. Leader expertise as a moderator of the effects of instrumental and supportive leader behaviors. *Journal of Management,* 1983, *8,* 173–185.

PODSAKOFF, P. M., TODOR, W. D., and SKOV, R. Effect of leader contingent and non-contingent reward and punishment behaviors on subordinate performance and satisfaction. *Academy of Management Journal,* 1982, *25,* 810–821.

POLMAR, N., and ALLEN, T. B. *Rickover: Controversy and Genius.* New York: Simon and Schuster, 1982.

PRAHALAD, C. K., and DOZ, Y. L. Managing managers: The work of top management. Seventh NATO Conference of Leadership, St. Catherine's, Oxford, July 12–17, 1982.

PRICE, K. H., and GARLAND, H. Compliance with a leader's suggestions as a function of perceived leader/member competence and potential reciprocity. *Journal of Applied Psychology,* 1981, *66,* 329–336.

PURYEAR, E. F. *Nineteen Stars.* Washington, D.C.: Coiner Publications, 1971.

QUINN, R. E., and CAMERON, K. Organizational life cycles and shifting criteria of effectiveness: Some preliminary evidence. *Management Science,* 1983, *29,* 33–51.

QUINN, R. E., and HALL, R. H. Environments, organizations, and policy makers: Towards an integrative framework. In R. H. Hall and R. E. Quinn (Eds.), *Organization Theory and Public Policy: Contributions and Limitations.* Beverly Hills, CA: Sage Publications, 1983.

REITZ, H. J. Managerial attitudes and perceived contingencies between performance and organizational response. Paper presented at the Academy of Management, Atlanta, 1971, 227–238.

RESTON, J. Who advises Reagan? *New York Times,* April 26, 1983.

RILEY, M. W., and FLOWERMAN, S. H. Group relations as a variable in communications research. *American Sociological Review,* 1951, *16,* 174–176.

ROBBINS, S. P. *Organization Theory: The Structure and Design of Organizations.* Englewood Cliffs, NJ: Prentice-Hall, 1983.

ROBBINS, S. P. The theory Z organization from a power-control perspective. *California Management Review,* 1983, *25,* 67–75.

ROBERTS, N. C. Transforming leadership: Sources, processes, consequences. Paper presented at the Academy of Management, Boston, 1984.

ROCHE, G. R. Much ado about mentors. *Harvard Business Review,* 1979, *57*(1), 17–28.

ROSENTHAL, R. A., and JACOBSON, L. *Pygmalion in the Classroom: Teacher Expectation and Pupil Intellectual Development.* New York: Holt, Rinehart & Winston, 1968.

RUCH, R., and GOODMAN, R. *Image at the Top.* New York: Free Press, 1983.

RUSMORE, J. T. Executive performance and intellectual ability in organizational levels. Advanced Human Systems Institute, San Jose State University, 1984.

RUSTOW, D. A. Ataturk as a founder of state. In D. A. Rustow (Ed.), *Philosophers and Kings: Studies in Leadership.* New York: Braziller, 1970.

SCHIFFER, I. *Charisma: A Psychoanalytic Look at Mass Society.* Toronto: University of Toronto Press, 1973.

SCHRIESHEIM, C. A., and KERR, S. Theories and measures of leadership: A critical appraisal of current and future directions. In J. G. Hunt and L. L. Larson (Eds.), *Leadership: The Cutting Edge.* Carbondale: Southern Illinois University Press, 1977, pp. 9–45.

SCHRIESHEIM, C. A., and VON GLINOW, M. A. The path–goal theory of leadership: A theoretical and empirical analysis. *Academy of Management Journal,* 1977, *20,* 398–405.

SCHULTZ, D. Managing the middle-aged manager. *Business Management,* 1974, *7,* 8–17.

SCHWAB, D. P., and DYER, L. D. The motivational impact of a compensation system on employee performance. *Organizational Behavior and Human Performance,* 1973, *9,* 215–225.

SCHWARTZ, B. George Washington and the Whig conception of heroic leadership. *American Sociological Review,* 1983, *48,* 18–33.

SCOTT, W. R. *Organizations: Rational, Natural, and Open Systems.* Englewood Cliffs, NJ: Prentice-Hall, 1981.

SHAPIRA, Z. Expectancy determinants of intrinsically motivated behavior. Unpublished doctoral dissertation, University of Rochester, 1975.

SHAPIRO, E. C., HASELTINE, F., and ROWE, M. P. Moving up: Role models, mentors, and the patron system. *Sloan Management Review,* 1978, *19* (3), 51–58.

SHERIDAN, J. E., KERR, J. L., and ABELSON, M. A. Leadership activation theory: An opponent process model of subordinate responses to leadership behavior. In J. G. Hunt, U. Sekaran, and C. A. Schriesheim (Eds.), *Leadership: Beyond Establishment Views.* Carbondale: Southern Illinois University Press, 1982, pp. 122–141.

SHILS, E. A. Charisma, order, and status. *American Sociological Review,* 1965, *30,* 199–213.

SHULL, F. A., JR., DELBECO, A., and CUMMINGS, L. L. *Organizational Decision Making.* New York: McGraw-Hill, 1970.

SIEHL, C., and MARTIN, J. The role of symbolic management: How can managers effectively transmit organizational culture? Seventh NATO Conference on Leadership, St. Catherine's, Oxford, 1982.

SIMON, H. A. *The New Science of Management Decision.* New York: Harper, 1960.

SIMS, H. P. The leader as manager of reinforcement contingencies: An empirical example and a model. In J. G. Hunt and L. L. Larson (Eds.), *Leadership: The Cutting Edge.* Carbondale: Southern Illinois University Press, 1977, pp. 121–137.

SMIRCICH, L., and MORGAN, G. Leadership: The management of meaning. *Journal of Applied Behavioral Science,* 1982, *18,* 257–273.

SMITH, H. *The Russians.* New York: Ballantine, 1975.

SOLBERG, C. *Hubert Humphrey: A Biography.* New York: Norton, 1984.

SORENSEN, T. *Kennedy.* New York: Bantam Books, 1966.

SPECTOR, P., and SUTTELL, B. J. An experimental comparison of the effectiveness of three patterns of leadership behavior. Technical Report Contract NONR 89003. Washington, D. C.: American Institute for Research, 1957.

STOCKDALE, J. B. The principles of leadership. *American Educator,* 1981, *5* (4), 12, 14, 15, 33.

STOGDILL, R. M. *Leader Behavior Description Questionnaire—Form XII.* Columbus: Ohio State University, Bureau of Business Research, 1963.

SUTTELL, B. J., and SPECTOR, P. Research on the specific leader behavior patterns most effective in influencing group performance. Annual Technical Report, Contract NONR 89003. Washington, D. C.: American Institute for Research, 1955.

TARNOWIESKI, D. *The Changing Success Ethic.* New York: American Management Association, 1973.

TOBIAS, A. *Fire and Ice: The Story of Charles Revson—The Man Who Built the Revlon Empire.* New York: Morrow, 1976.

TOLAND, J. *No Man's Land: The Story of 1918.* London: Methuen, 1982.

TRICE, H. M., and BEYER, J. M. Charisma and its routinization in two social movement organizations. School of Management, State University of New York at Buffalo, Working Paper No. 593, 1984.

TROTSKY, L. *Trotsky's Diary in Exile.* Cambridge, MA: Harvard University Press, 1963.

TRUMAN, H. S. *Memoirs.* New York: Doubleday, 1958.

TSUI, A. A role set analysis of managerial reputation. Paper presented at the Academy of Management, New York City, 1982.

TSURUMI, R. R. American origins of Japanese productivity: The Hawthorne experiment rejected. *Pacific Basin Quarterly,* 1982, *7,* 14–15.

TUCHMAN, B. *The March of Folly.* New York: Knopf, 1984.

TUCKER, R. C. The theory of charismatic leadership. *Daedalus,* 1968, *97,* 731–756.

TUCKER, R. G. The theory of charismatic leadership. In D. A. Rustow (Ed.), *Philosophers and Kings: Studies in Leadership.* New York: Braziller, 1970.

VAILL, P. B. Toward a behavior description of high-performing systems. In M. W. McCall, Jr. and M. M. Lombardo (Eds.), *Leadership: Where Else Can We Go?* Durham, NC: Duke University Press, 1978, pp. 103–125.

VON AUW, A. *Heritage and Destiny.* New York: Praeger, 1984.

VROOM, V. H. *Work and Motivation.* New York: John Wiley & Sons, 1964.

WALDMAN, D. A., BASS, B. M., and EINSTEIN, W. O. Effort, performance, and transformational leadership in industrial and military settings. School of Management, State University of New York at Binghamton, Working Paper 84-78, 1984.

WALEY, A. *Three Ways of Thought in Ancient China.* London: Allen and Unwin, 1939.

WALL, J. F. *Andrew Carnegie.* New York: Oxford University Press, 1970.

WEBER, M. *The Sociology of Religion.* Beacon, NY: Beacon Press, 1922/1963.

WEBER, M. *The Theory of Social and Economic Organizations* (T. Parsons, trans.). New York: Free Press, 1924/1947.

WEISS, H. M. Subordinate imitation of supervisor behavior: The role of modeling in organizational socialization. *Organizational Behavior and Human Performance,* 1977, *19,* 89–105.

WEISS, H. M. Social learning of work values in organizations. *Journal of Applied Psychology*, 1978, *63*, 711–718.

WEISS, H. M., and SHAW, J. B. Social influences on judgments about tasks. *Organizational Behavior and Human Performance*, 1979, *24*, 126–140.

WILNER, A. R. *Charismatic Political Leadership: A Theory*. Princeton, NJ: Princeton University, Center for International Studies, 1968.

WOLFENSTEIN, E. V. *The Revolutionary Personality: Lenin, Trotsky, Gandhi*. Princeton, NJ: Princeton University Press, 1967.

WOODWARD, J. *Industrial Organizations: Theory and Practice*. Oxford: Oxford University Press, 1965.

WORTMAN, M. S. Strategic management and changing leader-follower roles. *Journal of Applied Behavioral Science*, 1982, *18*, 371–383.

YANKELOVICH, D., and IMMERWAHR, J. *Putting the Work Ethic to Work*. New York: Public Agenda Foundation, 1983.

YUKL, G. A. *Leadership in Organizations*. Englewood Cliffs, NJ: Prentice-Hall, 1981.

YUKL, G. A., and NEMEROFF, W. Identification and measurement of specific categories of leadership behavior: A progress report. In J. G. Hunt and L. L. Larson (Eds.), *Crosscurrents in Leadership*. Carbondale: Southern Illinois University Press, 1979.

YUKL, G. A., and VAN FLEET, D. D. Cross-situational, multimethod research on military leader effectiveness. *Organizational Behavior and Human Performance*, 1982, *30*, 87–108.

ZALD, M. N., and ASH, R. Social movement organizations: Growth, decay, and change. *Social Forces*, 1966, *44*, 327–341.

ZALEZNIK, A. The dynamics of subordinancy. *Harvard Business Review*, 1965, *43* (6), 59–70.

ZALEZNIK, A. Management of disappointment. *Harvard Business Review*, 1967, *45* (6), 59–70.

ZALEZNIK, A. Managers and leaders: Are they different? *Harvard Business Review*, 1977, *55* (5), 67–80.

ZALEZNIK, A. The leadership gap. *Washington Quarterly*, 1983, *6* (1), 32–39.

ZALEZNIK, A., and KETS DE VRIES, M. F. R. *Power and the Corporate Mind*. Boston: Houghton Mifflin Co., 1975.

ZANDER, A., and CURTIS, T. Social support and rejection of organizational standards. *Journal of Educational Psychology*, 1965, *56*, 87–95.

Index